PUBLICATIONS OF THE EUROPEAN UNIVERSITY INSTITUTE
PUBLICATIONS DE L'INSTITUT UNIVERSITAIRE EUROPÉEN
PUBLICATIES VAN HET EUROPEES UNIVERSITAIR INSTITUUT
PUBBLICAZIONI DELL'ISTITUTO UNIVERSITARIO EUROPEO
DET EUROPÆISKE UNIVERSITETSINSTITUTS SKRIFTER
VERÖFFENTLICHUNGEN DES EUROPÄISCHEN
HOCHSCHULINSTITUTS

8

BADIA FIESOLANA - FIRENZE

The Management of Industrial Conflict in the Recession of the 1970s: Britain, Germany and Italy

Papers of a Colloquium held at the European University in November 1978

Edited by

EZIO TARANTELLI and **GERHARD WILLKE**
with the editorial assistance of David Shonfield

SIJTHOFF: Alphen aan den Rijn
KLETT-COTTA: Stuttgart

BRUYLANT: Bruxelles
LE MONNIER: Firenze

1981

219513

I.S.B.N. 90 286 2561 5 Sijthoff

Stabilimenti Tipografici « E. Ariani » e « L'Arte della Stampa » – Firenze
Manufactured in Italy - Imprimé en Italie

Table of contents

INTRODUCTION

THE MANAGEMENT OF INDUSTRIAL CONFLICT DURING THE RECESSION OF THE 1970s

by

EZIO TARANTELLI

1. Overview *

After the French May of 1968, the oil embargo of 1973 and the Iranian crisis of 1979, the magic triangle of economic liberalism — consenus, equilibrium, stability — was transmuted into a cross: conflict, disequilibrium, instability. Without much success, governments and central banks asked those rusty weapons, their econometric models, to predict stag-flation, J curves, recycling of oil surpluses, and multipliers in xenocurrency markets. Even the equilibrium solutions of the textbook box of a closed economy — income; consumption, investment — had become indeterminate: if the rate of (expected) profit diminishes, then investment diminishes but the propensity to consume may increase. The net effect on income is *a priori* indeterminate. Once he is out of the box of the old Hicksian IS-LM curves, the first year economics student can't go wrong at the exam. Even the professor doesn't know the answer. His crisis is the crisis of economics.

The 1929 crisis was a crisis of aggregate demand while it may be said that the crisis of the second half of the 1960s and of the early 1970s was a crisis of consensus. What are the main aspects or, shall we say, the " stylized facts " of this crisis?

* I want to thank C. Saunders and D. Shonfield and my colleagues at MIT, T. Barocci and H. Katz, for having read a first draft of the manuscript and for their useful comments and suggestions. I remain solely responsible for any remaining error.

Let me list five or six of the stylized facts.

1. The conflict was roughly contemporaneous in all Western industrialized countries beginning with the increase in social unrest in Britain and the Vietnam war in the United States in the second half of the 1960s, the student movement of the French May of 1968, the workers' movement in the Italian " hot autumn " in 1969, and in September of the same year in Germany, the industrial unrest in the Scandinavian countries, Japan, Canada, Australia, New Zealand, etc. in the early 1970s; 2. The socio-political and not only plant level aspects of the crisis: from the revolt of blacks and other minority groups in the ghettos of Washington, Chicago, Detroit, etc., from the feminist movement and student protest in many industrialized countries, to the immigrants' strike wave in Germany in 1973. Not only does the crisis break out more or less simultaneously in all Western countries, but its features are pervasive: it is multi-dimensional; 3. The way in which the conflict developed at the grass roots level and was only later taken on (and often appropriated) by social institutions including trade unions; 4. The egalitarian character of the conflict, which manifested itself in the trade unions by a tendency towards equal absolute (rather than percentage) across the board wage increases including, in Italy, the increases stemming from the cost of living escalator clause; 5. The shorter-lived upswings of the national trade cycles (with the major exception of the USA since the last quarter of 1975), high youth unemployment and the increase in the deficit of the State as a percentage of GNP in Western countries. 6. Last but not least, the widely different movements of labour turnover rates and real wages in different countries and the differing speeds at which national economic policies accepted the burden of adjustment of their balance of payments disequilibria after the oil embargo of 1973. Thus, while more consensus-prone countries like Germany, Japan and the USA were able to lower real wages and employment following the first oil crisis, more conflict-prone countries like Italy, Britain and France experienced lower labour productivity and higher wage and price inflation. [1]

---

[1] I have asked (unfortunately too late for inclusion in this book) Sellier and Silvestre to write two papers, respectively, on the management of the French industrial relations system and of the labour market in the recession of the 1970s. Both papers, which were delivered at the University of Florence in May 1980 and which will be published elsewhere, showed a remarkable degree of coherence with a number of the "connecting issues" related to the Italian and British case, which I will attempt to sketch in Section II.

It has been said that every society looks for explanations — or, rather, scapegoats — when things go wrong. Primitive societies blame evil spirits. The ancient Greeks offered sacrifices to their gods, Christians blamed man's sinfulness, and the enlightenment outmodel institutions. In our own times, economists have blamed the crisis of the 1970s on money, (Zis, 1976), or on the so called " too few producers " hypothesis, (Bacon and Eltis, 1976), on the recession hypothesis, (Crouch and Pizzorno, 1978), on the Kondratieff cycle, (Forrester, 1976), or on vague notions of economic and extra-economic origin, such as " rising expectations ", " aspirations gap ", " deprivation and/or frustration hypothesis ", " governability crisis ", the " overload theory " and " passion for equality ", (Goldthorpe et al., 1978).

2. The actors and the basic questions of the Colloquium

The actors and their respective roles, the questions, in a word, the stage of our Colloquium was organized with this scenario in mind. In particular, the scope of the Colloquium was the exploration of the effects of differences in the functioning of the labour market and the system of industrial relations in three European Common Market countries — Britain, Germany and Italy — concentrating attention on the particularly difficult moment of the crisis of the 1970s.

These three countries were also chosen in view of the extreme and opposing ways in which their labour market and systems of industrial relations function: we might say, from Germany to Italy, by way of Britain. The differences between these countries also include the different economic policies they followed. While, for instance, after the oil embargo, Italy still followed an expansionary policy, Germany endorsed restrictive fiscal policies in February and May 1973. In Britain, internal demand fell in the course of 1973 despite a worsening of the trade balance [2].

The analysis in this volume is based on two papers for each of

---

[2] For an analysis of monetary and fiscal policies as followed by these countries and for a number of comparative statistical data see Izzo and Spaventa, 1979.

the three national cases: one which concentrates principally on labour market problems, the other on the system of industrial relations. Further, we invited experts from both fields of enquiry and from different countries as well as from various international organizations, to participate in the discussion following the papers. Even though space precludes a detailed account of the many ideas and points of view which were expressed in the course of this discussion, this Introduction, its topics and the issues I choose to raise owe much to the Colloquium participants (a list of whom can be found at the end of this book).

The questions we asked the participants in the Colloquium were intended to give an indication of the ways in which the theme of the Colloquium might be dealt with. Obviously, we allowed each participant to choose freely from these themes in accordance with his interest and experience. The papers which follow describe many important aspects of te national cases we chose to explore.

For the reader's convenience, I attempt in the following section to organize the material contained in the six papers of this book into their main "connecting issues".

3. THE CONNECTING ISSUES OF THE PAPERS

3.1. *The "new" labour demand*

Hibbis (1976), has found a close connection between the evolution of strikes and changes in political power between classes and social groups. In particular, the greater the percentage of ministerial positions in the governments of several countries held by left wing forces which are thought to represent the working class (socialists, labour party, communists), the lower the strike level and in general, the level of industrial conflict. As Mazzocchi shows in his paper, beginning from the 1976-government which sprang from the alliance of the Communist party and the Christian Democrats, Italy registers a decrease in strikes for structural reforms, thus supporting Hibbs' thesis.

From the second half of the 1960s, industrial conflict in Italy was in great measure the result of an unsatisfied political demand for reforms, such as the attack on tax evasion, the demand for social services, the development of the less developed Southern regions (Mezzogiorno), etc. (Tarantelli, 1978). Between the end of 1976 and 1978, the new government allowed the central trade union organization greater possibility to collaborate with the government, with the effect of decreasing official strikes for structural reforms. But, as Mazzocchi shows, the number of spontaneous rank and file-initiated strikes, not due to the demand for structural reforms, does not diminish during the same period with respect to the early 1970s (July 1970 — June 1972).

This illustrates the degree of the difficulty that the central trade union organizations encountered in controlling the actions and obtaining the consensus of the rank and file. In fact, while trade unions, with strikes and demonstrations, asked for and obtained a reform of the social security system, a law protecting rights of workers and unions (*Statuto dei Lavoratori*, 1970) and a new and more complete system of indexation of wages (1975), they almost completely failed to achieve results with regard to problems such as housing and health services, which were an important part of their rank and file demand from the second half of the 1960s onward (see Valli's paper).

This new labour demand, which, to adapt Flanders' famous dictum, "has forced govenment to share control in order to regain it", also applies in the British case. Thomson distinguishes four levels of action into which this labour demand as been organized by the TUC, which has stated policy and institutional objectives of participation at each level: the economy, the sector or industry, the company and the plant. Especially after 1975, the TUC worked towards the establishment of decision making committees with tripartite direction. It sought to introduce committees for forward planning at company and plant level, and for collective bargaining, recognition measures, disclosure of information, time off work for trade union business, redundancy notification and institutional rights to joint regulation in health and job safety under the 1974 act of that name. Moreover, the government proposed union representation in the management of pension funds and employees' share in pension schemes.

The failure of the Bullock Report, and the White Paper of the British government (May 1978: statutory rights to the joint discussion of company strategy as it affects employees) show the importance that union demands had on issues of codetermination at the end of the 1970s. Further, as Thomson again shows, there has been growing union representation in administrative and judicial agencies which collectively set policy across much of the range of employment related issues (conciliation and arbitration, health and safety, equal opportunity race relations commission, etc.). These bodies have inherited a majority of the work of the Department of Employment, which has few policy decision left within its jurisdiction, all of them are tripartite, and all independent of the government.

The new labour demands (including the 35 hour work week and the trade-off between less work and more pay in Britain) have not only involved Britain but also Germany and Italy. For example, Saunders asks whether the egalitarian tendencies with regard to wage differentials can be explained by the fact that the more inegalitarian countries in Europe — Britain, France and Italy — have suffered the most from inflation and industrial conflict, while Germany, with the most egalitarian pay structure, has suffered the least. In the postscript to his article, Saunders comes back to this issue and notes that current strikes (January 1979) occurred among workers in the lower paid sectors. Like Mazzocchi for Italy, Saunders also suggests the need for a radical change in pay bargaining systems and attitudes in Britain, and, particularly, the need for some form of coordination of union pay claims which recognizes the consequences of each pay claim on the overall distribution of pay, prices and, in the case of public services, taxes.

Mazzocchi's paper demonstrates the difficulties of restructuring wage differentials through across-the-board equal (in absolute amount rather than percentage) wage increases and through the Italian escalator clause. The egalitarian policy in Italy seems to have functioned well in closing wage differentials between different sectors and (above all) differentials by skill within any given sector. The latter objective seems to have been reached in Italy. But its effect is to discourage skill incentives in the firm. Trade unions, in particular the Communist CGIL, have recently proposed (but not implemented) measures for the restructuring of wage differentials. This would imply a level of coordination of wage bargaining by central trade unions which, as Thompson shows, does not exist in Britain and has developed in Italy with periods alternating between centralized and plant level bargaining (see Mazzocchi's paper).

The new labour demand, and, in particular, the growing importance of non-wage and non-monetary matters of industrial relations was also underlined by Halbertstadt and Hughes during the discussion in the course of the Colloquium.

Kühl shows that, as a consequence of the labour market slack in the 1970s the German unions started to use the instrument of collective bargaining for employment policy goals, the protection of workers, and the humanization of work. This trend implies, in his view, that in the years to come the 45% yearly growth of labour productivity will be distributed between wages and leisure differently from how it has been in the past. In the 1980s, Kühl argues, in the presence of a growing labour supply, the job component of collective bargaining — i.e. jobcreation and protection of workers, skill and worpklaces — may have priority over wages and income policies. Again according to Kühl, the F.R.C. may approach severe conflict if the recently emphasized attempts to combat unemployment by means of a policy on working hours and a number of measures of job protection fail. In addition, there has been some evidence that the unions and the works councils might change their aims and actions from consensus to conflict-prone policies in order to fulfill the still increasing demands of workers for extensive protection.

Müller-Jentsch stresses the change in the issues at stake in conflicts. In Germany, in the 1960s labour disputes were exclusively wage disputes. In the 1970s, non-wage policy issues have achieved equal importance, at least in the manifest conflicts between capital and labour. As Müller-Jentsch notes, it was during the wave of unofficial strikes in 1973 that demands for improvements in working conditions first played a significant, though not primary, role. After that, qualitative demands also emerged in official strikes in Germany. In these instances, attention was focused on questions concerning the organization of the labour process, the social security of older employees, reclassification in lower wage brackets, and the devaluation of qualifications.

Another important change in Germany was the amendment of the Factory Constitution Act in 1972 and the Co-determination Act of 1976. The former meant that the unions had improved access to the individual plant and an extension of the rights of the works councils to participate in decisions pertaining to personnel and social matters (hiring, dismissing, short-time work, extra shifts, overtime, etc.). The Co-determination Act of 1976, on the other hand, did not grant union representatives full parity of representation but, as is well-known, did increase their number.

Another change in labour demands underlined by Müller Jentsch was the growing dissatisfaction on the part of relevant sections of the work force in large firms with the traditional interest representation system. A significant part of these changes, which also concerned the German hot issue of labour humanization, took place at plant level. It reinforced legislation extending union influence. Müller-Jentsch reports an opinion research institute which ascertained a "growing propensity towards class struggle" in Germany in the 1970s. And he adds, "during this period, there seems to have been an increase in workers'" awareness of their own interests — within the working class as a whole as well as in its various "factions' — as well as an increased willingness to join trade unions". Other signs of a "dynamic consciousness" were ascertained by the Institut für Sozialforschung in 1970. Müller-Jentsch also stresses the appearance, in the same period, of groups of workers who had played, at best, a subordinate role in the earlier strike history in Germany: foreign workers, in the unofficial 1973 strike wave.

3.2. *The limits of the social contract*

Most economists agree that incomes policies are ineffective beyond the short-run and that after the end of an incomes policy, money wages tend to recover the losses which have been registered in the period in which it was in force. Thomson quotes Crouch on this issue:

> "Corporatism appears at a moment when labour has reached such a strength that classic constraints are no longer operating nor are the techniques of compromise ... For the strategy to be pursued effectively, the basis for a reintegration of political, economic and ideological dimensions must also be present in wider structural developments in the society".

In the absence of such a strategy, the British government was forced to alternate periods of union collaboration with periods in which the government was left on its own. Thus, as Thomson notes for the British case, by midsummer 1977 the government was left on its own to pursue a 10 percent guideline, "backed up, not by parliamentary authority or union acceptance, but rather by administratively imposed sanctions on companines which broke the rule by not awarding government contracts and by refusing selective industrial grants".

A further feature of these later stages of incomes policies — which apart from tax reductions on wages and profits in some sectors partly resemble some of the initial measures of the Thatcher government — was the introduction of cash limits on expenditure in the public sector, thus creating a (monetarist) ceiling on pay increases. This attitude of the British government that failure of pay restraint on the part of the unions would force a resort to fiscal and monetary measures to limit inflation is also noticed by Saunders.

The limits of the social contract are underlined by Müller-Jentsch in relation to the German case. The Konzertierte Aktion succeeded in tying union wage policy to increases in productivity and prices only in the second half of the 1960s. On the contrary, in the early 1970s — after the first wave of unofficial strikes in 1969 — the Aktion had already lost its influence over the course of development of both negotiated and actual wages. It was only with mass unemployment, and as Kuehl argues, with the segmentation of unemployment which penalized certain groups of workers (foreigners, women, the unskilled, etc.) and the restrictive economic policies followed by the Federal Bank and the Federal Government, that this trend was reversed.

Mazzocchi also refers to the limits of the social contract in Italy (or, as I would put it for the Italian case, the social "exchange": a social contract with a non-contractable political residual). In substantial agreement with Korpe's analysis (1978), Mazzocchi suggests that the Italian unofficial social contract, which was obtained from 1976 to 1978 through the involvement of the Communist party (and its union, the C.G.I.L.) in the government, cost the Communists 4 per cent of the votes in the June 1979 election. If left wing parties support the government, says Mazzocchi, the strike profile decreases, but the parties then splinter. Several groups (in particular, in Italy the youngest part of the electorate, which gave the Radical Party an increase of 2 per cent — from 1 to 3 per cent — in the 1979 elections) detach themselves from the left when the left is at least in part drawn into the power complex. Left wing parties' (and in Italy, the Communist party's) attempts to regain lost votes may lead (with the end of the "social exchange") to the explosion of new centres of conflict (as could occur in Italy).

Beginning with the outspoken interview granted by the secretary general of the Communist union C.G.I.L., Luciano Lama, to the daily newspaper "La Repubblica" (January 24, 1978) — an interview in which Lama maintained that "wages are no longer to be considered as an independent variable" and which marked the moment of greatest integration of union policy with government policy — Valli analyzes the change in the industrial relations scenario up to the end of the 1970s. During the second half of 1978 and the beginning of 1979, there were increasing symptoms of a new marked change in the trade unions' policy. As Valli argues, this process has probably been accelerated by the discontinuity of the support given by the Communist Party to the government and by the governmental crisis of February 1979.

The growing discontent in the public administration and the consequent recovery of the power of the autonomous unions (i.e. the unions associated with the three main Italian confederations) have added fuel to the fire of industrial conflict in Italy. An example of this discontent was given by the explosion of wildcat strikes in hospitals in autumn 1978. The incapacity of the government to carry out the structural reforms (the attack on fiscal evasion, the inefficiency of public services, the inadequacy of social security, the lack of low-cost housing, etc.) which had been announced in July 1976 (that is immediately after the inclusion of the Communist Party in the government coalition) has been at the root of this.

3.3. *The tension between the rank and file and the trade unions*

The tension between the rank and file and the trade unions is also one of the main aspects or "stylized facts" of the crisis of consensus which I noted at the beginning of this paper and may be seen as one aspect of the "new" labour demand discussed earlier. This issue — a decentralized fragmented industrial relations structure — is central to the Thomson paper. Britain has the strongest semi-independent shop-floor union organization in the world. This, as Thomson points out, is not only a function of rank and file attitudes but also has to do with union structure and organization. The tension between union leadership and the rank and file, between the formal and the informal system of industrial relations, is a constant in Britain as in Italy (and, at times, in Germany) from the end of the 1960s to the present.

As Thomson argues, even in early 1979, it was obvious that the 1978 pay policy had been effectively destroyed and that the country was heading rapidly towards a wage explosion. The TUC was itself concerned by the sequence of events whereby unions were being overruled by the shop floor and many groups were openly flouting union advice on issues such as the permissible limits of picketing. These facts can be seen as a continuation of tensions in the relationship between union management and the rank and file which, prior to the pay policy of 1978, had through many union conferences given their leadership a mandate not to accept a further phase of formal incomes policy.

Similar lines of analysis can be found in the postscript to Saunders' paper, with a special emphasis on pay differentials. As Saunders points out, the January 1979 strikes came from workers in lower paid sectors, even though, as Thomson notes, they were also the result of the inter-union rivalry between unskilled workers — e.g. the TGWU car workers' motto "Second to None" — and the skilled groups. Even more recently in England, the union leadership has faced strong pressures from below to reject any cooperation with government-supported restrain. In addition, as Saunders points out, another dilemma appears for the unions: while in favour of raising relatively low pay, they are also anxious for the restoration of differentials for skill. Can these objectives really coexist? Saunders asks. Not only do different unions take different views on the priorities, but the opposing objectives conflict within many British unions.

Questions of this kind are discussed by Mazzocchi in reference to the Italian case. Across the board, equal (in absolute amount rather than percentage) pay increases have greatly reduced wage differentials in Italy. Mazzocchi notes that this reduction causes tension not only between non-manual and manual but also among manual workers (both skilled and unskilled).

As Valli points out, the tensions between trade unions and the rank and file have characterized the Italian industrial relations system throughout the 1970s, although in an admittedly discontinuous fashion. So, since 1970, there was a growing tendency to decentralize the unions' structure through the institution of the so-called "consigli di fabbrica", composed of plant level representatives directly elected by each group of workers, which replaced the preceding union-controlled plant level structures ("commissioni interne"). The unions eventually regained control in the course of the 1970s.

Tensions between the rank and file and the unions continue. For example, the less favourable indexation of wages (compared with the private sector) led in 1978 to a growing discontent in the public administration in Italy, and thus to a recovery of the power of autonomous unions and to the explosion of wildcat strikes. (The indexation problem has only recently been solved). During the contract renewals signed in July 1979, the losses of the Italian Communist party at the elections caused a desire for a comeback in a number of plants, above all in several branches of the metal-workers' sector and on the part of the more militant and combative groups of leftist workers.

As said above, there have also been tensions between rank and file and union management in the German case. Müller-Jentsch points out that there were changes in works' councils elections in recent years. In 1975 and 1978, opposition groups, mostly of the left, put up candidates in several large steel, metalworking and chemical firms against the candidates of the official trade union list, with surprising sucesses — sometimes up to 40 per cent of the votes. Again the return to the acceptance of the incomes policy guidelines in 1972-73 (after the phase of active, sometimes militant wage policy in 1970-71) had as a consequence a new wave of wildcat strikes for cost of living increases accompanied by sharp criticism of the unions.

However, as both Kühl and Müller-Jentsch point ont, militancy on the part of both unions and the rank and file declined substan-tially with the "phase of mass unemployment" in the autumn of 1974. Apart form the printers' strike in 1976, there were no major strikes in Germany for higher wages until the spring of 1978.

3.4. Bargaining fragmentation and centralization

During the period immediately after World War II, the structure of collective bargaining in Italy was very centralized. Due to the high level of unemployment and the trade unions' fear of its increasing, the unions tended to fix wage contracts on the basis of marginal firms' capacity to pay. As Mazzocchi points out, large companies were the beneficiaries of this situation. They used wage policy not only to maintain a high measure of control over their costs but also to maximize labour docility, minimize strikes and even to exert a considerable control over the development of the labour movement and to divide workers from trade union leadership.

This is the principal reason why from the mid-fifties onward, the CISL (the trade union of Christian socialist ideology with a majority of Christian Democrats), against the initial opposition of the Communist CGIL, began to favour a decentralized bargaining structure (which it "imported", together with the Keynesian model from the United States) which gives greater space both to sectoral and to plant level bargaining. Decentralized bargaining started in the Italian industrial sector at the end of the 1950s.

But, since the end of the 1950s, the new structure of collective bargaining centralized at the sectorial level but decentralized at the plant level has caused a sharp increase in wage differentials. This was largely the result of the fact that Italy's dual economy is characterized by a mix of industrial firms that are extremely differentiated regarding their technology, productivity and capacity to pay. The increase in wage differentials during the 1960s is, according to Mazzocchi, one of the main causes of the egalitarian philosophy adopted by the Italian unions at the beginning of the 1970s. As Mazzocchi shows, this philosopy, with its above mentioned across the board equal wage increases, has led to an excessive reduction of the skill differentials internal to many industrial firms, while at the same time there have remained excessive "unfair" differentials especially in the public sector. The relative dose of centralization and fragmentation of the bargaining structure necessary to bring some order into this state of affairs is at the present time the central issue of collective bargaining in Italy.

For the British case, Saunders notes that an essential feature of top-level bargaining is that the TUC should be in a position to obtain commitment from the constituent unions and the lower levels of pay bargaining. This means, he adds, a greater central union authority than has so far been achieved and, as he admits, is one of the most difficult objectives to achieve. He sees the decentralized structure of pay bargaining as a major factor in strengthening the inflationary momentum.

According to Thomson, the issue of a decentralized and fragmented industrial relations structure has been the major cause of governmental attempts to control the output of the industrial relations system by law, incomes policy and voluntary reorganization. But, he adds, the demands from the shop floor on the State and the economic system have proved impossible to satisfy and, to date, the resultant conflict has not been adequately institutionalized. The issue is therefore, as in Italy, at least as much political, behavioural and organizational as economic.

Müller-Jentsch's account of the German case has some striking points in common with the above mentioned Italian account by Mazzocchi. While the concept of a "central bargain" is contrary to British practice and principle, both in Germany and in Italy, union wage policy was characterized in the 1950s by strongly centralizing trends. Unlike Italy, these trends continued in Germany in the 1960s. But after the September 1969 strikes, criticism within the unions of their centralized wage policy met with wider response in Germany. As Müller-Jentsch points out, some trade unions saw themselves forced towards a more militant wage policy and a return to regional bargaining policy.
The regionalization of bargaining policy gave militant, progressive districts more room to manoevre in implementing their own wage bargaining ideas. Union bargaining policy became a "see-saw policy".

3.5. *The segmentation of the unemployed*

The problem of the segmentation of the unemployed, an important connecting issue of the papers presented at the Colloquium, is at the centre of Kühl's analysis. He shows that the resistance to increases in unemployment that led to massive political action of workers and unions in the 1970s also led to a segmentation of the unemployed into a number of hard to employ and low status groups who had little power to enforce their interests. The increase of immigrants', women's and unskilled workers' share of the unemployed as caused by the cyclical decrease in the demand for labour. But cyclical unemployment can clearly become structural unemployment if it involves successive generations of new or young labour force entrants.

Restrictive economic policies and decreases in the demand for labour are not the only causes of segmentation. In Italy, new young entrants' exclusion from employment (prevalently young entrants with high school and university degrees) has been the result of a sizeable reduction in the turnover rate. This reduction came from the blocking of dismissals imposed by unions to protect already employed workers (beginning from the *Statuto dei Lavoratori* in 1970) to the blocking of hires decided by firms as a market "vendetta". With reference to the German case, Müller-Jentsch suggests that although rationalization methods were showing their negative employment effects from the beginning of the 1970s, it has only been recently that the unions have seen themselves compelled to act defensively, when the rationalization pressure began to hit union core groups.

The central characteristic which has distinguished the German from the British system and, even more, from the Italian system regarding these problems, has been the extension and efficiency of the social security network. As Kühl affirms, in Germany from 70 to 90 per cent of the unemployed received unemployment insurance benefits. Müller-Jentsch argues that, as long as the system of social security (including unemployment compensation, compensation for short-time work, early retirement, retraining programs) works to counteract the negative social consequences of the crisis and the consequent rationalization, those directly affected are not compelled to seek radical solutions for their problem.

As Thomson shows, in Britain as well much of the legislation of the decade, which has been strongly influenced by the unions, has been oriented to creating greater jobs security and moving towards property right on the job. Both Thomson and Saunders offer data on special labour market and employment policy measures taken in Britain.

In Italy, the problem of labour market segmentation has not involved the unemployed, as in Germany and, in lesser measure, in Britain, as much as it has the employed, given the division between workers employed in the "official" and those in the "unofficial" sectors of the Italian "dual economy".

There have been measures to segment the unemployed also in Italy. For instance, as Mazzocchi points out, the *Cassa Integrazione Guadagni* has (at sizeable cost) guaranteed their wages to laid-off workers kept inactive on the job in those cases where dismissals would have provoked massive reactions on the part of workers and unions.

But the social security network in Italy is too inadequate to allow a fine tuning manoevre such as that analyzed by Kühl for the

German case. The result or the absence of an adeguate social security system in Italy has been the opposition of the rank and file and the union to dismissals of *any* kind. Firms have replied with an equally drastic reduction of hires. The Italian economic system has thus increasingly come to resemble what I have elsewhere called a "Pompean economy" (Tarantelli, 1978), that is, an economy with workers who are embedded like the dead in Pompei, fixed in factories that don't produce, don't hire and don't fire. The turnover rate (flow of hires and dismissals) has diminished considerably since 1969 and especially after the crisis of 1973 (from more than 35 to less than 15 per cent of industrial employment).

Valli suggests that the increase in labour market segmentation in Italy has been the result of the larger recourse of enterprises to "black labour" and other forms of precarious and unofficial labour. The increase in the share of what has come to be called in Italy the subterranean economy (*economia sommersa*) (piece work at home, subcontractiong, part-time, unregistered work in small establishments, etc.) has allowed firms to limit increases in labour costs, to evade taxes and to react against the increased rigidity in the use of the labour force at plant level and to resistances against dismissals, thus limiting trade union power.

The submerged economy, non-unionized, untaxed, has sustained productivity, employment and the competitiveness of the Italian economy and has confined ever larger shares of women and of youths with high school or university degrees to the less protected segments of the labour market or to unemployment.

As Hughes asserted several times in the course of the discussion, the increase in the unemployment rate in all three countries can be seen as a safety valve (all the safer where, as Kühl shows for Germany, the social security network functions adequately) in an international system which has reabsorbed industrial conflict, transforming itself into a "Kaleckian semi-slump economy".[3] Indeed it

---

[3] As is wellknown, the Polish economist Michael Kalecki, in an article written during the war, predicted a political trade cycle in the new Keynesian economy. In his view, the new Keynesian government would make a full employment policy by means of a budget deficit. But full employment makes the bargaining position of workers strong. "In this situation a powerful block is likely to be formed between big business and rentier interests, and they would probably find more than one economist to declare that the situation was manifestly unsound" (Kalecki, 1943). Thus, "sound finance" will restore unemployment again until the next election when the government returns to the vote-getting policy of full employment. This is the "semi-slump Kaleckian economy".

could be said that industrial conflict was "reabsorbed" — even more than "managed" — in the 1970s through the semislump Kaleckian economy which characterized all European countries — with the exception of countries characterized by a higher degree of consensus such as Austria, Sweden and Norway — beginning from the oil crisis of 1974.

When my colleagues at the E.U.I. kindly asked me to suggest a subject for this Colloquium, I gave both the topic and the title of this book. Actually, the title which I had initially suggested substituted the term "reabsorption" (from the Italian *riassorbimento*) for the term management. Since I was unable to come up with a translation of my Italian term which was more adequate than the literal one, the term management was used in the title. But today as I finish writing this introduction, I am more convinced that (aside from the linguistic problem) the word "reabsorption" through unemployment describes the facts of industrial conflict as they evolved in the 1970s more than the by now traditional, and largely obsolete, industrial relations paradigm — developed in the early 1960s of the élites' "management" through consensus (Kerr et al., 1960; Ross and Hartmann, 1960).

4. THE NON-CONNECTING ISSUES OF THE PAPERS, OTHER LIMITS OF THIS RESEARCH AND THE FAILURES OF THE DOMINANT THEORIES

In concluding this section, I wish to underline that the "connecting issues" of the papers included in this volume, which I have isolated in the preceding section, should not give the illusion of a high degree of harmony on the topics dealt with by the various participants. This would not be a reasonable expectation in a Colloquium of this nature which attempts to compare both industrial relations and labour market problems in three widely different institutional contexts and during the deepest crisis since the Great Depression.

Indeed, there was wide disagreement even between the two editors of this book on the interpretation of the papers which follow and even in the way the findings should be presented. Rather than attempting to come out with a false agreement between us and at the cost of some repetitions, this Introduction and the last

chapter on the Concluding Discussion were therefore conceived as
two completely separate and independent pieces with no cross responsibility.

In addition, several problems were dealt with by only one or a
few of the participants of the Colloquium.[4] Other important issues
are simply not discussed at all (i.e. employers' attitudes and reactions
to conflict at plant and national level; how the State's strategy
develops in the 1970s from an overall response towards a selective
and policy making strategy; the growth and changes in labour
legislation: codetermination, works councils *delegati*, shop stewards;
how the Industrial Relations Act failed, etc.).

While, finally, the attentive reader may find numerous, and illu-
minating points of contact between the connecting issues mentioned
in the preceding section and the main aspects of the crisis of the
1970s — the "stylized facts" mentioned in the Overview of this
Introduction — an analogous search among the central themes of the
papers presented here and the explanatory capabilities of the dominant theories will, in my view, prove illusive. Let me give, in
closing, a few brief examples. The monetarist hypothesis (Zis, 1976),
which is the only truly economic paradigm among the dominant
theories,[5] locates the cause of the industrial (but not of the socio-
political) conflict in events which occured *after* it happened. The
sizeable deficits in the American balance of payments occur, in the
early 1970s, *after* the wage freeze in England (1966), the French
May of 1968, the Italian hot Autumn in 1969, the Swedish strikes
(excluding the borderguards!) in 1970, the Japanese strikes and those
in other Western countries in the same period.

Bacon and Eltis' "too few producers'" hypothesis (1976) may
be plausible for Britain, perhaps for Sweden where fiscal pressure has
reached 65 per cent of national income, and (as the authors are never
tired of repeating!) for one city: New York. It does not hold, for
example, for the other two national cases discussed in this volume,
Germany and Italy, where recent empirical evidence has largely
discredited it (Castellucci).

---

[4] Only Müller-Jentsch, for example, discusses at some length "shop floor issues",
such as rationalization measures and work organization, the "manning rules" for jobs
using new technology and the IG Druck und Papier workers' resistance to these
rationalization measures.
[5] In fact, both Eltis' and Bacon's model (1976) and the well-known "Scandinavian model" (Okhrust, 1970) may be seen as variations of the monetarist model.

The so-called recession hypothesis of Soskice (in Crouch and Pizzorno, 1978), can explain the contemporaneity of industrial conflict in at most four countries (Germany, Italy, France and Britain) but not in the others mentioned at the beginning of this Introduction. The hypothesis is thus incomplete: it does not explain why the crisis took place in all other industrialized countries. Further, three of the four countries to which the hypothesis is supposed to apply (Italy, France and Britain) were no closer to full employment at the end of the 1960s than in many previous, and by far less conflictual, periods in their post-war history. Yet, "full employment" is supposed to be the detonator of industrial conflict in the recession hypothesis, after the "frustrations" of the workers in the "recession" (and the consequent incomes policies and lower real wage increases) of the second half of the 1960s.

As for the hypothesis of a Kondratieff cycle in the 1970s (Forrester, 1976), the empirical evidence is, with the exception of a few sectors with very advanced techonology, almost as shaky as the underlying theory.

There are in addition a large number of "national" theories which completely neglect the problem of explaining the first of the stylized facts of the Overview to this Introduction: the reason for the *contemporaneity* of the industrial (and socio-political) conflict in Western countries beginning in the second half of the 1960s. Each of these theories explains the conflict as a "national case", relative to the country under consideration. The reasons for the contemporaneous nature of the conflict are not even considered. These theories (of which the recession, and even more, the too few producers hypothesis constitute an example) are reminiscent of the ancestral practice of a great number of territorially proximate tribes, who in times of drought — or epidemic — which caused famines extending over vast geographical areas, attributed the meagreness of their respective harvests each to a different god.

5. IN LIEU OF A CONCLUSION

The entire literature on human resource development since the early 1960s has taught us that "education" is an asset in itself without counter-indications for anyone (Harbison, 1973). The more "human capital" the better. But, in my view, you cannot ask a worker to be both more educated and less imaginative about his role in the technical division of labour vis-à-vis his fellow workers, both more informed and more servile in the social division of labour vis-à-vis his employer, both more politicized and more accepting of the present division of power in society. The Keynesian era has brought about a rapid accumulation of physical capital but an even more rapid (as Schultz first noticed in 1961) accumulation of "human capital" through schooling, mass media, and second and third generation urbanization and immigration.[6] This difference in speed between the two, in the face of even more automated and dehumanized technical division of labour (Brauerman, 1974), produces conflict. Conflict, in turn — as in a "ratchet-effect" — is likely to raise the technical, social and political division of labour to the plateau on which the ever new worker has been capable of articulating his demand and organizing his strengths. This, as we have seen again in the 1970s, is no easy task. Thus, capitalism is condemned to grow painfully carrying its cross of inequality. The papers in this volume, I believe, add to rather than subtract from this view.

[6] Space precludes the development of these ideas (see Tarantelli). For an extended version of this hypothesis — which grew out of my fall term course on Comparative Systems of Industrial Relations at MIT — see also my "The Generational Leap Hypothesis and the Management of Industrial Conflict in the 1970s", Sloan School, MIT, 1980. These are also the two main sources for "Tarantelli's model" to which some of the participants in the Colloquium kindly refer. According to my "generational leap hypothesis", the contemporary nature of industrial conflict is the result of a conflict between the inherited technical organization of labour in firms — hierarchies, status, wage and normative differentials — and the new rank and file demands of the postwar and, more generally, post-Great Depression generations. Both of these generations participate, respectively, as a hole or in part, in the unprecedented growth of education, diffusion of mass media, increase of urbanization and immigration (above all, second or third generation) which follow the Great Depression and especially the post-war period. The "new" labour demand to which I referred in section 3.1, is founded on this growth and the consequent change in the organic composition of the work force. The crisis of the social organization of labour — the relationship between workers and entrepreneurs — is, in turn, the result of the crisis of the technical organization of labour.

BIBLIOGRAPHY

R. Bacon and W. Eltis (1976): *Britan's Economic Problem: Too Few Producers*, London, Macmillan 1976.

H. Braverman: *Labor and Monopoly Capital*, Monthly Review Press, New York, 1974.

G. Carli, E. Tarantelli (1979): "The Recycling of Opec Surplus Funds: A Proposal", in: *Banca Nazionale del Lavoro Quarterly Review*, 1979.

L. Castellucci: *The Growth of the Non-market Sector in Britain and Italy: a Comparison* (forthcoming).

C. Crouch and A. Pizzorno (1978): *Conflict in Europe*, London, Macmillan 1978 (see article by Soskice).

J. W. Forrester (1976): "Business Structure, Economic Cycles, and National Policy", *Futures*, June 1976.

J. Goldthorpe et al. (1978): *The Political Economy of Conflict*, Cambridge University Press 1978.

F. H. Harbison: *Human Resources as the Wealth of Nations*, New York, Oxford University Press 1973.

F. Hayek (1976): *Choice in Currency: A Way to Stop Inflation*, Institute of Economic Affairs 1976.

D. Hibbs (1976): *Long Trends in Strike Activity in Comparative Prospective*, Cambridge, Mass., Center for International Studies, MIT 1976.

L. Izzo and L. Spaventa (1979): "Macroeconomic Policies in Western European Countries: 1973-77", Paper prepared for a conference on "Macroeconomic Policies for Growth and Stability. The European Perspective", Kiel, June 20-23, 1979 (forthcoming in *Weltwirtschaftliches Archiv*).

M. Kalecki, "Political Aspects of Full Employment" (1943), in: *Selected Essays on the Dynamics of the Capitalist Economy*, London, Cambridge University Press 1971.

C. Kerr et al. (1960): *Industrialism and Industrial Man: The Problem of Labor and Management in Economic Growth*, Cambridge, Harvard University Press 1960.

W. Korpe: *The Working Class in Welfare Capitalism: Union, Work and Politics in Sweden*, London, 1978.

J. O'Connor (1973): *The Fiscal Crisis of the State*, New York, St. Martin Press 1973.

O. F. Okhrust (1970): *A Model of the Price — and Income Distribution Mechanism in an open economy*, 1970.

A. M. Ross and P. T. Hartmann (1960): *Changing Patterns of Industrial Conflict*, New York, John Wiley and Sons, 1960.

T. Schultz: "Investment in Human Capital", in: *The American Economic Review*, March 1961.

E. Tarantelli: *Il ruolo economico del sindacato e il caso italiano*, Bari, Laterza 1978.

G. Zis (1976): "Inflation: an International Monetary Problem or a National Social Phenomenon?", in: *Inflation in Open Economies*, ed. M. Parkin and G .Zis, Manchester University Press 1976.

Chapter I

THE BRITISH CASE

INDUSTRIAL RELATIONS IN BRITAIN DURING THE PERIOD OF THE RECESSION, 1974-1978

by

ANDREW W. J. THOMSON

1. INTRODUCTION

The current world recession must be seen in Britain as the latest and deepest of a series of cycles since World War II, rather than as a major break with past economic performance, as may be true of some countries. The recession has undoubtedly been severe in Britain, yet because the British post-war economic performance has been one of short "stop-go" cycles, recessions have to a considerable extent been discounted in industrial relations and labour market behaviour. Moreover, the concept of a recession must be qualified in at least three ways: first, the period has also contained the highest rates of inflation in modern British history; second, the term recession carries temporary connotations, whereas in Britain the present unemployment level is seen as having much longer-term structural implications; and third, the social and employment issues of the recession have tended to be overshadowed in industrial relations terms by the continuing debate on the role of the trade unions in society.

The hypothesis of this paper is fairly simple; it is that pay quetions, not unemployment, are the key issues of the period, that attempts have been made to persuade the unions to act as agents of social control by participating in incomes policies, that unions have gained greatly in influence as a quid pro quo for these attempts, that the success of the policies has been limited because the unions themselves are limited in the extent to which they can control their members. While the unions have certainly been keenly aware of the employment dimension, their members have preferred to concentrate on pay. However, this paper will concentrate on the institutional and behavioural aspects of these developments rather than on the detailed statistical trends in pay covered at greater length in the companion paper by Saunders.

Tables 1-3 provide a set of background indices for the paper. As can readily be seen from Table 1, output indicators show little growth during the decade to date, for although there was a short-lived boom in 1973, the two succeeding years were sharply recessionary, and little forward momentum has been achieved since then. Indeed on the labour market front unemployment has continued to rise, although the normal inverse correlate of vacancies has begun to recover and there are in fact substantial labour shortages in key sectors of the economy. However, the most striking aspects of the table are the inflationary indicators of prices, costs and earnings, which have advanced at a historically unparalleled rate for Britain, and for a brief period 1974-75 looked capable of reaching South American rates of increase. There followed three years of stabilization during which inflation was reduced to single figures, but a resumption of wage inflation from the last quarter of 1978 will lead to another increase in the rate of inflation.

Table 2 shows the rate of growth of trade union membership over the last decade. After little or no growth for twenty years, union membership rose from the late 1960s and now covers over 50 per cent of the labour force. Recent gains have largely been amongst females and white-collar workers; two other points worthy of note are that the public sector is twice as densely unionized as the private sector and that there has been an increasing concentration of membership into the larger unions, with the 25 largest unions accounting for 79.5 per cent of total union membership. Table 3 illustrates the recent growth in time lost through industrial conflict, even though the numbers of stoppages and the number of workers involved have remained much the same as during the 1960s. The reason for this has been that after a decade during which strikes were predominantly unofficial, short-ived and small-scale, the 1970s have seen a resumption of official industry-wide strikes which have lasted considerably longer on average. The range of employees engaging in industrial action has also widened, especially into various hitherto non-militant groups in the public sector, but the major cause of stoppages still remains overwhelmingly pay issues.

Table 1: ECONOMIC INDICATORS 1970-77

	1970	1971	1972	1973	1974	1975	1976	1977
A. *Macro-economic*								
Retail Price Level Annual Percentage Increase	6.4	9.4	7.1	9.2	16.1	24.2	16.5	15.8
Industrial Production (1975 = 100)	99.7	99.8	102.0	109.5	105.1	100.0	102.0	105.8
GDP at factor cost based on Expenditure data (1975 = 100)	92.2	94.4	95.7	103.4	101.7	100.0	103.6	105.0
Investment £m (1975 prices)	19845	20209	20240	21609	21164	20817	20489	19738
Real Personal Disposable Income (1975 = 100)	84.9	87.4	94.2	100.0	100.7	100.0	99.7	98.3
Balance of Payments, Current Balance £m	+ 731	+ 1090	+ 135	—999	—1855	—1137	+ 289	—1137
Sterling Effective Exchange Rate (Dec. 1971 = 100)	—	—	95.2	86.3	83.6	77.2	65.4	62.1
B. *Labour Market*								
Unemployment '000's (excluding school leavers)	602	776	855	611	599	929	1270	1378
Unemployment %	2.6	3.4	3.7	2.6	2.6	3.9	5.3	5.8
Vacancies '000's at July	295	193	208	453	323	135	120	15.3
Average Hours. All Industries - manual men - April	—	46.1	46.0	46.7	46.5	45.5	45.3	45.7
Shorttime working '000's at April	51	91	82	24	35	239	114	46
Average Earnings (January 1970 = 100)	106.7	118.7	134.0	152.1	179.1	226.6	261.9	288.5
Average Earnings Annual Percentage Increase	12.1	11.3	12.9	13.5	17.8	26.5	15.6	10.2
Labour Costs per unit of Output (1975 = 100)	48.6	53.2	57.9	62.1	76.7	100.0	111.3	120.4

Sources: Central Statistical Office Economic Trends. Department of Employment Gazette.

The period 1974-78 fits neatly into both a political and an incomes policy cycle as well as an economic one. The first two months of 1974 saw a major challenge to the incomes policy of the then Conservative Government, the fighting of a General Election on the slogan "Who Rules the Country?" and the inauguration of a Labour Government. At the time of writing, doom-laden parallels are being drawn between that period and the present, with the unions challenging the incomes policy of a government in the last year of its life amid fears of the same type of confrontation with the union movement which characterized early 1974. We therefore begin with a brief examination of the situation at that time.

The period from 1968 onwards saw a series of challenges by the unions to the government, initially to the Labour Government up to the 1970 election, and particularly its plans for labour law reform

Table 2: TRADE UNION MEMBERSHIP 1966-1977 (at year end

Year	Number of Unions	Membership'000's		Total	Percentage change since previous year
		Males	Females		
1966	622	8,003	2,256	10,259	— 0.6
1967	604	7,903	2,286	10,188	— 0.7
1968	583	7,829	2,362	10,191	—
1969	562	7,965	2,505	10,470	+ 2.7
1970	540	8,437	2,741	11,178	+ 6.8
1971	522	8,374	2,752	11,126	— 0.5
1972	504	8,445	2,905	11,351	+ 2.0
1973	515	8,443	3,005	11,447	+ 0.8
1974	501	8,579	3,176	11,755	+ 2.7
1975	492	8,721	3,462	12,184	+ 3.6
1976	462	8,816	3,560	12,376	+ 3.0
1977	480	8,953	3,753	12,707	+ 2.6

Source: Department of Employment Gazette, January 1979.

encapsulated in the White Paper "In Place of Strife", (1969)[1] but between 1970-74 to the Conservative Government.

The Conservatives in the "Downing Street Talks" of July 1972 attempted a precursor of the 1974 Labour Government's "Social Contract" by trying to draw the Trades Union Congress into limited joint regulation of macroeconomic policy in exchange for acquiescence in a voluntary pay policy. These talks failed, and the prelude to the commencement of our period was the Conservatives impose a statutory incomes policy from November 1972, which in its later stages was index-linked. This was deeply resented by the unions and a motion to take industrial action against the policy received considerable support at the 1973 Trade Union Congress (TUC). Moreover, the Conservatives were already highly unpopular with the unions as a result of the Industrial Relations Act of 1971. This had already

Table 3: INDUSTRIAL DISPUTE STATISTICS 1960-1978

Year	Number of Stoppages	Number of Workers Involved '000's	Days Lost '000's
1960-64 (av)	2,552	1,499	3,180
1965-69 (av)	2,380	1,215	3,929
1970	3,906	1,801	10,980
1971	2,228	1,178	13,551
1972	2,497	1,734	23,909
1973	2,873	1,528	7,197
1974	2,922	1,626	14,750
1975	2,282	809	6,012
1976	2,016	668	3,284
1977	2,703	1,166	10,142
1978	2,349	979	9,306

Source: Department of Employment Gazette, January 1979.

[1] The story of the Government's proposals is evocatively and amusingly told in Jenkins (1970).

produced several confrontations between the unions and the law, notably in a widespread sympathy strike after five shop stewards were imprisoned for not obeying an injunction under the legislation[2]. A third component of the internal situation under the Conservatives was the very considerable expansion of money supply in 1973 in order to achieve growth, most of which went into property and the banking system rather than industrial investment and which inevitably ran counter to the restrictive policies being pursued on the wage front. In all three respects the scene was therefore set for further clashes between the unions and the Government. Government's hope of a dash for growth was then crushed by the massive oil price rises of late 1973, which was the key factor precipitating the present recession.

The clash between unions and Government came with the miners' strike of early 1974, after a build-up in the last part of 1973. The country was put on a 'three-day week' in order to conserve coal stocks and ration electricity. The strike was a direct challenge to the incomes policy then standing at 7 per cent, and in spite of referring the matter to the Pay Board, the Government felt that the challenge was a sufficient threat to is auhority to justify calling an election. This it lost in spite of obtaining more votes than any other party, and the Labour Party came in with a minority government to face a very difficult industrial relations and economic situation.

Its immediate response was to seek to activate the Social Contract which had been negotiated in the TUC-Labour Party Liaison Committee during 1972-3. The Liaison Committee was itself a recently-formed body with the objective of bringing the unions and the party closer together, and it rapidly assumed a major role in policy-making. The incoming government raised pensions, froze rents, changed the structure of income tax and provided food subsidies in its first budget and immediately prepared a Bill to repeal the Industrial Relations Act. This was rapidly passed although some reversals on detailed points occurred in Parliament. In October, however, the Government sought and obtained an overall majority in Parliament in another General Election. Thereafter, the economic problems which had been threatening became immediate and pressing. The company sector developed massive liquidity problems,

---

[2] For a review of the Act see Thomson and Engleman (1975).

a weak currency and rapidly rising import costs produced a disastrous balance of payments situation, and a pay-explosion followed the end of the formal incomes policy as various groups sought to reclaim what they saw as lost wages. The Government too was now climbing rapidly and from this point onwards the Social Contract had to take second place to the battle for economic viability. After this very brief synopsis of recent events in Britain, we now turn to a rather more detailed examination of the industrial relations issues of the period, first in respect of pay, second in respect of specific reactions, or lack of them, to the recession, and third in respect of legal and structural aspects which are discussed within the context of a move to corporatism.

2. THE INDUSTRIAL RELATIONS OF PAY

"Hardly anywhere else in the world is pay a political issue in the way it is in England. To be sure, collective bargaining and its offspring, inflation, are problems known in other lands, and Frenchmen and Germans are as interested in their bellies, and even in their pay packets, as your average Englishman. But pay — who gets what compared with whom — does not dominate political debate or even conversations in pubs, to the degree that it does with us. The British fixation with pay, the English vice, derives in large part from problems which are exceptional in their degree, if not in kind. Remuneration is determined by a system which is at the same time powerful and unfair; its proceeds are legitimised neither by the arbitrariness of market forces nor the rationality of political institutions but rather results from the competitive activities of a multitude of bargaining agencies; and because it is competitive in spirit, anarchic in procedure and unacceptable in its result what we laughingly call 'free collective bargaining' packs an exceptionally inflationary punch".

(*The Guardian*, 20 October, 1978)

The above comment is representative of a good deal of editorial agonizing as the present incomes policy cycle appears close to its end. It also reflects the sense of disillusion, sometimes close to despair, with which the subject is viewed. Britain has had an almost continuous series of more or less formal incomes policies with short intervals characterized by wage explosions. In trying to contain 'free collective bargaining' almost none has come close to the goals set out for it, as Table 4 indicates, and the 1974-78 cycle is no exception.

We have noted that the Conservative Pay Policy of 1972-74 was greatly resented by the trade unions and that challenge to the policy by the miners' union precipitated a General Election and the return of a Labour Government faced by very considerable economic problems on a number of fronts. On the pay front the Conservative policy could not be overturned until legislation was passed and until this happened the TUC accepted the existing policy. Threshold-awards involving automatic wage increases triggered by price increases did something to sweeten the policy, although prices did nevertheless rise faster than wages during this phase of incomes policy. The Government was in a difficult position; it had effectively abdicated responsability for any policy on pay to the TUC under the Social Contract and it therefore had to leave any action to the TUC once Conservative policy had expired in midsummer. The TUC in fact issued a statement, "Collective Bargaining and the Social Contract", in June 1974, in which it argued that there was little scope for increasing personal consumption overall but that living standards should be maintained; a scheme of eight negotiating recommendations to this effect was presented to the unions.

The outcome of these recommendations was, however, average increases of some 30%; this, as the TUC made clear in its 1975 statement, "The Development of the Social Contract", "was a general levels of settlements significantly above the guidelines endorsed by Congress" [2]. It also recognised that wages were contributing significantly to price inflation, by now running at over 20 per cent or at least twice that of other industrial countries. Why then had wages shot up ahead of prices and in apparent disregard of other economic forces? The TUC's anwer was as follows:

> "Following the restoration of voluntary collective bargaining a number of increases recognised as special cases were made in the public sector to deal with longstanding injustices and manpower difficulties stemming from statutory controls. These included spe-

[3] p. 15.

cial reviews of nurses' and teachers' pay; postmen and transport workers also received special increases ... Later in 1974 long-overdue improvements in the region of 30 per cent were made in the pay of local authority manual workers and NHS ancillaries to bring minimum rates into line with the TUC's low pay target of 30 pounds. However, these increases were used as a basis for comparability increases in other parts of the public sector beyond the low pay target level; and the miners' settlement of over 30 per cent of 1975 had repercussions in electricity supply and elsewhere" [4].

Here we have a number of reasons concerned largely with catch-up increases in the public sector (although similar things happened in the private sector to a much lesser extent) and the use of comparability either to maintain wage relativities, whether the initial advance comes from weakness (e.g. low pay groups) or strength (e. g. the miners). The public sector is not, of course, subject to market pressures in the same way as the private sector, and a we shall reflect later one of the notable features of the recent past has been the growth of public sector militancy.

By mid-1975 the Government was still assuming the TUC to be responsible for pay and had taken no action of its own. At this point, therefore, the TUC stepped into the policy vacuum and suggested an incomes policy of a flat rate increase of six pounds per week for adults up to a cut-off point where the high paid would get nothing. Its arguments for this amount, which was equivalent to some 10 percent, were those of simplicity and benefits for the low paid [5]; the policy was duly accepted by the September Congress by 6.9 million votes to 3.4 m. More important, however, was the symbolic precedent of a trade union movement voluntarily and unilaterally imposing an incomes policy. Indeed, the White Paper announcing the policy formally included the TUC statement as an appendix [6]. In many respects this must represent the high water mark of influence on a major issue of economic policy of any union movement in the world. *The Economist*, no friend of the unions, commented: "Perhaps power corrupts, but the power the TUC has enjoyed in the last

[4] TUC (1975), p. 12-13.
[5] The low-paid as a group did not, in fact, gain, mainly because by no means everybody received the six pounds. See Dean (1978) p. 44.
[6] Cmnd 6151 (1975).

18 months has educated and moderated more than it has corrupted" [7].

As Table 4 indicates, the policy worked to the extent that the rate of increase in earnings was halved during the period up to mid-1976. The setting-up of the 1976-77 policy involved a bargaining exercise between the Government and the TUC in which the Government offered tax reliefs in return for wage restraint and the TUC negotiated upwards from three to five per cent the permissible wage increase for the tax concessions. Nevertheless, there was agreement between the two sides, although the TUC did warn the Government that it wanted a return to free bargaining the following year. This round was quite exceptionally successful in persuading employees to accept a considerable cut in their standard of living of about 4 per cent. The tax concessions and other benefits could not come close to compensating a situation where inflation, largely engendered by the drastic fall in the value of the pound by some 35 per cent in late 1976, was running at twice the rate of earnings increases. It was thus probably inevitable that with falling living standards there should be considerable unrest within the union movement, and by midsummer 1977 many union conferences had mandated their leaderships not to accept a further phase of formal incomes policy. This was carried overwhelmingly but the Congress did agree to continue to accept the 'twelve-month' rule, an important part of the pay strategy since 1975 which involved a year's gap between pay claims. The Government was left on its own to pursue a 10 per cent guideline, backed up not by parliamentary authority or union acceptance, but rather by administratively imposed sanctions on companies which broke the rule, by not awarding government contracts and by refusing selective industrial grants. A further feature of these later stages of incomes policy has been the introduction of cash limits on expenditure in the public sector, thus creating an effective ceiling on pay increases. The 1977-78 round was, in spite of the lack of union endorsement, reasonably successful, keeping earnings increases to 14.2 per cent; these were surprisingly few challenges to the policy, and the most serious, that of the firemen, was not directly backed by the TUC. Productivity bargaining was permitted, and this enabled the miners' union, the most feared opponent of incomes policies, to be placated, although only after some rather byzantine internal manoeuvres by those in the union sympathetic to the

[7] *The Economist* (September 6th, 1975) p. 17.

Table 4: BRITISH INCOMES POLICIES 1965-1978

		Percentage Increases at Annual Rates	
		Weekly Earnings	Retail Prices
1. April 1965-June 1966	Norm 3-3½%	7.6	5.1
2. July, 1966-June 1967	Standstill to end 1966. Severe restraint to June 1967. Norm zero	1.7	2.5
3. July 1967-March 1968	No norm but 4 criteria for increases - productivity, low pay, manpower demand, serious anomalies	8.8	2.8
4. April 1968-Dec. 1968	Ceiling 3½%. Continuation of criteria	7.9	5.5
5. Jan. 1969-Dec. 1969	Ceiling 3½%. Continuation of criteria	8.3	5.1
6. Dec. 1969-June 1970	Norm 2½%-4½%. Weakening of policy. Wider criteria	15.8	8.2
7. June 1970-Dec. 1970	No pay policy	12.8	7.3
8. Dec. 1970-Dec. 1971	'N-1' policy of successive reductions of 1% in major settlements. Public Sector only	9.4	9.0
9. Dec. 1971-Nov. 1972	'N-1' policy, but effectively broken by miners' strike early 1972	17.0	8.5
10. Nov. 1972-April 1973	Wage freeze	8.4	10.4
11. April 1973-Nov. 1973	£1 per head + 4%. Ceiling £ 250 per year	14.8	9.8
12. Nov. 1973-June 1974	7% or L 2.25 per head, whichever greater. Also possible cost-of-living payments	17.1	19.9
13. June 1974-July 1975	No formal policy. Increases to be based on cost of living	29.0	25.3
14. August 1975-July 1976	£ 6 per head up to £ 8500 annual income	14.0	12.9
15. August 1976-July 1977	5%, £ 2.50 minimum £ 4 maximum	8.8	17.6
16. August 1977-July 1978	'Weak' guideline of 10%. 12 month interval between settlements. Productivity bargaining	14.2	7.9
17. August 1978	5%. Productivity bargaining Exceptions for low-paid workers		

Source: Various Issues of Department of Employment Gazette.

Government. But the drama continued; the Government decided not
to hold a General Election in October 1978, and this meant pursuing
another round of incomes policy, this time set at 5 per cent [8].

However, the 1978 policy immediately ran into much worse
difficulties than that of 1977, and indeed was effectively broken by a
combination of political and industrial pressures. The TUC and the
Labour Party both voted comprehensively against any continued
restraint, although this did not prevent discussion between the Government and the TUC with the objective of producing a very
general statement of the need to fight inflation, without any indication of numerical norms or guidelines. Had this been agreed, the
TUC intended to issue notes for the guidance of negotiators essentially proposing that the impact on prices should be a key issue in
the formulation of claims. But in the event, and at least partly
through unexpected absences, the TUC General Council failed to
endorse the proposed agreement on a 14-14 vote. The Government
was therefore thrown back on its main sanction, the blacklisting of
companies. In the 1977-78 pay round, a considerable number of
companies were put on the blacklist, and over sixty remained on it at
the end of the round; nevertheless none were major national companies. But soon after the start of the 1978-79 round, two key companies, Ford and British Oxygen, both broke the 5 per cent guideline.
Ford with a settlement around 17 per cent after an eight week
strike. This transgression could not be ignored. However, the sanctions so imposed on Ford raised a storm of protest from all quarters,
employers, unions, opposition parties and the Labour party's own
left wing. The Conservatives proposed a motion in the House of
Commons attacking the sanctions and managed the rare feat of securing the backing of all the minor Opposition parties as well as the
abstention of some left-wing members. The sanctions policy was
therefore defeated and had to be unequivocally withdrawn by the
Government. This Parliamentary undermining of the policy was
shortly followed by demands for increases of over 20 per cent in
road transport, and with other strikes imminent over a wide range of
the public sector; it was obvious early in 1979 that the pay policy
had been effectively destroyed and that the country was heading
rapidly towards a wage explosion.

[8] Cmnd 7293 (1978). Note the continued reference to inflation as the major
subject of the White Papers.

The TUC was itself concerned at the run of events whereby unions were being led from the shop floor and many groups were openly flouting union advice on issues such as the permissible limits of picketing. As a result, and with an eye on the obligation to hold a General Election during 1979, the Government and the TUC issued a joint statement on industrial relations. The main points were: the introduction of an annual tripartite national assessment of economic prospects; the recognition of the need to provide assurances of comparability and fair treatment for public service workers to obviate the need for taking industrial action; and an inflation target of 5 per cent for 1982. Equally and perhaps more important were three guides issued by the TUC and appended to the statement on subjects where public concern at union practices had grown, namely negotiating and disputes procedures, the conduct of industrial disputes and the closed shop.

No mention was made of any incomes policy or any pay norm, a clear acceptance by the Govenment that its 5 per cent policy was no longer viable, even if it was not officially repudiated, and that the 1979 pay round must be allowed to run its course; nevertheless, the concept of a permanent but loose incomes policy seemed implicit in much of the statement. It remains to be seen what the effect of the 'Concordat', as it has been called, will be; inevitably it was met with considerable scepticism. Even so in 1970 and 1974, the Government has been seen to lose credibility and control in the area of industrial relations, which has yet again proved itself to be the main Achilles Heel of government authority in Britain.

Why then, has the Government persisted in the face of such opposition, and the apparent lessons of past history, since most economists have argued that incomes poicies are ineffective beyond the immediate short run? Though the National Institute for Economic and Social Research, in the latest review to be carried out on incomes policies have reduced the rate of wage inflation during the period in which they operated, this reduction has been only temporary. Wage increases in the period immediately following the ending of the policies were higher than they would otherwise have been, and these increases match losses incurred during te operation of the incomes policy [9]. "Other economists of a monetarist persuasion have been

---

[9] Henry and Ormerod (1978) p. 39.

even more damming, calling them counter-productive. However, Governments do not usually agree with these judgements, at least during the operation of policies. Thus the Government's introduction to its 1978 inflation document: 'In the past year, inflation has come down from 17 per cent to around 8 per cent, the lowest for almost 6 years. This dramatic success has been partly due to a higher exchange rate and stable commodity prices. The Government's monetary and fiscal policies have also played a vital role. But it was the firm pay policies over the past three years, and the responsible cooperation by employer and trade unions in observing them, which made the achievement possible'" [10]. Moreover, public opinion polls have always shown a clear majority in favour of incomes policies.

Beyond this, one obvious reason for persisting with such policies is fear of the problems of 're-entry' to free collective bargaining; that the pent-up demands to regain lost living standards, to re-establish differentials and to express new aspirations will result in an inflationary jump like those of 1969-70 and 1974-75. An international review by Dodge of ocllective bargaining issues suggested that catch-up for uncompensated past inflation appears to be the most important determinant of aggregate wage behaviour [11]. The difficulty with this approach is that the longer the return to collective bargaining is left, the worse the re-entry problem becomes. But Governments, for example Labour from 1974-79, seem to hope that some more general and permanent agreement can be arrived at which will prevent any such explosion from taking place.

Secondly, governments do not, or for political reasons cannot, trust market-forces. The Phillips curve is effectively discredited as a policy instrument; indeed, the NIESR article quoted above found earnings to behave perversely in relation to unemployment [12], although this probably has a lot to do with the gains in the public sector during the last decade rather than reflecting an actual reversal of accepted economic principles. In any case most British governments feel that the political and perhaps economic cost of obtaining wage moderation purely through deflation would be too high. The 1970 Conservative and 1974 Labour Governments both started out by disclaiming any intention of introducing an incomes policy but

[10] Cmnd 7293 (1978) p. 2.
[11] Dodge (1978).
[12] Henry and Ormerod (1978) p. 39.

the end of their period of government has been embittered by the defence of an incomes policy. But there have also been suggestions that earnings have in any case very little to do with market forces. The same NIESR article found considerable empirical support for the proposition that money wage movements are generated from the desire by employees to adjust real net pay to a target value. Such a proposition would obviously require a good deal more validation before being generally accepted, since it certainly does challenge established econonmic principles. However, if it has any credibility within government circles it would indicate trying to short-circuit these desires by deflating expectations through an incomes policy and its counterpart, a successful prices policy. Indeed, there have attempts since 1974 to concentrate on the prices side of the equation rather than the wages side, and the TUC is currently pressing for this as the major means of inflation control.

Thirdly, the Government is also worried about the economic impact of wage inflation, such as the effect on the pound, the effect on employment,[13] and not least the social and industrial dislocation resulting from a sharp increase in industrial conflict. Ultimately, the Government does not trust the trade unions to keep their promise to bargain responsibly; as the then Prime Minister noted in his speech to the 1978 Labour Party Conference, he had never met a trades union negotiator who thought that his demands were irresponsible. But even more, the Government fears the rank-and-file workers and recognises that in a situation of free collective bargaining, unions could exercise very little pressure to be 'responsible' upon their members, since so much of the key bargaining in the private sector is outside the hands of full-time union officials [15]. This is perhaps the heart of the pay problem in Britain and thus deserves some further elucidation.

[13] Ibidem.
[14] A recent report of the Independent Treasury Economic Model Club indicated very beneficial effects of an 8 per cent increase in earnings rather than one of 12 per cent. Growth in 1979 and 1980 is increased by 1-1 1/2 per cent, employment is increased by 100,000, price inflation is cut by 2 per cent, and real disposable income is virtually unaffected because of higher output and employment (*The Guardian*, October 8, 1978).
[15] There is unfortunately no single unambiguous way of measuring the structure of bargaining or the extent of fragmentation. However, a Department of Employment survey estimated that of manual males in manufacturing, 45.0 per cent were covered by national plus supplementary agreements, 24.1 per cent by national agreements only, 14.8 per cent by company, district or local agreements only, and 16.1 per cent were not covered. (Department of Employment Gazette, February 1974).

The issue of a decentralized fragmented industrial relations structure has been the major cause of governmental attempts to control
the output of the system by law, incomes policy, and voluntary
reorganization, mainly because of the opportunities it gives for the
heavy pressures of "coercive comparisons" between workgroups,
the expression of a strong sense of status through wage levels and a
challenge to managerial control. As Fox has said:

> "Rank-and-file employees (in Britain) do not, on the whole,
> accept management leadership in the work situation; they do not
> see themselves as members of a works community; and they
> rarely appear to act on the principle that their own welfare is
> bound up with the economic health of the enterprise in which
> they are employed ... Circumstances since the Second World War
> have powerfully promoted union organization on the shop-floor
> which has carried the adversary love-trust relationship into the
> workplace it-self ... In the event, 'arms-length contractualism'
> broke through on an ever-widening front when sustained full
> employment for nearly three decades enhanced shop-floor power
> sufficiently to make its practical expression possible. The exper-
> ience created expectations, organizational practices, and shop
> steward powerbases that have not been destroyed by subscequent
> unemployment" [16].

The result is "the fact that Britain has the strongest semi-independent shop-floor union organized in the world" [17].

This is only partly a function of attitudes such as Fox describes,
but also has to do with union structure and organization. There are
only some 4,000 full-time national trade union officers in Britain,
dues are often less in real terms than they were before World War II,
and run on shop steward organizations have become increasingly
strong. In addition to some 300,000 unpaid stewards, i.e. many more
union officials are paid by the employer than by the union, and in a
large number of situations stewards have taken over negotiating roles
previously carried out by national officials.

The formal structure of unionism, in contrast to the flexibility of
shopfloor organization, remains extremely complex. To over-simplify,
craft unions in the nineteenth century took only the skilled workers
in most industries leaving the less skilled to be taken into general

[16] Fow (1977), p. 20.
[17] Ibidem, p. 44.

unions, in the early part of this century, but as time went on boundaries and areas of representation became blurred; the last two decades have seen the growth of white-collar unionisation, usually with the same inter-union competition and confused structure that was already manifest in the manual area. The result has been a multiple unionism in almost all large companies which has prevented adequate establishment level representation or control by any or all or the national unions and has led inevitably to power accruing to informal shop steward organizations. Table 3 indicates the extent of multi-unionism for manual and non-manual groups separately, although taken together the average extent of multi-unionism within any establishment would not be as great as adding the separate figures together. On the other hand, the table only deals with individual establishments; multi-plant companies, and these employ the great majority of employees, might have to deal with more unions in total, to say nothing of rivalries between different plants.

The result of these structural and attitudinal factors is that a great deal of local level bargaining takes place outside the 'official' system; indeed a good deal of it is competitive bargaining between

Table 5: MULTI-UNIONISM IN LARGE ESTABLISHMENTS
Percentage by size of Establishment

Manual

Number of Unions	500-999	1,000-2,499	2,500 and over
None	9	5	2
1	23	14	11
2	15	15	13
3	19	18	17
4	13	12	11
5	9	11	7
6-7	8	15	15
8-10	2	6	18
11-20	0	2	4
Unspecified	4	3	2

Cont. Table 5: MULTI-UNIONISM IN LARGE ESTABLISHMENTS
Percentage by size of Establishment

Non-manual

Number of Unions	500-999	1,000-2,499	2,500 and over
None	35	24	7
1	22	16	11
2	16	19	22
3	13	23	33
4	4	8	4
5	2	3	9
6-7	2	2	4
8-10	0	1	7
11-20	0	0	0
Unspecified	7	5	4

Source: Commission on Industrial Relations Study N. 2, Industrial Relations at Establishment level: A Statistical Survey (HMSO, London, 1973) Tables 16 and 20.

the various occupational groupings in the company. Thus many of the well publicised labour difficulties in Britain's car industry can ultimately be traced to the rivalry between the Amalgamated Union of Engineering Workers, representing most of the skilled workers, and the Transport and General Workers Union, representing most of the less skilled. There are two basic problems; the first is that the boundaries between skills have become so uncertain, especially where the traditional indicator of demarcation, the apprenticeship system, is not a reliable guide. Thus a Panel of Investigation trying to examine this issue in a specific instance noted "it would be more realistic if the parties avoided the use of the term skilled with its connotation of a traditional qualification and were to agree to a classification related to the realities of the job and the experience of the people involved" [18]. Such a formula inevitably leaves room for almost end-

[18] A.C.A.S. (1975), p. 12.

less argument. The second is over pay differentials; the semi-skilled have made inroads into the traditional skilled differentials, and in some cases have caught up with or even passed the skilled groups. Thus in parts of British Leyland direct production workers have been on the same rate as skilled workers, based on an argument that high pay is a necessary compensation for the boredom and monotony of the job, and in keeping with the TGWU car workers' motto of "Second to None". The motto is itself an eloquent reflection of the inter-union rivalry. The skilled workers for their part can point to much longer training, the fact that the skill differential, although attenuated, still exists, and fairly widespread shortages of certain key skills. Indeed to take the British Leyland example again, the highly skilled toolroom workers have formed themselves into a splinter group thereatening to break away from the existing bargaining structure in order to reassert a differential over the production workers.[19]

The Leyland case is perhaps exceptional but "the British fixation with pay" quoted at the start of this section has much to do with the fragmentation of collective bargaining and the loss of consensus in respect of pay relationship. Enormous anomalies exist within as well as between occupations, establishments and local labour markets; incomes policies did not cause these, but have exacerbated them by freezing them, or by permitting differential opportunities. The situation which one Labour Government Minister recently likened to "occupational tribal warfare", was evocatively stated in sociological terms by Fox and Flanders a decade ago:

> "Work groups capable of mobilizing the necessary power have broken through a relatively larger area of regulation and imposed a relatively smaller one more favourable to themselves. And when faced with gaps in the normative system in respect of certain of their aspirations, groups with sufficient power have introduced their own. In both situations the revision and creation of norms has been improvised and piecemeal, has rested on a very small area of agreement and has not been related to larger units of regulation. This splintering of the normative order

---

[19] The story of the rivarly between the two groups mentioned here is best expressed in *Financial Times* (22 September, 1977); more generally, the concepts of occupational status and riavlry are taken up in Brown, Brannen, Cousins, and Saunphier (1972), and Wedderburn and Crompton (1972).

within the establishment and the piecemeal, hotch-potch additions to it, all determined by the accidents of power distribution
rather than by agreed principles of any sort, has greatly increased
the probability of disorder and loss of control ..." [20].

Shopfloor power of the sort just described often goes beyond
shop steward power, never mind official trade union power, and is
thus extremely difficult to control once group cohesiveness has been
built up. Nevertheless, it has appeared possible for an incomes policy
to cut across the leapfrogging rivalry of different groups and thus to
restore order. In particular, the early phases of an incomes policy
have usually been characterised by some reassertion of control within
the union movement as the shopfloor is persuaded that the national
interest demands restraint. In the meanwhile, it is hoped by the
authorities some more definitive framework for resolving pay issues
can be sought.

A final reason for continuing incomes policy is the rather special
position of the public sector, with almost a third of all employees
and almost completely unionised. Bargaining is much less fragmented, but the pressures of comparability are none the less
intense. Up to the present decade the public sector was relatively
quiescent, in spite of the turbulent histories of some of the public
sector industries such as coal. But in the late 1960s the public
sector collectively began to feel that it was being discriminated
against and that Government was not living up to its obligation
to be a 'good employer', primarily that comparability with the
private sector would be maintained.[21] Unfortunately, incomes policies
conflicted with comparability especially due to the delays built into
comparability assessment procedures, and because governments
could ostensibly more easily control public sector settlements. Wage
drift, grading drift, 'phoney' productivity agreements, and non-wage
benefits were all felt to be much more favourable in the private
sector, and this led to a considerable increase in militancy in the
public sector.

The major analysis of public and private sector pay has been by

[20] Fox and Flanders (1969) p. 164.
[21] For a more extensive account of developments in the public sector, see
Thomson and Beaumont (1978).

Dean, although only for male manual groups.[22] He showed that over the period 1950-1970 the ratio of private to public sector pay varied between 105 and 100; it was kept within this narrow band by the forces and institutions of comparability. In the 1970s, however, the pattern whereby the two sectors moved in relative unison changed dramatically and by 1975 the ratio had fallen to 89, i.e. there was a rapid improvement to the relative pay of the public sector male manuals vis-a-vis their private sector counterparts, mostly contained in the 1974-75 period.

However, since then there has been a move back in favour of the private sector. Table 6 gives a fuller description of relative movements between the two sectors during the 1970s; it will be seen that the gains for men were larger than those for women (indeed there was a private sector advantage for non-manual women). This may be due in part to the differential operation of the Equal Pay Act of 1970, whose objective had already been largely implemented in the public sector in the 1960s. The 1978 figures will show a further improvement in the pay of the private sector, but probably not sufficient to eradicate the relative gains of the public sector throughout the decade. Moreover, the major claims of the 1978-79 threatened wage explosion are in the public sector and a swing back in its favour seems probable on the evidence of the 1969-70 and 1974-75 releases from incomes policies. Perhaps the most important feature of the period, however, is the loss of synchronisation between the two sectors, with the private sector doing better in periods of incomes policy because of the tighter controls in the public sector while the policy is operating, followed by gains for the public sector when the policies end. If, as is possible, this results not only in the traditional line of causation from the private sector to the public sector based on comparability, but also a feedback from public sector gains to the private sector, it will have important implications for wage determination and inflation.

The apparent new independence of the public sector in the wage determination process has been partly due to the newly-developed militancy, partly because there were not the market pressures which helped keep down private sector earnings, and partly because of the very real power of some public sector unions. If the miners struck,

[22] Dean (1975 and 1977).

Table 6 - PUBLIC AND PRIVATE SECTORS

Average gross weekly earnings

Full-time men aged 21 and over, and full-time women, aged 18 and o

	Average (L.)						
	1970	1971	1972	1973	1974	1975	197
Manual men							
Central government	21.8	25.5	27.7	30.3	36.2	49.7	58.:
Local government	21.1	24.0	26.5	30.8	35.2	48.4	56.(
Public corporations	37.6	30.2	34.5	39.8	45.8	62.4	72.:
Public sector	25.8	28.6	32.4	37.3	43.3	59.0	68.:
Private sector	27.0	29.8	32.9	38.4	43.7	43.5	64.(
Non-manual men							
Central government	36.0	39.7	44.4	46.3	56.6	69.3	88.!
Local government	35.5	39.2	44.8	49.5	55.5	72.4	88.:
Public corporations	34.6	38.8	43.8	47.9	54.7	72.7	85.{
Public sector	35.3	39.2	44.5	48.2	55.6	71.7	87.'
Private sector	34.9	39.0	43.0	48.1	53.9	66.5	78.:
Manual women							
Central government	13.2	15.9	18.3	19.9	26.4	37.2	44.
Local government	11.7	13.8	15.6	18.4	22.0	31.4	37.'
Public corporations	18.3	19.4	22.5	24.8	28.3	42.0	50.(
Public sector	13.5	15.7	18.0	20.1	25.0	35.5	42.(
Private sector	13.3	15.1	16.9	19.7	23.2	31.2	38.(
Non-manual women							
Central government	19.3	21.4	24.3	25.5	30.4	42.6	53.'
Local government	24.8	26.7	30.5	33.8	38.1	52.8	65.'
Public corporations	18.1	20.2	23.3	25.9	30.3	41.8	51.
Public sector	21.2	23.2	26.6	28.8	33.2	46.8	58.
Private sector	15.2	17.3	19.0	21.7	25.4	33.6	40.

Source: Dèpàrtèment of Employement Gazette, Dècember 1977. The data are taken from th

entage increases: 1970 to 1977
se pay for the survey pay period was not affected by absence.

970	Percentage increase over previous year							April of each year
	1970-1971	1971-1972	1972-1973	1973-1974	1974-1975	1975-1976	1976-1977	1970-77 at an annual rate
4.4	17.0	8.6	9.4	19.5	37.3	17.7	10.1	16.7
9.4	13.7	10.0	16.7	14.3	37.5	15.7	6.1	15.9
8.2	9.4	14.2	15.4	15.1	36.2	15.9	8.2	6.10
3.9	10.9	13.3	15.1	16.1	36.3	15.6	8.4	16.2
2.9	10.4	10.4	16.7	13.8	24.7	17.4	13.9	15.7
3.9	10.3	11.8	4.3	22.2	22.4	27.7	6.1	14.7
2.7	10.4	14.3	10.5	12.1	30.5	22.0	5.0	14.7
3.5	12.1	12.9	9.4	14.2	32.9	18.0	9.0	15.3
3.2	11.0	13.5	8.3	15.4	29.0	22.3	6.3	14.9
6.5	11.7	10.3	11.9	12.1	23.4	17.6	10.6	13.2
7.3	20.5	15.1	8.7	32.7	40.9	18.5	7.3	20.0
0.0	17.9	13.0	17.9	19.6	42.7	18.2	7.8	19.2
5.7	6.0	16.0	10.2	14.1	48.4	20.5	10.1	17.2
5.2	16.3	14.6	11.7	24.4	42.0	18.3	7.6	18.8
3.3	13.5	11.9	16.6	17.8	34.5	23.7	12.2	18.4
7.0	10.9	13.6	4.9	19.2	40.1	26.1	6.1	16.7
0.9	7.7	14.2	10.8	12.7	38.6	24.4	7.9	16.2
7.0	11.6	15.3	11.2	17.0	38.0	22.5	11.3	17.8
2.7	9.4	14.7	8.3	15.3	41.0	24.8	7.4	16.8
6.1	13.8	9.8	14.2	17.1	32.3	20.8	13.5	17.2

nual New Earnings Survey.

as they did in 1972 and 1974, they could bring the country to a halt; the same would be true of electricity workers, water workers and possibly railway workers while others could cause great inconvenience to the public.[23] There is little doubt that if free collective bargaining were only operated in the private sector, governments would be prepared to live with any economic results. They dare not, however, allow unrestrained collective bargaining in the public sector because of its potential impact on both wage levels and social stability, and although setting cash limits on particular areas of public expenditure has so far proved a useful supplement to incomes policy, it would be unrealistic to suppose that they could be operated for long without any equivalent form of control in the private sector.[24] It is indeed an unfortunate irony that the incomes policies which have made a considerable contribution to militancy in the public sector are not only seen as the only solution to that militancy, but must be generalised throughout the economy, with all the attendant difficulties of enforcement, in order to obtain even a minimal degree of acquiescence in the public sector.

3. The Reaction to the Recession

For all the above reasons, incomes policies have been continued, and given their very high visibility have served to keep the question of pay in the forefront of public consciousness. However, the account so far does not entirely explain why there has not been more of a social outcry about the employment impact of the recession. Nor does it explain the attitudes of the workforce, why they have been so keen to pursue issues of pay and to take apparently little account of the existence of the recession.

First, it is unfair to suggest that the union movement has done nothing. Its annual economic reviews have been full of the employ-

[23] Strong groups can use economic power, but weak groups in the public sector can use public sympathy to obtain 'catch-up' awards. The nurses and teachers were examples in 1974 and there are several groups which have been singled out as "special cases" in the current round, including policemen, firemen, doctors and university teachers.

[24] This is, in fact, the Conservative Party's policy, but few commentators think it a feasible one.

ment problem, and possibly the dominant theme at the 1978 Congress was the threat of the micro-processor revolution. Moreover, much of the legislation of the decade, which has been strongly influenced by the unions, has been oriented to creating greater job security and moving towards property rights in the job. Unfair dismissal, time off to look for work, redundancy payments and procedures, guaranteed pay for short-time working, maternity rights and changes in employment contract obligations all help the individual employee. On the labour market front the unions have been particularly influential in the key agency in this area, the Manpower Services Commission on which they have three representatives on the governing council.[25]

Table 7 shows the numbers of people covered by the MSC and the Department of Employment's (DE) special measures in 1977 and 1978, which can be seen as a specific response to the recession over and above the already considerable growth in expenditure and activities in more general labour market activities, especially training and employment search. The total expenditure of MSC, including some on behalf of the DE, was some 543 millions in 1977-78, as compared to 125 millions in 1974-75[26]; even allowing for inflation this amounts to more than doubling of expenditure. To comment briefly on the major pro, the Job Creation Scheme (and its recent successor, the Special Temporary Employment Programme), enables projects of benefit to the community to be put forward to carry out work which would not otherwise be done and must be approved by the relevant union. The Temporary Employment Subsidy is designed to maintain employment where redundancies would otherwise take place by providing employers with a subsidy of £ 20 per week per job at risk for up to a year, with a possibility of an extension of a further six months of 10 per week. The basic objective of the Work Experience Programme is to provide unemployed young people aged between 16 and 18 with a chance to gain first-hand experience of working life, and especially the skills and disciplines involved.

[25] Thus Elliott has said of the TUC's performance on the MSC: "... a well drilled TUC team can run rings round the more diverse and less well disciplined people from the CSI and other interests, who find it hard to mount campaigns against the TUC on items like alleviating unemployment, however well briefed they may be by their own back-up staff" (Elliott (1978) p. 56).
[26] MSC, Annual Report 1977-78.

Table 7: SPECIAL LABOUR MARKET MEASURES 1977 AND 1978

	March/April 1977	March/April 1978
Special Programmes		
Job Creation Programme	31	48
Work Experience Programme	8	28
Community Industry	4	5
Training Measures		
MSC special courses for young people	4	4
Training places supported in industry	31	27
Employment Subsidies		
Temporary Employment Subsidy	193	173
Youth Employment Subsidy	13	8
Small Firms Employment Subsidy	—	4
Job Release Scheme	10	10
Total	294	307

Source: Manpower Services Commission Annual Report 1977-78.
Note: The term special measures is that of the MSC, not the author.

As another aspect of the employment dimension, there has also been a union reaction to the recession in using collective bargaining to create jobs by reducing the length of the working life and working week and increase holidays. It must be said, however, that in spite of a great deal of discussion of this issue [27], it has very much taken second place to pay increases as a bargaining demand. The miners were able to reduce their age of retirement from 65 to 62 in 1977 as a means of inducing them not to challenge the pay policy, and in several of the 1978-79 bargaining round claims there have been demands for a 35-hour week, but with very few exceptions

[27] Especially in the TUC Annual *Economic Reviews* and two articles, in the *Department of Employment Gazette* (March and April, 1978).

these have been dropped in favour of pay. Again there tends to be something of a clash between the top and the bottom of the union movement, since while the TUC can argue that a cut of 500,000 in unemployment could be achieved by a move to a 35-hour week [28] and seek to make this a major focus of union activities, there would be difficulties in obtaining this without some loss of potential gross pay from the point of view of the negotiating groups, while employers and to some extent the Government fear that any cut in standard hours would merely be recouped in overtime at premium rates of pay. Unions have, in fact, tried to cut overtime levels for many years, but they remain persistently high, being viewed by the rank and file as a means of raising pay beyond the constraints of incomes policies and adherence to low basic rates. There is also the possibility, given present levels of over-capacity and under-working in British industry, that reductions in time worked would not be compensated by increases in number of jobs. Nevertheless, at least at the national level, this is seen by the TUC as a major component of its anti-recession policy, and it is also one which it has sponsored at the European trade union level.

Second, unions must ultimately respond to the expressed desires and priorities of their present members rather than pursue general social policies, and these desires have geneally been very narrow and sectional in orientation. It would be wrong to think that the recession has had no influence on the workgroup level of organisation; wage drift, a major issue in the 1960s, has greatly diminished in the 1970s, and over 60 per cent of redundancies have been due to deficient demand for the employer's product rather than technological or oranisational change. Nevertheless, it has normally been the case that the groups making demands on the system at any level are not those who will suffer directly from any unemployment caused, and where unemployment is threatened, powerful groups have been quick to use the political process to try to save their jobs by governmental action.

Third, from the point of view of individual workers, there have been several resons for ignoring the recession and being unwilling to accept continuing incomes policies. The decline in the standard of living for most in 1976-77 was a major interruption in expectations which had assumed at least real income maintenance every year and

[28] TUC Economic Review (1978) p. 12.

indeed had been led to expect faster rates of growth by the political parties than actually occurred. British workers had constantly been asked to sacrifice the short-run for longer-term gains, and they did accept the leadership of their unions and fairly stringent controls for the first two years of incomes policy, but it was too much to expect that they would continue to do so, given the strategic power of numerous groups to break through the guidelines. Exacerbating this unwillingness has been the structure of taxation, since there is a high marginal rate of taxation even for relatively poorly-paid workers.[29] The TUC has tried to educate workers into the concept of the 'social wage' whereby in 1975 for each worker the government spent £ 15 per week on direct services.[30] However, workers have proved very resistent to this; they have a high preference for personal take-home pay over government expenditure, and the rapid rise in overall government expenditure up to 1976 had resulted in sharply higher taxes.

Finally, some at least of the policies pursued in trying to ameliorate unemployment may have worsened the problem of wage inflation by reducing the potential employment cost of wage demands. Unemployment pay has been earnings-related since the mid-1960s, and the various social security benefits for the unemployed, together with the structure of pay and tax, can in some circumstances mean that it is financially better to be unemployed than employed, although this would be true in the long term for only a very small proportion of the working population.[31] Job security has also been greatly increased: this began with the Redundancy Payments Act 1965, whereby those not replaced in their job obtain a length of service-related lump sum; the Industrial Relations Act 1971 introduced the concept of compensation or reinstatement for unfair dismissal, which has been further strenghthened by later legislation; and the Employment Protection Act 1975 derived its name from a number of

[29] The major case that increasing taxation has played a considerable part in wage inflation has been put by Jackson, Turner and Wilkinson (1972). An analysis of public attitudes on incomes policies and price increases can be found in two studies by Behrend (1973a and 1973b).

[30] TUC (1975) p. 11.

[31] The relationship between benefits, tax and pay is a very complex issue, and is particularly complicated by the existence of a "poverty trap", whereby an increase in pay can result in a drastic reduction of means-tested benefits to the point where the marginal rate of is over 100 per cent. For the most authoritative discussion see Royal Commission on the Distribution of Income and Wealth (1978), especially chapter 4.

additional security measures, notably rehiral after maternity, short-term lay-off pay, and preferential treatment in employer insolvency. These pieces of legislation have helped to create a property-right in the job which both makes it more difficult to lose a job and in a range of circumstances provides compensation for any such loss. If there is other work available, it can be quite lucrative to lose a job. There is also the difficult issue of the financing of strikes; although recent work by Gennard indicates that although most strikers pay the brunt of the costs of industrial action themselves [32] they are at least assured that their dependents can be supported by the state. Thus if wage bargaining is envisaged by the parties in terms of a trade-off between costs and benefits, the balance of advantage has moved in favour of employees for these as well as other more technological and structural reasons.

4. THE MOVE TO CORPORATISM

The other main factor deflecting industrial relations attention away from the recession during the 1974-78 period has been the attempt to incorporate the unions in decision-making at all levels at which key economic decisions are made. There have been several reasons for the move towards corporatism, but the attempt to use the unions to control wages by offering them as a quid pro quo a larger share in decision-making (and its concomitant responsibilities) has been an important component. In Crouch's words:

> Corporatism ... appears at a moment ... when labour has reached such a strength that classic constraints are no longer operating nor are the techniques of compromise securing what dominant interests consider to be adequate control over subordinates' actions. For the strategy to be pursued effectively, the basis for a reintegration of political, economic and ideological dimensions must also be present in wider structural developments in the society.[33]

In effect, Governments, to adapt Flanders' famous dictum, have been forced to share control in order to regain it.[34] Inevitably,

[32] Gennard (1978).
[33] Crouch (1977), p. 34.
[34] Quoted in Royal Commission on Trade Unions and Employers' Assciations (1968) p. 555.

part of the reason for growth of union influence came from
within the Labour Party, in which the unions have a dominant
voting influence if they care to exercise it, and which they did
exercise to an increasing extent from the late 1960s onwards as they
became worried about the challenge by the state to laissez-faire collective bargaining. But more important has been the TUC-Labour
Party Liaison Committee, which was set up in 1972 to bring the
industrial and political wings of the labour movement closer
together, and which transmitted union desires to the Party and
almost directly into policy. Even so, the pressures which generated
greater union influence and the move towards corporatism have not
been restricted to the Labour Party. It was the Conservatives who
set up the first agency to monitor incomes, the Cohen Committee, in
1957; who introduced the National Economic Development Council
as a means of providing interest group participation in macro-economic policy discussion; who introduced the industrial tribunals as
local employment-related tripartite courts, and first created specialis-
ed higher labour courts; who inaugurated the Manpower Services
Commission as a tripartite and largely independent manpower co-
ordinating agency, and who tried further incorporation as a blandish-
ment for a voluntary incomes policy in 1972. Conservative attacks
on the corporate state and rule by 'quangos' (quasi-autonomous
national governmental organisations which are not part of the
civil service),[35] must thus be tempered by considerable participation
in the process of their creation. Quangos go well beyond the
employment related orbits to policy making and administration in
almost every area of government, but have nevertheless been perhaps
most heavily criticised in the industrial field.

Another reason that union influence in the process of government
has increased more in the period under review than at any other time
is that the unions have made a concerted effort to achieve this and
have tried in recent years to develop a coherent strategy of involvement as part of their broader perspectives of industrial democracy.
Thus the TUC identified four levels for industrial policy — the
economy, the sector or industry, the company, and the plant, and has
stated policy and institutional objectives of participation at each.[36]
We will briefly report at least the institutional aspects of this frame-

---

[35] Holland and Fallon (1978).
[36] TUC (1977) pp. 75-98.

work for planning. At the economy level, in addition to the NEDC for policy coordination, the TUC has sponsored the creation of the National Enterprise Board in 1975 as a state holding company with tripartite direction and is pressing for a tripartite Industrial Investment Bank to channel funds in accordance with the overall industrial strategy. At the sectoral level, over 30 Sector Working Parties were created in 1976 to examine strategies and bottlenecks for particular industries to complement the existing 19 Economic Development Committees. These sets of bodies are again tripartite, and the main purpose of the conference noted above was to assess their effectiveness. At the company and plant level the TUC saw three sets of developments. First, in the area of forward planning, the main instrument was seen as planning agreements, originated on a voluntary basis under the Industry Act of 1975, but so far unsuccessful in that only one has been concluded, the ill-fated Chrysler agreement which was overtaken by the Peugeot takeover of Chrysler's European interests. However, any future Labour Government is likely to introduce a greater element of compulsion.

In the second area, that of collective bargaining, there were numerous gains in legislative rights for unions as well as individual employees, mainly under the Employment Protection Act of 1975, some of them admittedly built on similar provisions in the 1971 Industrial Relations Act. Recognition, disclosure of information, time-off work for union business, redundancy notification, and the extension of terms and conditions came in this Act, but an important development in another field was institutional rights to joint regulation of health and safety under the 1974 Act of that name. The possibility of union representation on pension funds has been proposed by the Government but not yet implemented,[37] if it were there would be considerable implications for the operation of the capital market. There is also the possibility of an increased amount of employee share-ownership within their own companies after tax concessions in the 1978 Budget which essentially removed the onerous income tax liabilities which had previously made such shemes unattractive.

The third area, and the most publicly controversial, is industrial democracy. The TUC initiated the debate on board level representation in 1973 (with some assistance from Britain's accession to the

[37] Cmnd 6514 (1976).

European Economic Community) and it became a part of the Social Contract. However, the Government was unsure how to implement the TUC demand, and referred the matter to the Bullock Committee with very restrictive terms of reference, which asked the Committee how best to rather than whether to implement representation on the board. The Bullock report [38], closely following the TUC line, evoked such a furore from industry and such a lukewarm response from many unions that immediate legislation was not feasible. Indeed, the TUC at its 1977 Congress modified its position to incorporate the wide-spread union view that extended collective bargaining would be better than board level representation, by adopting a resolution which looked in both directions. The Government in turn produced a Wite Paper in May 1978 promising a slow move towards representation on company boards, but possibly more importantly, statutory rights on the joint discussion of company strategy as it affects employees, together with a much more flexible approach to structures.[39] The document notes: "In setting out its proposals for a statutory procedure, the Government reiterates that it wishes — and would much prefer — to see employee participation proceed by voluntary agreements between employers and the representatives of their employees. It is not the intention to impose a standard pattern of participation on industry by law [40].

So far we have merely examined the economic decision-making functions but of almost equal importance is representation on administrative and judicial agencies which collectively set policy across much of the range of employment related issues. The Manpower Services Commission (1973) has been mentioned, but it was followed by the Advisory Conciliation and Arbitration Service (1974) with a wide range of functions described in its name, the Health and Safety Commission (1974), the Equal Opportunity Commission (1975) and the Race Relations Board (1976). These bodies have taken over the majority of the work of the Department of Employment, which has few policy decisions left to it; all are tripartite, and all are independent of government. There are also the tripartite courts with the industrial tribunals at the bottom, the Employment Appeal Tribunal (1975) as their appellate body, and the Central Arbitration Committee (1975) to interpret aspects of law requiring arbitral judgement.

[38] 1977.
[39] Cmnd 7231 (1978).
[40] Ibidem, p. 2.

Although these latter bodies had forerunners, the amount of work and influence involved has increased manyfold as a result of the 1974-76 legislation.

To sum up this institutional structure, although there are clearly gaps between theory and practice on the planning side and it would be very difficult to evaluate the weight of union influence on, say, the judicial decisions, there can be little doubt that the unions are now firmly ensconced on a wide range of key agencies. They have also attempted to influence more general economic policy; in this they have been less successful, since external forces have tended to determine governmental decision-making, even though we noted TUC domination of pay issues between 1974-76.

All this extension of influence has been beneficial in a number of ways. It has produced union acquiescence in legal or arbitral decision-making over a range of issues that would earlier have been potential subjects of conflict, it has enabled unions to share responsibility as well as power, and it has shown that it is possible to make policy on a tripartite disagreement, such as the issue of recognition within ACAS. Much of the extension of influence is perfectly compatible with both participatory democracy and Labour Party policy anyway, without needing to justify it in terms of a trade-off with pay policy acquiescence. There are also counter-arguments, mainly to the effect that corporatism, and especially its union influence dimension, are inimical to parliamentary sovereignty, individual freedom, and economic markets. But a further criticism must be that if corporatism is intended to produce a quid pro quo in terms of a consensus amongst key groups, this is unlikely to be effective without acquiescence from the shop-floor. Almost all the effective incorporation to date has been above the level of the Company or the establishment, where the operating decisions are made, where employees feel the need for some degree of control over their working environment, and where much of the real power in industrial relations lies. However, at these levels adversary relations are still dominant, as the earlier quotation from Fox made clear.

5. CONCLUSIONS

The significant industrial relations themes in Britain have not essentially changed as a result of the recession; nor has the recession done much to resolve them. They are still dominated by the competitive scramble over relative pay, the disruptive power which is generated in this process, and the attempt to seek both temporary and permanent solutions through stratagems such as direct controls and incorporation of the major agencies into the higher levels of policy-making. Such attempts have had only limited success, primarily because the principal agencies, union and employer groupings, are institutionally weak in relation to their subordinates, whatever their influence on the national scene. Nor does dependence on market forces promise much greater success. This was a period of the contemporaneous existence of unprecedently high increases in earnings and the highest unemployment rates for forty years. At the very least wages have therefore responded extremely slowly to labour market slack, and have totally lost touch with productivity. Moreover, the approach of using tight monetary controls carries with it the possibility of disrupting the present political tolerance of unemployment to say nothing of risking irreversible de-industrialisation. In short, the model of British industrial relations here presented has much in common with Tarantelli's conflict model and Halberstadt's competition model described elsewhere in this volume. The demands from the shop floor upon the state and the economic system have proved incapable of satisfaction and to date the resultant conflict has not been adequately institutionalised.

The issue is, therefore, at least as much behavioural and organisational as economic. Crouch has argued that "the institutions of the classic bourgeois state are incapable of providing an adequate regulation of interests when so many of these interests are organised and incapable of containment by economic regulation alone. Inflation is one major outcome of such a situation".[41] He sees the answer as a greater integration of interests; in the industrial relations field this involves "i) transcending the 'trust gap' ii) transcending particularism iii) tackling problems of relations between leaders and members of labour organisations".[42] In practice this imlpies that incorporation in the future must be made relevant at those levels where the great mass of employees spend their lives, namely at the level of the shop floor. What appears to be an emergent system of bargained corporatism cannot be based only on national level institutions. For

[41] Crouch (1978) p. 237.
[42] Ibidem, p. 233.

all the problems that industrial democracy will cause in structural re-organisation and redefinitions of attitudes, it is also likely to be the best means of creating the cohesion of purpose and role legitimacy currently missing in many British enterprises. To hark back to the classic article of Fox and Flanders, it is necessary to create the building blocks whereby new systems of normative relations can be established.[43] This approach also implies that governments cannot easily impose solutions. The role of the state will continue to expand at higher levels in attempts to plan change to achieve economic growth and overcome unemployment, to institutionalise conflict, and to achieve consensus in the management of the economy. But the state cannot control or even easily influence the creation of these building blocks; ultimately these are tasks for managers, union officials, and employees.

[43] Fox and Flanders (1969) p. 176.

BIBLIOGRAHY

ACAS (Advisory Conciliation and Arbitration Service) (1975): Report n. 1,
    *Panel of Investigation on a Dispute between British Leyland Cowley and
    AVEW and TGWU concerning Mechanical Rectifiers.*
P. B. Beaumont and A. W. J. Thomson (1978): *Collective Bargaining in the
    Public Sector: A Study of Relative Gain*, London, Saxon House 1978.
H. Behrend (1973a): *Incomes Policy, Equity and Pay Increase Differentials.*
    Edinburgh, Scottish Academic Press 1973.
H. Behrend (1973b): *Attitudes to Price Increases*, London, National Economic
    Development Office 1973.
R. K. Brown et al. (1972): "The Contours of Solidarity: Social Stratifica-
    tion and Industrial Relations in Shipbuilding", in: *British Journal of
    Industrial Relations*, March 1972.
Cmnd 3880 (HMSO, 1969): *In Place of Strife* 1969.
Cmnd 6151 (HMSO, 1975): *The Attack on Inflation* 1975.
Cmnd 6514 (HMSO, 1976): *Occupational Pension Schemes: The Role of
    Members in the Running of Schemes* 1976.
Cmnd 7231 (HMSO, 1978): *Industrial Democracy* 1978.
Cmnd 7293 (HMSO, 1978): *Winning the Battle Against Inflation* 1978.
R. Crompton and D .Weddeburn (1972): *Workers' Attitudes and Technology,*
    Cambridge, Cambridge U.P. 1972.
C. Crouch (1977): *Class Conflict and the Industrial Relations Crisis.* London,
    Heinemann Educational Books 1977.
C. Crouch (1978): "Inflation and the Political Organization of Economic
    Interests", in: F. Hirsch and J. Goldthorpe (eds.), *The Political Economy
    of Inflation*, London, M. Robertson 1978.
W. W. Daniel and E. Stilgoe (1978): *The Impact of Employment Protection
    Laws*, London, PSI 1978.
A. J. H. Dean (1975): "Earnings in the Public and Private Sectors 1950-75",
    in: *National Institute Economic Review*, Nov. 1975.
A. J. H. Dean (1977): "Public and Private Sector Manual Workers' Pay
    1970-77", in: *NIER*, Nov. 1977.
A. J. H. Dean (1978): "Incomes Policies and Differentials", in: *NIER*, Aug.
    1978.
Department of Employment Gazette: (issues of February 1974, March and
    April 1978).
D. Dodge (1978): "Collective Bargaining Issues and Public Policies: Wages".
    OECD Conference, Washington, 10-13 July 1978.
Economist (The): (issue of September 6, 1975).
J. Elliot (1978): *Conflict or Cooperation? The Growth of Industrial Democ-
    racy*, London, Kogan Page 1978.
S. R. Engleman and A. W. J. Thomson (1975): *The Industrial Relations Act: A
    Review and Analysis.* London, Martin Robertson 1975.
Financial Times (22 Sept. 1977): "Leyland Cars Between Two Grindstones".
A. Fox (1977): "Corporation and Industrial Democracy: The Social Origins of
    Present Forms and Methods in Britain and Germany", in: *Industrial
    Democracy: International Views.* Papers at an SSRC International Confer-
    ence, Cambridge 1977.
A. Fox and A. Flanders (1969): "The Reform of Collective Bargaining: from
    Donovan to Dirkheim", in: *British Journal of Industrial Relations*, July
    1969.

J. Gennard (1978): *The Financing of Strikes.* London, Macmillan 1978.

Guardian (The): (issue of October 8, 1978).

S. G. B. Henry and P. A. Ormerod (1978): "Incomes Policy and Wage Inflation: Empirical Evidence for the U.K. 1961-77", in: *NIER*, Aug. 1978.

P. Holland and M. Fallon (1978): *The Quango Explosion: Public Bodies and Ministerial Patronage,* London, Conservative Political 1978.

D. Jackson et al. (1972): *Do Trade Unions Cause Inflation?*, Cambridge, Cambridge U.P. 1972.

P. Jenkins (1970): *The Battle of Downing Street,* London, Charles Knight 1970.

Manpower Services Commission: *Annual Report 1977-78.* OPCS (S. Parker, R. Thomas, N. Ellis and W.E. S. McCarty) (1969): *Effects of the Redundancy Payments Act,* 1969.

Report of the Committee of Enquiry on Industrial Democracy (Bullock Report): Cmnd 6706; HMSO 1977.

Royal Commission on the Distribution of Income and Wealth: *Lower Incomes,* London, HMSO 1978; cmnd 7175.

Royal Commission on Trade Unions and Employers' Associations (1968): *Selected Written Evidence,* London, HMSO.

Trade Union Congress (1975): *The Development of the Social Contract* 1975.

T.U.C. (1977): *The Trade Union Role in Industrial Policy* 1977.

T.U.C. and Government (HMSO, 1979): *The Economy, the Government and Trade Union Responsibilities* (Joint statement) 1979.

T.U.C. *Economic Review* (1978).

PAY DISTRIBUTION AND DIFFERENTIALS IN BRITAIN AND OTHER WESTERN COUNTRIES DURING THE 1970s

by

CHRISTOPHER SAUNDERS

This paper concentrates upon one aspect only of the management of industrial conflict in the 1970s: the distribution and development of pay (wages and salaries).[1] Further, my object is to see the British experience in the context of experience in some other Westren industrial economies, to look for significant similarities and differences. At the same time, a special feature of British experience in the 1970s is the almost continuous, and highly complicated, series of incomes policies through which governments and — with varying degrees of reluctance — the Trades Union Congress have sought to exercise some control over the extremely decentralized system of collective bargaining. The policy story is analysed in Dr. Thomson's paper in this volume; in my contribution I try to relate the actual development and distribution of pay to the sequence of policies and conclude with some reflections on the problems raised in Britain by the efforts to control the bargaining process.

1. THE WESTERN INFLATION OF THE 1970s

The background is the common Western experience of accelerated inflation during the 1970s. I suggest that there were essentially

[1] The term "pay" or "earnings" means the direct remuneration before tax of both wage-earners (manual, or "blue-collar") and salary earners (non-manual, or "white collar"), both groups being described as "workers". Except where otherwise

two points of inflexion in the international inflation curve of the last
decade. The first, it may be said, began with the events of 1968 in
France. After the students had raised the curtain in May, the French
union confederations — taking a little time to grasp the opportunities presented by an insecure government — were the first in the
European round of two-digit general pay increases (the agreement of
the rue de Grenelle later in the year). The "hot autumn ' of 1969
followed in Italy and it was not long before the unions in other
Western countries mounted the stage. In 1970, Britain, Germany,
Italy, France again, the Netherlands, Japan, all experienced pay
increases in excess of 10 per cent (but not the United States, which
appears up to now to have escaped two-digit pay increases). The
reasons for this widespread acceleration of pay increases from 1968
onwards are by no means clear.

Specific reasons can be found in some countries (e.g. reactions
from previous phases of rather severe restraint may help to explain
developments in Britain, Germany, France, Italy) but the process of
international transmission needs much more study. In any case, the
strong pay-push acquired momentum before a second impulse was
given by the general rise in commodity prices which began in
1971-72 and was accentuated by the OPEC action of October 1973.
Thus the Western inflations may be regarded as arising from the
interaction of internal and external factors.

The wave of large pay increases continued. During the nine years
1968-77, increases of more than 10 per cent a year occurred:

— in France in 9 years;

— in Italy in 8 years (over 20 per cent in 5 years);

— in Britain in 7 years (over 20 per cent in 3 years);

— in Japan in 7 years (over 20 per cent in 2 years);

— in Netherlands in 7 years;

— in Germany in 3 years (only in 1970, 1973 and 1974).

The overall pay increases from 1968 to 1977 in the six larger
industrial countries are shown in Table 1, together with data on

specified, "pay" does not include the social charges paid by employers (social security
contributions and other compulsory or voluntary payments which enter into the
employers' total labour costs).

prices, labour costs per unit of output, productivity and output. The figures relate to manufacturing only; more comprehensive information might modify the story in some respects. Also it must be noted that the series are not fully comparable (see the notes to the table); for comparisons, they cannot be taken as more than orders of magnitude. We take 1968 as the base year in view of the tentative historical outline suggested above and to provide a long enough trend to escape some of the ambiguities that can arise from short-period movements.

The divergence of inflationary experience between these six countries over the nine years is remarkable: the range of nominal pay increases in national currencies stretches from multiples of nearly 2 in the United States to 4 and 5 in Japan and Italy. In this respect, Britain takes its traditional place in the middle of the road with a multiple of over 3 — close to the (unweighted) average for the six countries. The range of increases in consumer prices — although everywhere less than those in pay — is still very wide: in this respect, Britain takes the not very creditable lead with a multiple of 2.75, and Germany, with a multiple of 1.6, comes last.

In terms of increases in *real* pay, which on average rose by about half as much as nominal pay, Japan and Italy come first, real pay almost doubling. For Japan, this corresponds, as could be expected, with a very similar increase in productivity and output. But in Italy, the increase in real earnings substantially exceeded that in productivity or output — suggesting a rising share of industrial wage earners "in manufacturing product, and perhaps in national income. In the United States, by contrast, the increase in real earnings was amazingly small, much less than in productivity, suggesting a substantial change — the reverse of that in Italy — in factor shares.[3]

Britain, where nominal pay rose by about the average amount, stands out with the smallest increase in real pay, in productivity and in output. The divergence in Britain between the increases in the monetary indicators of pay and costs, on tht one hand, and the indicators of movements in the "real" economy — in output and productivity — is much greater than elsewhere: the statistical evi-

[2] As noted on table 1, the Italian earnings statistics relate only to wage-earners (manual workers).
[3] The US earnings data also relate only to " production and related workers", but other statistical series suggest these workers increased their real earnings at least as much as other groups in the labour force.

dence suggests that the hold of the "money illusion", unjustified by economic performance, is strong everywhere, but seems strongest in Britain. In this unfortunate result, the particularly fragmented and competitive British pay bargaining system, despite the official restraints, may well have played a major role.

The combination of nominal pay rises with labour productivity is expressed in the rise of labour costs per unit of output in manufacturing. The divergence in unit labour costs has its obvious implications for international equilibrium; but the consequences are not entirely mechanical. The changes in unit labour costs are shown in Table 1; column (4) sets them out first in national currencies. But from the point of view of international competitiveness, these figures tell us little since throughout our period exchange rates have been in almost constant flux; indeed variations of exchange rates have been, in part, used in efforts to correct the disequilibria resulting from divergence in domestic inflation.[4] So in column (5) the unit cost indexes are all converted to indexes in current US dollars. The result is to alter the relative movements between countries. Britain and Italy, which — apart from the United States — experienced the greatest trade deficits have to some extent reduced their cost disadvantage by devaluation, although their cost increases in dollars remain relatively large. But the United States, with the smallest increase in unit labour costs in dollars, did not avoid the recent large trade deficits. And Japan, with the biggest increase in dollar costs, is still recording large trade surpluses (after recovering with great rapidity from the rise in oil prices).

I cannot hope to answer all the questions that arise from these statistical comparisons (and among the questions must be the true comparability of the statitsics). But two rather obvious conclusions stand out. The first is the absence of any simple mechanical relationship, across countries, between the rate of increase in nominal pay and general economic performance, especially foreign trade performance: many factors other than pay increases determine changes in competitiveness. The second conclusion is this: if we confine our attention to the problems of international disequilibrium and the balance of competitive power, ignoring all the other distressing con-

---

[4] I will not try here to enter the controversy about the efficiency of changes in exchange rates as a balancing instrument; it will of course be recognized that such changes may accentuate divergences in relative rates of domestic inflation as well as having some corrective effect on balances of payments.

sequences of rapid inflation, then it is the *divergent* national rates of inflation rather than their rapidity which appears as a main factor in our present difficulties. How far the greater rapidity of inflation has accentuated the divergencies deserves more study; at first sight, it seems that, although divergencies in inflation rates were subjects of concern evn in the happy days of 2, 3 or 4 per cent annual inflation (as against around 10 per cent in the 1970s), those divergencies were not then, for the most part, insuperable obstacles to international equilibrium.

2. PAY AND POLICIES IN BRITAIN IN THE 1970s [5]

Against this background, we may now return to examine more closely the evolution of pay in Britain during the 1970s, and the ways in which the pay negotiators responded to the policies promulgated at the top level and described by Dr. Thomson elsewhere. Table 2 displays, year by year, a number of relevant indicators. (The series are not quite the same as those used for Britain in Table 1, where choice of data was restricted by the need for some degree of international comparability. In particular, the figures for Britain in Table 2 cover effectively the whole economy, not only manufacturing industry).

The first clear fact is that a doubling of the rate of increase in nominal pay so far in the 1970s, compared with the 1960s, accompanied a drop by one-third in the rate of increase in real pay. From 1970 to mid-1978, average *nominal* earnings of all workers, blue-collar and white-collar, were tripled (15 per cent a year); average *real* earnings rose by 15 per cent, or 1.8 per cent a year — against 2.5 per cent a year over the 1960s. The growth rates of total output (GDP) and of labour productivity also fell by about one-third.

But the eight years have seen a variety of ups and downs in the evolution of all these indicators: the cyclical boom of 1972-1973, the downturn from early 1974 till the end of 1975 and the subsequent very modest recovery which continues if at a somewhat faltering pace. (The temporal pattern is fairly close to that in most other

[5] A more detailed account (up to 1976) is given in Saunders, Marsden et al. *Winners and Losers: pay patterns in the 1970s* (PEP and CCES University of Sussex, September 1977).

Western industrial countries, although the most recent recovery leaves Britain in mid-1978 with a volume of output still only about 14 per cent above the level of 1970).

Four phases may be distinguished.

i) 1970-1972

The year 1970 opened with the dismantling by a new Conservative government of the controls imposed by the Labour government since 1966. Nearly three years of free pay bargaining followed. The run of two-digit pay increases began almost at once, despite hopes and assurance of "moderation". The usual reaction from a period of enforced restraint was one reason, but there were others: Britain joined the international cyclical boom and was affected by the accompanying rise in commodity prices. Despite the wage-price spiral which began to take hold, real earnings increased; indeed nearly two-thirds of the increase in real earnings over the whole of the 8 years from 1970 to 1978 occurred in 1972 and 1973.

ii) 1972-1974

The rapidity of the nominal pay increases, and the evidence that the boom in the economy was coming to an end, forced a reluctant government into renewed controls — compulsory controls, since the unions refused at that time to enter into an explicit agreement for voluntary pay restraint. With modifications, the controls remained in effect until early 1974. The norms for this phase of policy were based on an average increase in collectively agreed pay levels of about 7 per cent a year. The actual rise in earnings up to the end of 1973 was at the rate of about 12 per cent a year. Most of the difference, however, can be explained by accepted deviations from the norm: some existing contracts had to be honoured; the pay rules provided exception for various anomalies; pay increases for women in accordance with equal pay legislation were permitted; additional overtime and increases under payment by results systems during the boom period were accepted; promotions and job changes caused inevitable increases in average earnings. These allowable and uncontrollable factors — to some extent at least taken into account when the norms were fixed — might together account for 4 or 5 per cent a year increases above the norm. So the figures do not suggest conclusively a large number of runaway infringements of the law.

In addition, towards the end of 1973 the pay policy provided for a form of price indexation known as the "threshold": pay agreements could incorporate automatic increases if the retail price index crossed the "threshold" of a 7 per cent rise in a year — a price increase which then seems to have been regarded as unlikely.

iii) 1974-1975

Early 1974, however, saw a disruptive strike by the coalminers, following the OPEC increase in oil prices, and the fall of the Conservative government. The new Labour government was compelled to abolish the statutory pay policy, which was replaced by nothing more than a TUC statement of "guidelines" to pay negotiators; but no norm was enunciated. Meanwhile, the automatic "threshold" indexation system had been incorporated in a large proportion of pay agreements — and the threshold was crossed in the spring of 1974. There followed nearly a year and a half of continuous and rapid pay increases raising average earnings for a time in the middle of 1975 by about 30 per cent a year [6] — in a period when output and productivity were stagnant or falling and unemployment rising. The whole increase in nominal pay was passing directly into unit labour costs and most of it into prices — the price rise being accentuated by the increase in import prices, not only of oil — and so back into further pay increases. As Table 2 shows, the rise in nominal pay was almost wholly offset in this period by the rise in prices: real pay increased by only 1-2 per cent a year.

iv) 1975-1978

History repeated itself. This time it was a Labour government, and the union leaderships themselves, who were forced into a new round of pay policy from August 1975. The policy preserved the form of a series of voluntary agreements for periods of one year only, but annually renewed, with successive difficulty and various modifications, until the third agreement expired in August 1978. It was this series of agreements which, on the initiative of the TUC, was known as the "Social Contract" (linking pay restraint with government commitments in other policy areas of interest to the unions).

---

[6] The fastest recorded annual rate of increase since the immediate aftermath of the *first* world war.

There followed almost at once a very substantial slowing down of increases in pay and prices (certainly assisted by a less violent rise in sterling import prices, despite the decline of sterling exchange rates). The norms, and the permitted exceptions varied in the successive annual agreements, and incorporated differing provisions aimed at improving the relative positions of the low-paid and, in general, at compressing the dispersion. And in 1976 and 1977 the pay policies were accompanied by reductions in the incidence of income tax designed to compensate for pay restraint.

In the three years of the Social Contract, taking increases from July to July to accord with the agreements, average earnings (on the same basis as the annual or quarterly averages given in Table 2, column 1) rose as follows:

1) July 1975 to July 1976   14 per cent

2) July 1976 to July 1977   9 per cent

3) July 1977 to July 1978   14 per cent

It is difficult to calculate with precision how far these pay increases were compatible with the norms. In the first period, the norm was a flat-rate increase of £ 6 a week (for full-time adults) which would be not far from 10 per cent. After allowance for permitted and uncontrollable deviations, the actual rise of 14 per cent probably indicated no substantia infringement. It included — as in other periods — a number of productivity agreements the results of which have not been precisely tested. The same applies to the second period when the more complicated — and more restrictive — rules probably implied a norm increase of a 4½ to 5 per cent; and also to the third period when the norm was a more generous straight 10 per cent increase, and when general economic recovery was increasing the amount of overtime worked — although not reducing unemployment.

Thus the hard-struck agreements between the union leaderships and the government were on balance well observed. The rate of price inflation slowed down from the alarming annual increases of 25-30 per cent experienced for a time in 1975-76 to the 8 per cent of recent months.

It must be stressed, too, that the effect of the series of Social Contract agreements was to bring about, for the first time in post-war history, a temporary fall in average *real* pay. For more than a year, from the summer of 1976 to the end of 1977, average real pay fell by about 5 per cent. The decline left average real pay at the end of 1977 slightly below the level it reached in 1973 and 1974. The tide turned at the beginning of 1978 when the more relaxed provisions of the third Social Contract agreement allowed pay increases once again to overtake prices. By mid-1978, real pay was increasing at an annual rate of over 5 per cent — faster than at any previous time in the 1970s.

3. PAY DISTRIBUTION AND DIFFERENTIALS IN THE 1970s

We come now to some aspects of pay distribution and its evolution. The issues for discussion here are: does the British distribution differ from that in other countries? How has it been affected by the income policies which were, in part, designed to influence distribution?

As aspects of pay distribution, we must distinguish the concept of *dispersion* (the spread of pay levels within a labour market) from that of *differentials* (differences between the average pay of particular groups in the labour market — e.g. between men and women, or between different occupations or industries).

Comparative pay distributions

First, is the *dispersion* of pay in Britain more, or less, egalitarian than that in comparable countries?

Data in Table 3 provide a first approach to an answer, selecting a few highlights from research in progress. Some comments are needed on the statistics:

i) The latest year for which anything like a reasonably comparable analysis can be made is 1972. For that year we can draw on the splendid work of the Statistical Office of the European Communities who persuaded the then six members of the Community to collect comprehensive, and (so far as possible) uniform, data on pay distributions in *industry*. We can compare these data with those collected for Britain annually since 1970.[7] But the comparison is somewhat

---

[7] The British surveys cover all sectors of the economy but we use for comparison the data for industry only.

uneasy, since the longer established British surveys differ in some details of method and classification from those used by the Community.

ii) Both the Community and British surveys treat as four separate "labour markets" manual and non-manual workers and males and females.

iii) As two summary measures of dispersion, I have used both the coefficient of variation (the standard deviation expressed as a percentage of the median) and the ratio of the highest to the lowest decile.

The conclusion from Table 3 is that, *in 1972*, the British pay dispersion, by either measure, stands out as the most "inegalitarian" for *manual* workers among the six countries, followed closely by France and Italy (except for females in the Netherlands [8]). For *non-manual* workers, the comparison is less clear: depending on the measure used, Britain, France and Italy all show high, and not very different, degrees of inequality compared with Belgium, the Netherlands (at least for men) and Germany. In all four labour markets, by both measures, Germany has the most equal distribution of pay. Belgium and the Netherlands generally fall into an intermediate position. The relative equality of pay in German industry is supported by data for earlier post-war periods.[9]

The high degree of inequality in the British industrial labour markets — again remembering that we refer to 1972 — may appear surprising, even within this limited selection of countries. Most comparative studies of distributions of personal or household incomes put France as distinctly more unequal.[10] But it must be remembered that our comparative figures are restricted to earnings from full-time *employment*, and to such earnings in the *industrial* sector. They thus represent only part of the French pay dispersion. A

[8] Because of the low participation rate of women in the Netherlands, an exceptionally large proportion of the female workers there are juveniles.
[9] See, for example, UN/Economic Commission for Europe *Incomes in Post-War Europe* (1967), giving comparative data for the mid-1960s (see especially Table 6.13) for wage and salary earners and Lvdall, *The Structure of Earnings* (Oxford 1968), especially Table 5.7 for around 1960.
[10] E.G. OECD *Economic Outlook, Occasional Studies*, July 1976. A French critique (*Economie et Statistique*, Dec. 1976) suggested that the methods used in the OECD study, based on fiscal assessments, may have somewhat overstated the degree of inequality.

different dispersion might be found for France if we could include earnings in the public administration, in the public and private service sectors, and in agriculture, not to mention incomes in the independent professions.

We have looked at the dispersion for each of the four separate "labour markets" in each country. Are the conclusions modified when we look at the *differentials* between the labour markets? In some respects they are indeed modified.

Consider first the important differentials between average manual and average non-manual pay. The two groups are not, of course, self-contained or non-competing, but convention, education and qualifications do set up certain barriers to movement between them (as well as within each group). We must note, too, the very wide range of occupations, especially within the non-manual group which comprises both top managers and young secretaries and clerks.

Table 1: RATIO OF NON-MANUAL TO MANUAL PAY 1972

	Males	Females	Total
Great Britain	1.31	1.18	1.20
Germany	1.34	1.31	1.29
Netherlands	1.43	1.20	1.37
Belgium	1.45	1.32	1.41
France	1.81	1.39	1.67
Italy	1.82	1.50	1.75

Sources: As for Table 3, but taking monthly (GB weekly) earnings for both manual and non-manual workers.

A very clear distinction emerges between the "Latin" and the "Anglo-Teutonic" countries (with Belgium and the Netherlands nearer the Anglo-Teutonic end of the range). In this respect, the British appear the most egalitarian; the relatively large inequalities *within* each labour market are in part offset by the relative equality between them. But in Germany the equality within each market is reinforced by the equality between the markets. In France and Italy, too, the wide intra-group dispersions are strengthened by the large differentials between them. These differences are hard to explain and not enough is known about how long they have persisted on their pattern. It does appear, nevertheless, that a large part of the difference between countries lies in the high relative pay of managers and specialists in France and Italy as contrasted with Britain and, although less conspicuously, with Germany. A "sociological" explanation offered by Phelps Brown [11] is that in France authority needs to be susstained by large differences in material rewards, while in Germany the hierarchy of authority is accepted as the natural order without such large monetary distinctions. Alternatively, one might suggest that educational qualifications gained outside the firms are more widely recognized in money terms in France than in Germany (or in Britain). The differences in relative pay of manual and non-manual workers suggested by the figures call for closer study of an issue that could be of some importance for the management of industrial relations.

When individual earnings in all four labour markets are merged, combining the effects both of the dispersions within each market as well as of the differences in average pay levels between them, Brittain, France and Italy emerge (in 1972) as the relatively inegalitarian countries among the six, Germany as the most equal, and Belgium and the Netherlands in an intermediate position. The wide *dispersion* in Britain, accompanying relatively narrow differentials, appears to be explained by the exceptionally wide dispersion of earnings in Britain *within* each occupational group.

These conclusions are based, as mentioned before, on data on pay distribution in industry for 1972 (Eurostat). For Italy, Mazzocchi is discussing more recent developments in his paper, emphasizing that the seventies have witnessed a considerable decline of differentials and dispersion due to the unions' explicit policy to reduce pay differentials. Flat rate increases and above all the 'scala mobile' after 1975 have led, according to Mazzocchi, to a "drastic narrowing of differentials".

[11] Phelps Brown, *Inequality of Pay* (Oxford 1977) page 34. The same difference between France and Germany, based on detailed comparison of specific jobs in a few firms, is found in a French study (Silvestre, "Industrial Wage Differentials: a two-country comparison", in: *International Labour Review*, December 1974).

Developments in British pay distribution during the 1970s

Our comparisons so far have stopped short at 1972. For Britain, we can bring the information up to date. Table 4 shows, for Britain, the changing pattern of pay distribution in the separate labour markets (the ratios of the deciles and quantiles to the median being used as measures of dispersion year by year) for each year from 1970 to 1978. It this case, since we are concentrating upon British experience, I give the more comprehensive and convenient figures of *weekly* earnings based on data for *all sectors* of the economy combined, and for *adult* workers (hence some differences from the British figures in Table 3).

First, we should comment upon one of the largest single changes in the British pay structure in the 1970s — a change not usually regarded as a constituent of "incomes policy" (perhaps because of doubts about its anti-inflationary effect?). This is the rise in *women's pay compared with men's* brought about by the Equal Pay Act of 1970 — the most notable piece of long-term legislation affecting pay distribution.

In 1970, and for many years before, the ratio of women's to men's pay in Britain was exceptionally low by Western European standards. The ratio steadily increased, from 54 per cent in 1970 to 65 per cent in 1977 (median weekly earnings of manual and non-manual adults combined; both ratios are higher — 62 and 74 per cent respectively — for hourly pay, since women on average work shorter hours). Of course, there remains a significant differential (still rather greater than the comparable ratio in other West European countries), due in part to the different occupational and industrial composition of the women's labour force — itself in part due to limited access of women to the higher-paid occupations — and in part perhaps to various ways of circumventing the law.

Particular interest may centre, next, on the question of how far the incomes policies of the period (or the absence of policy) might have affected the pattern of distribution of pay, as distinct from its rate of increase. The following points emerge from Table 4.

i) In 1970-1972, a period when incomes policy was in effect turned off, when average nominal pay was rising at 11-12 per cent a year, the dispersions hardly changed.

ii) But from 1972 to 1977, the dispersions narrowed significantly in each of the four labour markets. This narrowing, *grosso modo*, continued through the several phases of policy described above (including the "no-policy" period of early 1974 till August 1975 which saw the 25-30 per cent pay increases). Each phase of policy, it will be remembered, included some provisions aimed (through the flat-rate element in permitted increases) at bigger proportionate rises for the lower paid.

iii) However, the flattening of the distribution impinged in rather different ways on different positions in the pay structure. The results may be summarized by the ratios of the top to the bottom deciles:

Table 2: RATIO OF TOP TO BOTTOM DECILE

(Weekly earnings)

	1970	1972	1978	Change 1970-78	Change 1972-77
Manual men	2.19	2.17	2.10	— 0.09	— 0.12
Manual women	2.10	2.12	1.99	— 0.11	— 0.14
Non-manual men	2.84	2.82	2.61	— 0.23	— 0.23
Non-manual women	2.71	2.69	2.39	— 0.32	— 0.26

Source: Department of Employment Gazette.

iv) The smallest change during 1972-77 occurs in the best organized group of workers — manual men, who account for 60 per cent of the full-time labour force. There was a small increase (see Table 4) in the relative pay of the lower paid — the bottom quartile point rising from 67 per cent of the median in 1970 to 69 per cent in 1978. And the fall in relative pay of the top decile was also very small — only from 147 to 146 per cent of the median — distinctly less than in the other three labour markets. Although the extent of equalization was minor, it was not insignificant when we bear in mind that overtime pay, payment by results, etc., the variable effects of which cannot be exactly foreseen in collective agreements, are bound to affect the dispersions of manual men's earnings more than the earnings of other groups. (Thus the improvement in the economy in 1977-78 may have been responsible for the slight widening of the manual dispersion in 1978).

v) By way of historical background, Table 4 also gives the dispersion in *1960* for manual men (similar data for non-manual workers were not collected). This shows that the 1960s were, at both ends of the pay scale, a period of slightly *increasing* inequality (in those years, pay policies were not, on the whole, directed towards equalization). The subsequent equalizing, during the 1970s, represented hardly more than a return to the pattern of 1960.[12] Thus it is difficult to maintain that the degree of equality reached by 1977 — for manual men — represents a particularly abnormal or unprecedented situation; just as the international comparisons did not reveal the British industrial pay structure as exceptionally egalitarian.

vi) The biggest change is the decline in the relative pay of the higher paid non-manual men, which began even in the free bargaining period of 1971-72, but was intensified by the subsequent limits on the absolute amount of increases. From 1970 to 1978, the pay at the top decile point for non-manual men (around the median point for, e.g. senior managers), or even at the top quartile (e,g. engineers, salaried architects, senior police officers) remained almost unchanged in real terms. Curiously, the flattening was not notably stronger in 1975-1976, when the incomes policy should have had its strongest equalizing effect (increases at all levels being limited to a flat-rate of £6 a week), than at other times.

vii) A similar but more irregular narrowing occurred among *non-manual women*. Among *manual women*, there was also a marked reduction during the 1970s in the relative earnings of the higher paid, but a smaller increase in the relative pay at lower levels. This may be because the progressive general increase of women's pay relatively to that of men under the equal pay legislation acted as a substitute for the low-pay provision of the pay codes. The narrowing of the dispersion in the 1970s, like that for manual men, reversed a widening during the 1960s.

How far does this narrowing of the dispersions affect Britain's place in the international comparisons made for 1972 in the previous

---

[12] Indeed to find a *substantially* wider dispersion among manual men than that in 1972 or 1977, we have to go back to the wage census of *1906*. (See *Department of Employment Gazette*, May 1978, page 520, which shows dispersions from the wage censuses of 1886, 1906, 1938 and 1960).

section? We have no later data for the other five countries [13], so can compare the British position in 1977 only with that in the other countries in 1972. Unless the dispersions in the other countries changed significantly, Britain is unlikely to have altered its place in the rank ordering.

The white-collar: blue-collar differential

I turn next to the change in the differential between *manual and non-manual* workers — a differential which, as shown in the previous section, was already relatively small in 1972. This differential diminished further after 1972, especially for women.

Table 3: RATIO OF NON-MANUAL TO MANUAL WORKERS' AVERAGE PAY IN GB
(Median weekly pay, adults only; whole economy)

Men	1970	1.23
	1972	1.23
	1978	1.19
Women	1970	1.24
	1972	1.23
	1978	1.13

Source: Department of Employment Gazette.

The relative inequality in the separate labour markets in Britain was softened by this small differential between the average pay of manual and non-manual workers. The further small narrowing of this gap in Britain contrasts with a certain widening in Germany since 1972 when it was also very small.[14] In this respect, Britain's egalitarian position may have been reinforced.

Skill differentials

Much agony and conflict has been caused in Britain by the much-discussed erosion of pay differentials between workers with different qualifications. Some of this is reflected in the changed dispersions

---

[13] Except for the Netherlands where there was a slight narrowing.
[14] Statistisches Bundesamt, Fachserie M, Reihe 15.

analysed above. It is, however, hard to assess the extent of this erosion in any summary form.

Regrettably, a drastic (and not very well-timed) reorganization in 1973 of the British official system of occupational classifications prevents any consistent and complete analysis of changes in relative occupational pay through the 1970s, as well as comparisons with earlier periods. Thus the familiar and internationally well-recognized grouping of manual workers into skilled, semi-skilled and unskilled groups has disappeared; efforts by ourselves, and others, to reconstruct it from the detailed descriptions now used have so far been unsatisfactory. Similarly, the occupational grading of non-manual occupations has been almost unrecognizably transformed.

We can, however, make use of data for manual workers in the engineering industries which retain the traditional 3-fold grouping (for long the formal basis for the pay system although much complicated by later developments in occupational gradings).

The engineering data may be summarized as follows (instead of using the conventional ratio of skilled to unskilled workers' pay, I prefer the ratio of each group's pay to the mean for all workers, mainly because the unskilled group represents so small a proportion of the total):

Bigger proportionate increases for the low paid have had a marked effect on the industry's pay structure. But the erosion of skill differentials at the top has hardly been dramatic.

TABLE 4 : SKILL DIFFERENTIALS IN ENGINEERING GREAT BRITAIN

(Ratio of pay to mean for all workers)

	1970	1978	% of total employed 1976
Skilled	1.07	1.06	50
Semi-skilled	0.96	0.96	44
Unskilled	0.77	0.83	6
Total	1.00	1.00	100

Data relate to weekly pay, including overtime, of adult men in mechanical and electrical engineering, vehicles, and ship-building in June of each year.

Source: Department of Employment Gazette.

In the motor industry, disputes have been especially notorious (although by no means always concerned with pay differentials). In this industry the differentials have in fact been narrowed rather more than in other branches of engineering. But one reason, which may have more general implications for pay structures, has been the shift in motor manufacturing from payment by results to time-rates (or "measured day rates") in 1972-75 (in an effort, partly, to reduce the conflicts at shop floor level which too often accompany payment by results systems). The shift to time rates had to be "bought" by bigger wage increases and this affected mainly the semi-skilled, who make up the teams on the conveyor belts; fewer of the skilled men were moved on to time rates.[15] Thus the overall ratio of skilled workers' pay to the general average fell between 1970 and 1976 from 1.09 to 1.02, while that of the semi-skilled rose from 0.96 to 1.00.

By way of contrast, it may be noted that in Germany skill differentials among manual workers, in industry generally, have been well maintained through the 1970s.[16] One reason commonly given is that the skilled workers have tended to dominate the German industrial unions by virtue of their higher membership rates. Thus, although the unions have upheld, in principle, the aim of more favourable treatment for the lower paid, in practice pay negotiations have centred on the skilled rate and the rates for other grades have been determined by traditional relativities.

Pay and taxes

Only casual references have been made in this paper to the effects on pay and its distribution of changes in the incident of tax (which can be taken to include workers' contributions to social security), particularly in relation to the bargaining of tax reductions for pay restraint effected by the Chancellor of the Exchequer in 1976 and 1977. It is impracticable at this stage of an over-long paper to discuss in detail the combined effects of pay and tax changes on post-tax pay distribution.[17] However, the overall effects are summarized

---

[15] This is shown by detailed figures which separate time workers from workers on payment by results.

[16] Data from Statistisches Bundesamt, op. cit.

[17] For a fuller discussion see Saunders, Marsden et al., *Winners and Losers* (PEP/Sussex University, September 1977) from which Table 5 is derived. The latest data refer to 1976 but changes in 1977 would affect the results very little.

in Table 5, which combines the effects of changes in pay with changes in both the tax structure and in prices.

Table 5: SPECIAL EMPLOYMENT MEASURES
(The number of people covered by the special employment and training measures in Great Britain)

	Number covered	Date of count
Temporary Employment Subsidy	121,100	November 30,1978
Short-time working compensation scheme	7,237	November 30, 1978
Small firms employment subsidy	11,754	September 30, 1978
Job Release Scheme	18,742	December 5, 1978
Adult Employment Subsidy	397	December 7, 1978
Job Introduction Scheme	236	November 30, 1978
Youth Opportunities Programme	55,000	November 30, 1978
Community Industry	4,977	November 9, 1978
Special Temporary Employment Programme	5,000	November 30, 1978
Job Creation Programme	5,000	December 7, 1978
Training places supported in industry	35,486	October 31, 1978

This table shows:

i) At all pay levels, the incidence of tax increased during the 1970s by between 4 and 6 per cent of gross income at each quantile point. This was, of course, the result of "fiscal drag" as the rise in nominal pay brought lower incomes into the tax system, and higher incomes into higher rates of tax. "Fiscal drag" more than offset the tax remissions that were made in several budgets during the 1970s. Thus changes in the structure of tax rates and allowances hardly affected the distribution. Such redistribution as took place resulted from the redistribution of pre-tax earnings.

ii) The increases in real pay before tax were much reduced all round when tax is taken into account. Changes in real pay after tax range between 1970 and 1976 from a rise of 10 per cent for the bottom decile of manual men to a 1 per cent decline for the top decile of non-manuals. As Dr. Thomson points out, the increases in social benefits and collective consumption which the tax increases helped to finance were not generally regarded as adequate compensation for limited increases in disposable income.

4. SOME CONCLUSIONS FOR FUTURE INCOMES POLICIES

Three things emerge from these comparisons. First, the British pay structure is among the more inegalitarian among the countries reviewed. Second, developments in the 1970s, including the not very powerful equalizing provisions of the incomes policies, have had some effect — but quite a small one — in raising the relative pay of the lower paid and a rather larger effect on reducing relative pay at the top white-collar levels. Third, no simple association can be established, among our six countries, between relative inequality of pre-tax pay and relative economic performance or competitiveness. However, it could be significant that the more inegalitarian countries — Britain, France and Italy — have suffered the most from inflation and industrial conflict, while Germany, the most egalitarian, has suffered the least. (It can of course be pointed out that the causal relationship may go either way, and also that many other factors are involved in inflation and industrial relations, besides the shape of the pay structure).

The situation at the time of writing is that the government has attempted to get union agreement to continued restraint and a new norm — indeed the surprisingly severe norm of a 5 per cent rise in the 12 months from August 1978, although with allowances for productivity agreements and extra increases for the lower paid. The Government has also hinted that failure of pay restraint would force a resort to fiscal and monetary measures to limit inflation. The union leaderships have refused support to any formal restraint, their declared policy being a return to "free collective bargaining".

The union leaderships are caught between opposing forces. On the one hand, they are subject to intense pressure from thes Government to commit themselves as specifically as possible to restraint in pay claims. The union leaders recognize perfectly well the chaos that might otherwise follow — as it did in 1974-75 — in view of the fragmented and uncoordinated system of collective bargaining. Nor are the unions entirely unanimous in supporting a return to free bargaining: at the TUC conference in September 1978, the leaders of three major public sector unions, many of whose members are among the lower-paid workers, spoke in favour of a specific commitment to restraint.

On the other hand, the union leaderships face strong pressures from below to reject any cooperation with government-supported restraint. These pressures derive from groups of high-paid workers whose differentials have suffered in recent years; from lower-paid groups who lack confidence in the "low-pay" provisions of the pay codes; and from shop stewards and local groups who have found that pay policies restrict their powers of getting better plant bargains.

Another dilemma appears for the Unions: while in favour of raising low pay, they are also anxious for the restoration of differentials for skill. Can the objectives be reconciled? Not only do different unions take different views on the priorities, but the opposing objectives conflict *within* many unions.

It has become increasingly clear that under the present bargaining system no sensible solution is possible. The negotiators who effectively determine earnings are not only able, but are encouraged by the system, to maintain the illusion that their bargaining concerns only the workers and employers directly involved, without regard to the effects on other negotiations. This may be rational behaviour at the group level, since those who get a good bargain first do gain at least a temporary advantage.

The solution of leaving pay determination to "freely operating market forces" is unrealistic in a situation where supply and demand factors are outweighed by constellations of market power; a confrontation of monopolies, strongly enough organized to resist competition, is no market.

In these circumstances, it seems to me clear that the solution must lie in the introduction — or return — of some *authority*, not only over the average rate of increase of pay but over the distribution of pay.

There may be no realistic possibility of a drastic transformation of the bargaining system in the immediate future. But it is possible that the experience of the last few years is beginning to prepare the ground for better ways of solving the conflict between the short- run interests of competing groups and the efficient management of pay changes in the economy as a whole.

Views on the mechanisms for a solution must differ. But I would suggest the following as a personal expression of opinion of what should be done within the crucial area of incomes policies.

i) Two elements in policy — the short-term and the long-term — must be distinguished.

ii) the *short-term* element is the macro-economico anti-inflationary element on which most incomes policies in Britain have been forced to concentrate. This implies some kind of "norm" and a set of principles to be applied to each round of pay settlements in the light of the general economic situation. Some points seem clear:

a) These norms cannot be imposed simply by government fiat. They require the agreement of the organizations concerned and thus involve an element of top-level bargaining.

b) One essential feature of such top-level bargaining is that the leadership of the TUC should be in a position to commit the constituent unions, *and* the lower levels of pay bargainers as well. This means a greater recognition of central union authority than has so far been apparent — and is one of the most difficult objectives to achieve. The concept of a "central bargain", although long established in some other European countries, is contrary to previous British practice and principle. But more recent experience is, perhaps, gradually rendering the idea — in practice if not yet in principle — less unacceptable to a tradition-bound trade union movement.

c) One implication of a central bargain is that pay settlements should be conducted more or less simultaneously in the major bargaining groups; at present they are spread practically over the whole year; there are endless opportunities for each group to use the gains made by preceding groups as justification for its own demands. This appears to be a major factor in strengthening the inflationary momentum.

d) It is clear that the government is bound to be involved in any such centralized pay bargaining both because of its vital importance for the economy as a whole, and because the government is directly or indirectly involved in the pay levels of 30 per cent of workers — in the nationalized industries and the rest of the public sector.

e) Whether it is also necessary for government to have the power to prohibit by law extensive pay increases is a more difficult issue. My own view is that such powers should be taken, in order to protect the mass of workers from the still possible abuse of market power by an individual group.

iii) But we have seen from experience how the application of a necessarily rather inflexible short-term norm, especially when it is forced upon pay bargainers by emergency action, ignores (with only a few exceptions) the resolving of distributional tensions. Hitherto, the issue has been evaded, if not successfully, by the assumption that the resulting tensions will be relieved later when the "good old days" of free bargaining return. But if that hope is illusory, as it may well be, then better machinery is needed for the determination, in an acceptable manner, of at least the major differentials in pay. That is the *long-term* element in what I would regard as an effective incomes policy. It is unrealistic to imagine that the complex problems of setting pay differentials between skills or occupations can be solved by central bargaining year by year. A much longer-term approach is necessary. Probably the most practical organizational innovation would be to establish a form of arbitrating body to which disputes over differentials could be referred [18]. This is not to say that the determination of an acceptable pattern of pay distribution is a simple matter, needing only the application of impartial judgment. The considerations are exceedingly complex — "tradition" (but tradition since when?), "equity" (on which views will necessarily differ), efficiency, "comparibility" (with whom?) ... But it is possible that such a body could, no doubt over a long period, gradually establish a set of generally acceptable principles and that it could acquire a measure of authority which would be accepted. This would surely be preferable to the present lack of system, under which individual disputes are settled in part by power conflicts, and in part by reference to a variety of arbitral or conciliatory bodies, each adopting its own set of principles.

iv) Finally, it must be recognized that the short-term and long-term solutions, the macro-economic and the distributional, are bound together. Unless inflationary overall increases in illusory money terms can be restrained, allowing policy to be directed towards a reasonable growth of real income, there is no prospect of resolving the distributional tensions.

---

[18] Not wholly an innovation, since the National Board for Prices and Incomes performed this kind of function in part during the late 1960s.

Christopher Saunders

TABLE 6: COMPOSITION OF UNEMPLOYMENT
(Percentage of total unemployed, Great Britain, June/July 1978)

	Managerial & professional	Clerical	Other non-manual	Skilled manual	Semiskilled manual	General labourers	Total
(a) by occupation							
Males	7.8	8.5	2.8	14.4	24.7	42.0	100
Females	8.7	30.8	14.2	3.0	21.6	21.7	100
(b) by duration of unemployment (in weeks)							
	—4	—8	—13	—26	—52	over 52	Total
Males	21.6	13.2	8.7	14.6	16.4	25.4	100
Females	29.9	16.3	9.1	15.8	15.3	13.6	100
(c) by age (in years)							
	<18	18-24	25-34	35-54	55-59	60-	Total
Males	15.3	21.3	19.6	24.6	6.7	12.5	100
Females	28.9	34.2	15.3	16.4	4.9	0.3	100

TABLE 7: SHORT-TIME WORKING
(Percentage of manual workers working short-time in October of each year)

1973	1974	1975	1976	1977	1978
0.2	1.4	2.9	0.9	0.9	0.7

The peak figure in 1973-78 was 4.4% reached in April/May 1975.
(This excludes figure of 20% reached in Jan. Feb. 1974 when part of industry was closed down by a coalminers' strike).

Data relate to manual workers in manufacturing only, and to those working short-time (or stood off for the whole week), under arrangements with the employer, in specific weeks.

Fig. 1: *Engagements and discharges (and other losess): manufacturing industries in Great Britain*

Four quarter moving average *

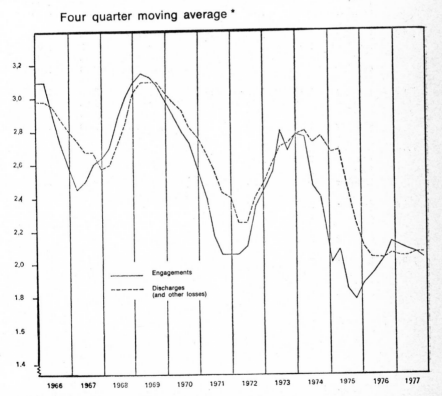

* The four quarter moving average has been compiled from the number of engagements and discharges (and other losses) in a period of four weeks expressed as a percentage of the estimated numbers of employees in employment.

SOURCE: *Department of Employment Gazette, May 1978.*

Table 8: LABOUR TURNOVER RATES

Four quarter moving average * of total engagements and discharges (and other losses): manufacturing industries in Great Britain

Year	Reference months**	Total engagements	Total discharges (and other losses)	Year	Reference months**	Total engagements	Total discharges (and other losses)
1966	January	3.10	2.93	1974	January	2.78	2.78
	April	3.10	2.98		April	2.77	2.80
	July	2.90	2.95		July	2.47	2.73
	October	2.73	2.88		October	2.40	2.77
1967	January	2.58	2.80	1975	February	2.00	2.67
	April	2.45	2.75		May	2.08	2.69
	July	2.50	2.68		August	1.85	2.45
	October	2.60	2.68		November	1.78	2.25
1968	January	2.63	2.58	1976	February	1.88	2.10
	April	2.70	2.60		May	1.93	2.03
	July	2.88	2.73		August	2.03	2.03
	October	3.00	2.85		November	2.13	2.05
1969	January	3.10	3.03	1977	Feb.	2.10	2.03
	April	3.15	3.10		May	2.08	2.03
	July	3.13	3.10		August	2.05	2.05
	October	3.08	3.10		November	2.00	2.05
1970	January	2.99	3.03				
	April	2.90	2.98				
	July	2.80	2.93				
	October	2.73	2.83				
1971	January	2.57	2.77				
	April	2.40	2.67				
	July	2.17	2.57				
	October	2.05	2.43				
1972	January	2.05	2.30				
	April	2.05	2.15				
	July	2.10	2.15				
	October	2.35	2.30				
1973	January	2.43	2.38				
	April	2.55	2.60				
	July	2.80	2.70				
	October	2.68	2.73				

* The four quarter moving average has been compiled from the numbers of engagements and discharges (and other losses) in a period of four weaks expressed as a percentage of the estimated numbers of employees in employment.

** On which the moving average is centred.

Source: Department of Employment Gazette, June 1977.

TABLE 9: INDICATORS OF INFLATION FOR SOME WESTERN COUNTRIES
(Indexes for 1977 (x968 = 100))

Rank order of countries in brackets

	(1) Hourly earnings in manufacturing	(2) Consumer prices	(3) Real earnings in manufacturing	(4) Labour costs per unit of manufacturing output National currency	(5) Labour costs per unit of manufacturing output in S	(6) Labour productivity in manufacturing	(7) Industrial production
France	312 (4)	205 (4)	153 (3)	197 (4)	198 (5)	168 (2)	143 (2)
Germany	226 (5)	156 (6)	145 (4)	169 (5)	290 (1)	151 (4)	140 (3)
Italy	492 (1)	255 (2)	193 (1)	335 (1)	237 (3)	153 (3)	134 (4)
UK	339 (3)	275 (1)	123 (5)	306 (2)	223 (4)	126 (6)	112 (6)
US	189 (6)	174 (5)	108 (6)	151 (6)	151 (6)	132 (5)	128 (5)
Japan	425 (2)	230 (3)	185 (2)	213 (3)	283 (2)	203 (1)	167 (1)
Average (unweighted)	330	216	151	229	230	156	137

Notes: Col (1) *Wage earners only* in Germany, Italy, and US. Basic hourly *rates* in France and Italy, *Monthly* earnings in Japan.
Col (4) Wages and salaries (plus social charges paid by employers in Italy, UK and US) per unit of manufacturing output.
Col (6) Output volume per man-hour (wage earners only in Italy and US) in manufacturing.

SOURCE: *National Institute Economic Review, August 1978 (data derived mainly from OECD Main Economic Indicators).*

Table 10 - UK: Indicators relevant to inflation 1960-78 (Whole Economy)

	(1) Weekly earnings	(2) Retail prices	(3) Real earnings	(4) Employment	(5) GDP	(5) Labour productivity	(7) Labour cost per unit of output	(8) Unemployment % of labour force
A. Index numbers (1970 = 100)								
1960	53	67.2	79	98	77	79	67	1.5[2]
1970	100	100	100	100	100	100	100	2.6[2]
1971	111.3	109.4	101.7	98.5	101.5	103.0	110.1	3.4[2]
1972	125.1	117.2	106.7	98.5	104.7	106.3	120.4	3.7[2]
1973	142.5	128.0	111.3	100.9	111.1	110.1	130.1	2.6[2]
1974	167.5	148.5	112.8	101.4	109.2	107.6	161.1	2.6[2]
1975	212.3	184.4	115.1	100.8	107.1	106.3	210.1	4.0[2]
1976	245.5	215.0	114.1	100.3	109.4	109.1	233.6	6.4[2]
1977	270.4	249.1	108.6	100.9	112.1	111.2	252.3	5.8[2]
1977/Qr. I	263.0	238.2	110.4	100.7	112.4	111.6	249.4	5.6[2]
1977/Qr. II[a]	267.4	249.0	107.4	—	—	—	—	5.6[2]
1978/Qr. I	291.3	260.9	111.7	100.9	113.8	112.8	272.2	5.9[2]
1978/Qr. II[a]	308.4	268.0	115.1	—	—	—	—	5.7[2]
B. Change from previous year (per cent)								
1971	11.3	9.4	1.7	-1.5	1.5	3.0	10.1	
1972	12.4	7.1	4.9	—	3.2	3.2	9.4	
1973	13.9	9.2	4.3	2.4	6.1	3.6	8.0	
1974	17.5	16.0	1.3	0.5	-1.8	-2.3	23.9	

	(1)	(2)	(3)	(4)	(5)	(6)	(7)
1975	25.7	24.2	2.0	—0.6	—1.8	—1.2	30.4
1976	15.6	16.6	—0.9	—0.5	2.1	2.6	11.2
1977	10.2	15.9	—4.8	0.6	2.6	1.9	8.0
1978/Qr. I*a)*	10.8	9.5	1.2	0.2	1.2	1.1	9.1
1978/Qr. II*a)*	15.3	7.6	7.2	—	—	—	—
July *a)*	14.2	7.8	5.9	—	—	—	—
Aug. *a)*	13.8	8.0	5.4	—	—	—	—

C. *Annual rates of change (per cent compound)*

	(1)	(2)	(3)	(4)	(5)	(6)	(7)
1960-70	6.6	4.1	2.5	0.2	2.7	2.4	4.1
1970-73	12.5	6.2	5.5	;3	3.6	3.3	9.1
1973-77	17.4	18.1	—0.5	—	0.2	0.4	18.1
1970-77	15.3	13.9	1.2	0.1	1.7	1.5	14.1

a) change from corresponding period of previous year.

Sources: col (1) Department of Employment index (old series) of gross weekly pay (wages and salaries) per employment index (old series) of gross weekly pay (wages and salaries) per employed person (agriculture, mining, manufacturing, construction, utilities, transport and some other services). From *Dept. of Employment Gazette; averages for period.*

col (2) Dept. of Employment index of retail prices (*Dept. of Employment Gazette*); *averages for period.*

col (3) col. (1) divided by col (2).

col (4) Total civil employment (*Economic Trends. Annual Supplement 1976*) and *Dept. of Employment Gazette*; averages for period.

col (5) Revised estimates of national accounts at 1975 prices (*National Income and Expenditure, 1967-77*).

col (6) col (5) divided by col (4).

col (7) Total labour costs (wages and salaries plus social charges falling on employers (*National Income and Expenditure 1967-77*) per unit of GDP.

col (8) *National Institute Economic Review.*

Table 11: MEASURES OF DISPERSION OF PAY IN INDUSTRY IN VARIOUS COUNTRIES 1972

	Manual a)		Non-manual b)	
	Coefficient of variation	Ratio top to bottom decile	Coefficient of variation	Ratio top to bottom decile
MALES				
Great Britain	31.6	2.04	49.2	2.58
Belgium	24.0	1.78	37.0	2.54
France	30.9	2.04	49.0	3.14
FR Germany	22.2	1.80	29.2	2.13
Italy	27.5	2.10	47.7	2.99
Netherlands	23.9	1.78	40.3	2.60
FEMALES				
Great Britain	27.9	2.00	38.1	2.07
Belgium	21.8	1.77	33.5	2.15
France	26.6	1.81	43.2	2.40
FR Germany	21.4	1.74	30.4	2.08
Italy	25.9	1.92	39.2	2.40
Netherlands	33.3	2.52	42.8	2.92

Notes: data relate to direct remuneration of workers, of all ages (juveniles estimated for GB) in mining, manufacturing (including gas, water and electricity supply) and construction. Manual workers: hourly earnings; non-manuals: weekly or monthly earnings.

a) Ouvriers or Arbeiter   b) Employés or Angestellte

Sources: Except for Great Britain, Statistical Office of the Communities, The Structure of Earnings in Industry 1972 (Social Statistics, Special Series, 1976). For Great Britain, Department of Employment New Earnings Survey, 1972.

Table 12: GREAT BRITAIN: DISPERSION OF WEEKLY EARNINGS BY QUANTILES (as per cent of median)

(Whole economy; full-time adults only)

	Manual					Non-manual				
	Lower decile	Lower quartile as %	Top quartile of median	Top decile	Median L.	Lower decile	Lower quartile	Top quartile as %	Top decile of median	Median L.
Men										
1960	70.6	82.6	121.7	145.2	14.2	—	—	—	—	—
1970	67.3	81.1	122.3	147.2	25.6	61.8	77.1	130.8	175.1	31.4
1971	68.2	81.8	122.1	146.5	28.1	61.7	76.5	131.2	174.4	34.3
1972	67.6	81.3	122.3	146.6	31.3	61.7	76.8	131.3	173.7	38.5
1973	67.3	81.4	121.6	145.3	36.6	61.6	76.7	130.9	172.7	42.8
1974	68.6	82.2	121.0	144.1	41.8	62.9	77.6	130.2	171.6	48.5
1975	69.2	82.8	121.3	144.4	53.2	62.6	77.5	129.6	166.7	61.8
1976	70.2	82.4	120.8	144.9	62.1	62.5	77.8	130.5	167.5	73.9
1977	70.6	83.1	120.2	144.4	68.2	63.6	78.4	128.8	164.5	81.1
1978	69.4	82.4	121.2	146.0	76.8	62.9	78.4	127.9	163.9	91.8

Cont. Table 12: GREAT BRITAIN: DISPERSION OF WEEKLY EARNINGS BY QUANTILES (as per cent of median)

(Whole economy; full-time adults only)

	Manual					Non-manual				
	Lower decile	Lower quartile as %	Top quartile of median	Top decile	Median L.	Lower decile	Lower quartile	Top quartile as %	Top decile of median	Median L.
Women										
1960	72.0	84.6	117.8	138.3	7.6	—	—	—	—	—
1970	69.0	83.0	120.1	144.8	12.8	64.2	78.3	129.4	173.7	20.6
1971	70.2	83.6	120.4	143.0	14.6	65.0	78.8	128.2	169.9	23.1
1972	68.9	82.5	121.6	145.9	16.4	64.0	78.2	129.1	170.9	26.0
1973	69.2	82.8	121.5	144.4	18.9	65.6	79.2	129.0	169.5	28.7
1974	69.1	83.0	119.8	143.4	22.7	66.5	79.4	127.9	162.0 -	33.4
1975	68.4	83.3	119.6	141.4	31.0	66.5	80.3	127.2	171.5	45.7
1976	67.8	82.6	119.7	140.6	38.4	65.1	79.9	128.6	172.9	56.9
1977	70.3	83.3	118.3	137.8	42.6	68.1	81.7	126.8	165.6	62.4
1978	70.8	83.2	119.6	140.9	47.6	68.8	81.9	127.4	164.7	68.7

a) The temporary drop in these years may be due to a temporary under-representation of certain groups in the sample.

Notes: 1. Data based on a 1% random sample of individual workers.
2. Earnings are for a pay period including a given week in April of each year.
3. Adults are men of 21 and over, women of 18 and over.
4. Figures for 1972 and thereafter exclude workers whose pay was affected by absence (earlier figures include them).

Source: 1970-1977 Department of Employment: *New Earnings Survey 1977* Table 16 1960: *Department of Employment Gazette May 1978* p. 520 *and* J. R. Thatcher *in Journal of Royal Statistical Society (Series A)* 1968 Part. 2.

Table 13: GB GROSS (BEFORE TAX) AND NET (AFTER TAX) PAY AT QUANTILE POINTS

		Lower decile	Lower quartile	Median	Top quartile	Top decile
A. 1976 as % of 1970 in real terms						
Manual men:	Gross	118	116	113	112	112
	Net	110	109	107	105	104
Non-manual men:	Gross	111	111	110	110	106
	Net	105	105	104	102	99
B. tax as % of gross income						
Manual men:	1970	10	14	18	21	23
	1976	16	19.5	23	26	28
Non-manual men:	1970	13	17	21	24	26
	1976	17	22	26	29	30

Data relate to adult men with non-earning wife and two dependent children. Earnings include child allowances. ' Tax ' includes income tax and workers national insurance contributions.

ANNEX I

Postcript (end January 1979)

These afterthoughts are written at a time when the threats to smooth pay management in Britain — threats suggested in fairly mild terms in the paper (written in October 1978) — have become reality. In the last few weeks, there have been: a strike of drivers for road haulage contractors; a series of local strikes, after a one- day strike everywhere, by manual workers in many vital public services; a series of one-day strikes by railway drivers; and a strike by drivers of oil tankers. The extent of the damage to industrial production is not yet clear. We can add the suspension of the London *'Times'* and its associate newspapers since November as a result of failure to reach agreement in the introduction of new printing technologies.

We can single out some special features of these disruptions which are relevant to points made in the paper, and particularly to the emphasis in the paper on the problems of pay distribution.

a) The strikes have followed a year or two in which pay management, through an incomes policy supported, if without enthusiasm, by the union leaderships, together with some industrial recovery, appeared to have reversed the trend of inflation and to have resulted in the first significant increase in real earnings since 1975. The government's efforts to get the unions to maintain a "norm" of 5 per cent increases (with the usual additions for productivity agreements, etc.) have been resisted, in several cases successfully, by a number of bargaining groups as existing agreements expired.

b) In general, the current strikes (together with some preliminary pay claims by other groups approaching negotiations) come from workers in the lower-paid sectors. But this needs qualification. The lorry drivers on average earn about the average pay for men manual workers — but only at the cost of an average working week, with overtime, of about 53 hours; their basic rates, for a 40 hours week, are around 10 per cent below the general industrial average, and one of their fears is that EEC restrictions on driving hours will substantially reduce their opportunities for overtime. On the other hand, most of the public service manual workers now in dispute earn well below average pay, in terms either of actual earnings or of basic rates. Opportunities for "drift" through local settlements are obviously very limited for the public service. The railway drivers earn about the average basic rate and, with extensive overtime and shift work, are able to get rather more than average actual earnings. Their effort is directed towards restoring the differential which formerly attached to a skilled occupation — an effort which is resisted by the rest of the railway workers (who are organized in a separate union from the drivers).

c) On the railways (as with the Times newspaper) an important part of the problem is inability to reach agreements on pay associated with agreements on working methods to improve productivity.

d) The current disputes have brought to the surface the tensions, in certain unions, between the union leaderships and the memberships. Thus the lorry drivers' strike was initiated by local "wild" strikes which appear to have forced the hands of the unwieldy and conglomerate Transport and General Workers' Union. And the efforts by the union to direct the conduct of this ill-prepared strike were frustrated by a number of aggressive local groups.

e) The Labour government, with an election approaching, still clings to the hope that the union leaderships will be able to regain the authority to organize "responsible free collective bargaining" in place of what has been termed "free collective suicide"). Thus the cautious approach of the government towards the present disputes is in part motivated by the need to underpin the efforts to restore control by the union leaderships, some of whom are clearly alarmed by the breakdown of discipline.

Some of the recent disputes have made clear the need for much more effective preferential treatment of the low-paid (however these may be defined). For some of the better organized groups of low-paid workers, large *percentage* increases are now being forced by industrial action, and will continue to be got either by strikes or by negotiations. But this creates further problems. First, there are many low-pay groups (e.g. in agriculture, textiles, clothing, distribution, catering) which may have equal claims in equity but not in bargaining power. Second, and more important from the point of view of restraining the inflation rate, the question is whether claims for more or less equal *percentage* increases will spread throughout the better-paid (and well organized) groups. Indeed the first important agreements exceeding the government's 5 per cent plus policy came at the end of 1978 from better paid groups (the Ford motor company and others).

The need to achieve at least two of the objectives mentioned in Section 4 is obvious to the observer, and — which is more relevant — is beginning to be recognized among some union leaders:

i) The need for a radical change in pay bargaining systems and attitudes, and particularly the need for some form of coordination of union pay claims which recognizes the reactions of each pay claim on the overall distribution of pay, on prices, and, in the case of public services, on taxes. This is the only way in which the justified efforts to raise low-pay can succeed for more than a few months. But above all the higher-paid must restrain the use of their own bargaining power. All this involves a degree of centralization of bargaining and, therefore, more uniformity in settlement dates. Probably, as suggested in the paper, it could be assisted by establishing a single body to which disputes over differentials and pay systems could be referred.

ii) The need for a restoration of the authority of some unions over their memberships.

Such proposals are easy enough to write down. They are not likely to be carried out in the near future. However, the lessons to be drawn from the history of the last few years are not entirely discouraging. There have been periods — certainly short periods — during which union policies have been directed, not without success, towards the observance of general rules for pay settlements — although these general rules have not been sufficiently focused on the distributional problem. The question is whether a long-term and gradual reform of the pay system can emerge from the responses to immediate emergencies.

ANNEX II

Special measures to combat unemployment

The most important of the special measures to create employment is the Temporary Employment Subsidy introduced in August 1975. The purpose is to maintain employment in firms where dismissals for redundancy would otherwise take place. Under the scheme, the government provides employees with a subsidy of £20 a week (about one-quarter of average adult male earnings) for each job which the employer agrees to maintain. The subsidy is paid so long as the job remains at risk, but for a maximum period of 1 year (a supplement, at £10 a week, can be paid for a further 6 months if the job remains at risk). To receive the subsidy, a firm must not be insolvent or "near to insolvency".

The cumulative total application approved between August 1975 and March 1978 covered 408,000 workers (plus 66,000 for the £ 10 supplementary scheme). And the number supported at 31 March 1978 was about 173,000 (equal to 12 per cent of total unemployment at that date, or 0.7 per cent of the total labour force).

Of the total numbers involved, nearly a quarter are in the textile industry and another quarter in clothing and footwear.

It is claimed that the subsidy is highly cost-effective in the sense that the costs to the state are to a large extent counter balanced by reduced need for unemployment benefit, and extra taxes and social insurance contributions received from the workers involved.

A survey of results shows that workers under 25 held nearly a quarter of the subsidized jobs; that 12 per cent were declared redundant after the subsidies ceased; but that a third of the firms increased the total size of their labour force after the subsidies ceased.

Source: Department of Employment Gazette, May 1978.

102   *Christopher Saunders*

BIBLIOGRAPHY

Department of Employment Gazette: (issue of May 1978).
Economie et Statistique: (issue of Dec. 1976).
H. F. Lydall (1968): *The Structure of Earnings*. Oxford 1968.
OECD (1976): *Economic Outlook, Occasional Studies* (July 1976).
H. Phelps-Brown (1977): *Inequality of Pay*, Oxford U.P. 1977.
C. Saunders et al. (1977): *Winners and Losers: pay patterns in the 1970s* (PEP and CCES, University of Sussex, Sept. 1977).
J. J. Silvestre (1974): "Industrial Wage Differentials: a two-country comparison", in: *International Labour Review* (Dec. 1974).
Statistisches Bundesamt: *Fachserie M,. Reihe 15*.
U.N./Economic Commission for Europe (1967): *Incomes in Post-War Europe*, Paris 1967.

CHAPTER II

THE GERMAN CASE

INDUSTRIAL RELATIONS IN THE FEDERAL REPUBLIC OF GERMANY DURING THE 1970s

by

WALTHER MÜLLER-JENTSCH

1. CHANGES IN THE SYSTEM OF INDUSTRIAL RELATIONS

In view of the profound nature of the current economic crisis, with its far-reaching consequences for the social situation of wage-earners and salaried employees, the West German system of industrial relations is characterized by a remarkable stability and adaptability. Nevertheless, it is obvious that several changes of great consequence have taken place in the 1970s — changes which I would like to summarize briefly at the beginning of my paper.

The *first* conspicuous change concerns the *level of unionization*. While it exhibited a tendency to fall in the 1960s, this trend was reversed in the early 1970s. Ever since, there has been an almost continuous rise in the level of unionization. This trend continued even after the onset of the West German economy's most serious recession to date, which led to the decline in the total number of persons employed and, thus, of the number of potential union members (see Table 1). The remarkable thing about this development is that is holds true for all groups within the labour force (workers, salaried employees, women, foreign workers) and for most industries.

The most notable exception is the public service, which in contrast to other sectors of the economy, continues to show rising employment figures in the seventies, though it shows a slightly declining trend in the growth of unionization.

It was only the DGB (German Trade Unions' Federation) that profited by the rise in unionization; the professional organizations

Table 1: MEMBERS AND DEGREE OF ORGANIZATION OF THE GERMAN TRADE UNIONS' FEDERATION (DGB), 1961-1977

Year	Labour force [1]	Trade union members	Degree of organization [2]
1961	20 911 000	6 382 000	30.5
1962	21 187 000	6 430 000	30.3
1963	21 447 000	6 431 000	30.0
1964	21 653 000	6 485 000	30.0
1965	21 904 000	6 574 000	30.0
1966	21 926 000	6 537 000	29.8
1967	21 513 000	6 408 000	29.8
1968	21 506 000	6 376 000	29.6
1969	21 931 000	6 482 000	29.6
1970	22 395 000	6 713 000	30.0
1971	22 599 000	6 869 000	30.4
1972	22 681 000	6 986 000	30.8
1973	22 837 000	7 168 000	31.4
1974	22 734 000	7 406 000	32.6
1975	22 460 000	7 365 000	32.8
1976	22 348 000	7 400 000	33.1
1977	22 344 000 (first 6	7 471 000	33.4
1978	22 349 000 months)	7 752 000	34.7

[1] In employment plus unemployed.
[2] Ratio of trade union members to labour force; slightly overestimated, since trade union members include pensioners, which are not included in the figures for the labour force.

Source: 1977 and 78/79 Annual Report of The Council of Economic Experts (labour force); DGB membership statistics; own calculations.

that compete with it in certain areas — the German Salaried Employees' Union Deutsche Angestellten-Gewerkschaft and the German Civil Servants' Association Deutscher Beamtenbund — have instead merely been able to slow down the decline in unionization.

The *second* notable change concerns the level of *industrial conflict*. Compared with the 60s, the intensivity of the conflicts has increased markedly. This is clearly indicated by the rise in the number of workers involved in strikes; however, it is demonstrated even more conclusively by the increase in the number of working days lost through strikes. While the average number of workers involved in strikes per year has doubled since the 1960s, the number of working days lost has quadrupled(see Table 2). In addition, for the first time in the history of the Federal Republic, waves of unofficial strikes took place, particularly in 1969 and 1973 — both prosperous years. Another indication of the general intensification of industrial conflict was the increase in the number of large-scale lock-outs. While there was only one major lock-out in the 1960s, there have already been five in the '70s (two in the engineering industry, two in the printing industry and one in the steel industry). Quantitatively, the engineering industry, which accounts for about three-quarters of all working days lost, leads the list of strike-prone industries. It is followed by the printing industry, the public service and the chemical industry — all of which lag far behind. The traditional industrial sectors (mining, textiles, construction) account for only a very small percentage of the total working days lost.

A *third* change concerns the *issues at stake in conflicts*. In the 60s, labour disputes were exclusively wage disputes. In the 70s, non-wage policy issues have achieved a status of equal importance, at least in the manifest conflict between capital and labour. It was during the wave of unofficial strikes in 1973 that demands for improvements in working conditions first played a significant, though not primary, role. After that, qualitative demands also emerged in official strikes. In these instances, attention was focused on questions of the organization of the labour process, the intensification of output, the social security of older employees, re-classification in lower wage brackets, and the devaluation of qualifications. The latter have become urgent problems, in particular as a result of the most recent rationalization measures and measures in response to the crisis taken by management in the printing and engineering industries.

At the end of 1978 there was a labour dispute in the steel

Table 2: DEGREE OF UNIONIZATION OF SOME SPECIFIC GROUPS, 1961-1976 (in per cent)

Year	Workers DGB	Employees			Civil Servants			
		DGB	DAG	Total	DGB	GdP	DBB	Total
1961	39.9	11.4	7.3	18.7	34.4	5.7	42.7	82.8
1962	39.6	11.7	7.3	19.0	33.7	5.6	41.6	80.9
1963	39.1	11.7	7.3	19.0	33.7	5.8	41.3	80.8
1964	39.7	11.5	6.9	18.4	33.0	5.8	40.1	78.9
1965	39.4	12.0	6.8	18.8	32.7	5.7	39.5	77.9
1966	39.6	12.1	6.7	18.8	32.8	5.9	39.4	78.1
1967	40.6	12.3	6.8	19.1	33.4	6.1	40.0	79.5
1968	40.0	12.5	6.5	19.0	33.6	6.2	39.1	78.9
1969	39.7	12.4	6.2	18.6	33.6	6.2	38.6	78.4
1970	40.7	12.6	5.9	18.5	32.8	6.0	37.1	75.9
1971	41.7	13.2	5.8	19.0	32.6	6.0	35.4	74.0
1972	42.0	14.0	5.7	19.7	32.9	6.0	34.8	73.7
1973	43.4	14.6	5.6	20.2	32.1	5.9	34.1	72.1
1974	46.1	15.9	5.7	21.6	31.7	6.0	33.9	71.6
1975	48.8	16.5	5.6	22.1	31.5	6.1	34.1	71.7
1976	49.2	17.1	5.6	22.7	31.8	6.1	36.6	74.5

DGB: Deutscher Gewerkschaftsbund (German Trade Union Congress)
DAG: Deutsche Angestellten-Gewerkschaft (Union of salaried employees)
GdP: Gewerkschaft der Polizei (Union of police)
DBB: Deutscher Beamtenbund (Union of civil servants).

Source: H. Bayer and E. Treu, Conditions and Results of White Collar Unionism in West Germany 1960-1976. Paper presented to the « EGOS-Workshop on Labour Unionism in a Cross-National Perspective », Berlin 23-24 November 1978, mimeographed.

industry that lasted more than six weeks over the demand for the 35-hour week.

A *fourth* change is in the area of government *incomes policy*. Upon the recommendation of the Council of Economic Advisors, the *Konzertierte Aktion*, a high level capital-labour discussion group, was set up in the mid 1960s, during the first postwar recession in West Germany. This tripartite body, composed of trade-union leaders, representatives of the employers and members of the Government, was supposed to serve as a means of controlling the course of wage and price development. In practice, its only purpose was to tie union wage policy to increases in productivity and prices. The *Konzertierte Aktion* in fact succeeded in doing this during the first few years of its existence. However, in the early 1970s — after the first wave of unofficial strikes in 1969 — it had already lost its influence on the course of development of both negotiated and actual wages. This was reflected in a clear redistributive success by wage and salary earners at the expense of self-employed incomes between 1970 and 1975. It was only with mass unemployment and the restrictive economic policies followed by the Federal Bank and the Federal Government that this trend was reversed. In 1977 the unions also officially discontinued their participation in the work of this body. (The immediate cause for this step was the attempt by the employers to have the Co-Determination Act of 1976 declared unconstituional).

This brings us to the *fifth* important change, namely the modifications in co-determination at the plant and company level. In 1972, the Factory Constitution Act (*Betriebsverfassungsgesetz*) was amended. In practice, this meant improved access by the unions to individual plants and an extension of the rights of the Works Council (*Betriebsrat*) to participate in decisions pertaining to personnel and social matters (in particular with respect to hiring, dismissing, short-time work, extra shifts, overtime). The Co-Determination Act of 1976 did increase the number of union representatives on company supervisory boards; it did not, however, grant them full parity of representation. While the reaction of the unions to the Act tended to be critical, the employers, on the other hand, thought it went too far and brought suit to have it declared unconstitutional.[1]

---

[1] The Bundesverfassungsgericht (Constitutional Court) has since dismissed this action and certified the constitutionality of the co-determination rules (with unequal parity). The court left open the question of how far this would also be true of complete parity.

Sixthly and lastly, there were changes in the *Works Council elections* in recent years. In 1975 and 1978 opposition groups, mostly of the left, put up candidates in several large steel, metalworking and chemical firms against the candidates on the official trade union lists, with surprising successes (sometimes up to 40% of the votes). These protest votes expressed the growing dissatisfaction on the part of relevant sections of the work force in large firms with the traditional interest representation system. As a rule, the established works councils and the trade union leaderships have reacted to this challenge by expelling the opposition candidates from the union; it is only recently that they have begun to realize that this kind of action merely threatens still further their legitimacy as representatives of the interests of all workers.

Let us seek to summarize these various changes in West Germany's industrial relations system. The first striking thing is that the strengthening of the unions' organizational basis has gone along with a more militant bargaining policy, extended by qualitative demands. Whether there is a direct connection between these two phenomena is hard to decide; it is only if further factors are considered that plausible arguments on this can be made (see Section II). A notable part of the changes outlined are those at plant level: both the extension of co-determination rights and the conflicts between rival groups in the works council elections indicate a changed significance of the plant level institutions for the settlement of industrial disputes. Finally, in the relation between government and the unions, no clear-cut trend can be picked out: concessions on the one hand have been accompanied by restrictions on the other. Thus, legislation has extended union influence at company level, but the restrictive economic policy, devoted more to the goal of monetary stability than to that of full employment, has cramped the possibilities of action in the area of wages policy, of central importance to the unions.

2. Two phases of militant action

So far, in our discussion of the changes which have taken place in the 1970s and of the tendencies deduced from them, we have referred to the period as a whole, including both the years of full employment and those of mass unemployment. However, we must distinguish between these two phases. The two phases differ not so much with respect to the quantitative dimension of industrial conflicts, but rather in regard to the forms and objects of militant action. It can also be presumed that the underlying motives for the rise in the level of unionization are different in each phase.

The *phase of full employment* (up until the middle of 1974) was still characterized by the optimistic atmosphere of anticipation generated by the student protest movement, and by the general climate of reform of the Social Democratic/Liberal coalition government under Chancellor Willy Brandt. At that time, there was widespread public discussion of the necessity of social change and of the "humanization of labour". An opinion research institute ascertained a "growing propensity towards class struggle". During this period there seems to have been an increase in workers' awareness of their own interests — within the work-class as a whole as well as in its various "factions" — as well as an increased willingness to join trade unions.

In 1970 the Institut für Sozialforschung conducted a survey of 600 active union members having plant-level functions (shop stewards, members of Works Councils); they ascertained a "dynamic wage consciousness" on the part of just under half of those surveyed. The experience of increases in real wages over a period of years had led to the firm expectation on their part that such increases would continue in the future. For them, the demand for a share in the benefits of economic growth and increases in productivity was a matter of course. In cases where the unions did not act on this demand, active groups at the plant level achieved their wage objectives themselves through "wildcat" strikes.

The unions' traditional monopoly in representation and strikes was first spectacularly questioned in the "September strikes" in 1969. The unions, which in the recession years of 1966 and 1967 had not only fully adapted their wages policy to the official incomes policy guidelines, but also concluded wage agreements for more than empoyed persons strongly to the fore again. The fact that in this policy in the subsequent boom, which brought the wage claims of employed persons strongly to the fore again. The fact that in this situation company workforces were able independently to defend their wage interests calls for explanation.

In the fifties and sixties union wages policy was characterized by strongly centralizing trends; industry-wide collective agreements were the rule. The adjustment and adaptation processes that in many large firms regularly followed the large scale collective agreements not infrequently brought considerable increases over the collectively bargained rises. As a consequence, in the boom years the interest of many workforces became concentrated on what the works councils achieved in addition, in "second-round bargaining". This favoured the growth of communication systems in firms in which committed works council members and shop-stewards frequently played the key role. Through such informal group structures and information networks, experienced officials in firms are able to activate and mobilize the work force, when for instance the unions want monitory strikes in firms to support their wage negotiations. They can however also — as the September strikes showed — serve to initiate independent action by the workforce; with few exceptions, the leading figures in the September strikes were unionized works council members or shop-stewards.

After these strikes criticism within the unions of their centralized wages policy and their participation in the Konzertierte Aktion met with wider response. Following the loss of legitimacy they had experienced and in view of the growing opposition trends among the officials, some trade unions saw themselves forced towards a more miltant wages policy and a return to a regional bargaining policy. Though the union leaderships were thereby merely yielding to the pressure from below, without questioning in principle their policy hitherto, there were farther-reecing consequences for wage bargaining practice. The regionalization of bargaining policy gave militant, progressive districts more room to manoeuvre in implementing their own wage bargaining ideas. All round, union bargaining policy became seesaw policy. The September strikes were followed in 1970/1971 by a phase of active, sometimes militant wages policy, resulting in the highest wage rises in the existence of the FRG. The return to the acceptance of the incomes policy guidelines in 1972-73 had as a consequence a new wave of wildcat strikes for cost-of-living increases, this time accompanied by much sharper criticism of the unions. The following wages round in 1974 was again characterized by wage conflicts. In the mid-seventies the militancy slackened off again, under the influence of the most severe economic crisis since the end of the war.

Taken all round, the annual wage rounds were in the first half of the seventies accompanied more often than before by numerous monitory strikes, not infrequently ending in larger labour conflicts, to which the employers in part responded by large-scale lock-outs. With the increase in wage disputes, labour conflict in the Federal Republic lost its exceptional character. This suggests that there is a close connection between the more aggressively conducted wage conflicts by comparison with the sixties and the above mentioned "dynamic wage consciousness". Further resultant and accompanying phenomena of this development are:

a) a redistributive success unique in the history of the Federal Republic: the adjusted wage ratio rose from 1970 to 1975 by some four percentage points;

b) a rise in union affiliation: both membership figures and the level of unionization rose again in the early 70s;

c) the appearance of groups of workers that in the earlier strike history of the Federal Republic had played, at best, a subordinate role: foreign workers, who took an active and initiative role particularly in the 1973 strike wave, and public employees, who contributed largely to the rise in strike activity in the service sector.

While till the mid-seventies wage policy issues were clearly at the centre of the disputes, a development that in the second half of the seventies was to make wage interests take second place to productivity and jobs policy issues, was already apparent.

After the first break in the till then continuous growth of the West German economy, the 1966-67 recession, West German employers made greater efforts to rationalize work organization and the production process. Among the creeping rationalization measures in work organization were: the extended use of payment by results systems; the introduction of pre-set time systems (MDW) as an instrument of personal and work planning and of performance estimation; the better use of invested capital through the extension of shift-work; the introduction of special shifts and speed-ups. These measures frequently went hand in hand with technological rationalization, producing serious consequences particularly in the printing industry (replacement of lead typesetting by photographic methods) and in areas of the metal industry (introduction of micro-electronics).

The consequences of these rationalizations for the social position and work situation of employed persons were long concealed by the favourable labour market situation. As long as production expanded,

there was an accompanying rise in total employment, despite technological redundancies in individual industries. This increase was supplied mainly by foreign workers and women, in both cases mainly
unskilled. They felt the negative effects of rationalization earlier and
harder than the skilled workers initially still protected by the labour
market situation, who mostly belonged to the core workforce.

The groups hardest hit by the consequences of rationalization in
this phase — foreign workers, female, unskilled and marginal workers — are also marginalized groups within the trade unions; their
representation on the decision-making bodies is far below their proportion of the membership. By contrast with male skilled workers,
who as a rule constitute the trade union core groups, they have no
organizational leverage in defending their interests. It is significant
that it was those hardest hit by the rationalization offensive that
during the 1973 wildcat strike movement, which had begun as a
"wages counter-offensive", for the first time raised specific demands
for improvements in work conditions. The fact that demands of this
nature were finally also raised in an official steel and metal workers'
union (IG Metall) strike in 1973 in Baden-Württemberg was
mainly thanks to the initiative of the district leadership there, which
skillfully tied the various interests of individual worker groups (piece
workers, older workers, assembly line workers, workers with mon-
otonous jobs etc.) together into a package of demands that both set
bounds to the forced productivity policy of capital and helped the
union ideas of the "humanization of labour" to break through.

Things changed in the *phase of mass unemployment*. In the wake
of the onset of unexpectedly high unemployment in the Autumn of
1974, the militancy of the unions with respect to wage demands
declined notably. Except for the printers' strike in 1976, there were
no major strikes for higher wages until the spring of 1978. And even
that strike was decisively determined by the threat to qualifications
and jobs arising from the measures of technological rationalization
taken in the printing industry. As is indicated by the results of
recent surveys, relevant shifts took place during this phase within the
complex of worker interests which are potential objects of union
action and demands. The wage-policy demand patterns which had
been built up during the prosperity phase disintegrated and were
replaced by an orientation towards the protection of jobs and demands for measures to safe-guard job-related assets (income,
employment, qualifications).

These shifts in the direction of interests explain why the adaptation of wages policy to the crisis conditions by the unions, which
thereby accepted a deterioration of the distributive position gained in
the previous phase, met with much less criticism from the rank and
file than before. The threat to the union leaderships of loss of
legitimacy came less from the area of wages policy than from that of
protection of jobs and of assets. But even in this area the unions
were able to remain relatively inactive in the first crisis years, since
again it was primarily only "marginal groups" that were affected by
the dismissals. Of the strikes that broke out in the three years of
crisis (1975-1977), all, with one exception, were unofficial actions,
which did secure moral support from the official union organizations,
particularly at local and regional level, but were scarcely able to
rouse the trade unione centres out of their passivity.

Numerous smaller spontaneous strikes were directed against dismissals and plant shut-downs. It was characteristic of a number of
these unofficial strikes that they occurred in regions in which the
unemployment rate was high anyway, so that in the case of further
dismissals, the workers affected could scarcely count on finding other
employment opportunities. In such "hopeless" situations, the barriers to "wildcat" strikes are lower because the personal risks
involved in every work stoppage not authorized by the union — for
example, that of dismissal — are no longer very important. In some
cases these defensive reactions took the form of factory occupations,
a new phenomenon in the conflict history of the Federal Republic.

The occurence in 1978 of three big official strikes on non-wage
demands can be explained through the increasing threat as the crisis
proceeds to skilled workers and permanent staff from the rationalization measures. While the strike in the metal industry had as its
object a collective agreement that would prevent possible downgrading from higher to lower wage groups, which had become possible
with the rationalization measures, those in the printing and steel
industries centred round the protection of jobs for those employed
there. Both the printing and the steel industries, — both of them
among the best-unionized industries, had undergone a continuous
decline in employment in the seventies. Since a continuation of this
trend was to be feared, both unions saw themselves compelled to
protect the jobs of their traditional memberships. They did this in
different ways, in line with their differing traditions. The IG Druck
und Papier (print union) demanded manning rules for jobs using the

new technology: these should continue to be filled only by skilled print workers, i.e. the new jobs should be available for those liable to lose their old ones (the fact that on balance less new jobs would be created than old ones eliminated was accepted as inevitable). The IG Metall called for the 35-hour week: a reduction in working hours would prevent or delay the reduction in jobs (a longer-term goal was the introduction of an additional shift).

In all three strikes the aim was ultimately to prevent employers from using the available possibilities of rationalization to the full. How little compromise was possible with this objective is shown by the employers' reactions: in all three cases they responded to the strikes with large-scale lock-outs. It was this resolute resistance by the employers, politically and materially supported by the central employers' association, that brought about the limitation of union success, such as they were, to group-specific arrangemnets for limited periods.

Altogether, the second half of the seventies is characterized by the manifold consequences of crisis and rationalization that affect individual groups in the labour force with varying intensity and at different times. It is to be presumed that the general insecutiry hereby created as regards employment, income and skill levels has strengthened the motivation to join a union, especially since the Works Council member (as a rule regarded as the union representative in the firm) has to agree to dismissals and is involved in selecting those to be dismissed. Since the crisis situation has faced Works Council members with completely new problems, which can scarcely be dealt with by traditional methods of representation, it is understandable why on the one hand there were numerous conflicts in firms over the Works Council members' representation policies and on the other why trade unions took up matters that were earlier dealt with by the Works Council members, in more favourable economic and labour market conditions.

3. THE DUAL SYSTEM OF REPRESENTATION AND THE SEGMENTATION OF THE LABOUR MARKET

In spite of an increased tendency to conflict, and in spite of the extension of the range of issues at stake in conflicts in the '70s, the

West German system of industrial relations has, on the whole, displayed an amazing degree of structural stability and adaptability. Even the serious effects of the most recent economic crisis on the social situation of wage-earners (mass unemployment) have not shaken the system. The reasons for this relative stability lie in the effectiveness of two central mechanisms for conflict absorption or conflict restraint: the *dual system of representation of* interests and the *segmented labour market.* They lead to a) diffedences in the extent to which individuals are personally affected, b) a fragmentation of the experience of conflicts, and c) a particularization of the mode in which conflicts are conducted and resolved.

a) The dual system of representation of interests — which is guaranteed by labour law in the Federal Republic of Germany — facilitates a functional differentiation in the way in which conflicts are dealt with. At the *plant and company level*, the representation of the interests of wage-earners and salaried employees is effected through the *Works Council*, an institution which is provided for by law. At this level, practically the whole range of workers' interests can be made the object of labour-management negotiations. However, in representing interests at the plant level, the Works Council possesses only limited means of actively compelling management to meet demands reflecting these interests. Its only forms of leverage are the threat of the withdrawal of cooperation or of suits before labour courts. As they are forbidden by law to do anything which would disturb the internal peace of the plant, the Works Councils may not take any kind of militant action. At *industry level*, representation of interests is effected through the *trade unions.* To be sure, the unions have the right to use strikes and other militant forms as a means of sanction against management; however, their use of such forms is subject to limiting conditions (*last resort*; appropriateness of means — they must not pose a threat to the very existence of the other party; social appropriateness — strikes may only be conducted in order to achieve goals which can be met through collective-bargaining agreements; thus, political strikes are not considered "socially appropriate"). An additional element is the fact that in the past the unions concentrated almost exclusively on wage policy and did not challenge the autonomy of management with respect to investment decisions, changes in production technology and the organization of the labour process. While the most recent labour conflicts were characterized by non-wage demands, employers were still able through social policy concessions largely to fend off the restrictions on the rationalization possibilities that the unions were aiming at.

b) J. Kühl's paper says more about the segmented labour market. At this point, I would merely like to say that it results in workers being affected by economic change in group-specific ways. Thus the so-called marginal or problem groups (unskilled workers, women, foreign workers) were the first to feel the effects of "creeping rationalization" in the early '70s and were hardest hit by mass unemployment after the beginning of the economic crisis in the mid-'70s. They account for a disproportionately high percentage of the unemployed — especially of those workers who remain unemployed for long periods of time. In addition, since these groups are poorly represented in the trade unions, they do not have the same organizational leverage as skilled employees to defend themselves collectively against threats to their interests. Although the rationalization methods showed their negative effects from the beginning of the seventies, it is only recently that the unions have seen themselves compelled to active defence, when the rationalization pressures began to hit union core groups. The fact that the unions had let themselves in for splitting even their generalized non-wage demands like that for the 35-hour week or for the protection of social assets into special arrangements for groups or industries shows how deeply rooted in sectional interests and how far from representing class interests they are.

The fact that the labour conflicts have retained a group-specific character means that they have the potential to cause partial paralysis, but they do not challenge the system as a whole.

Aside from the two absorption mechanisms mentioned above, two additional factors must be named which contribute to the stability of the system: first, the "network of social security", and, second, the lack of social and political alternatives. As long as the system of social secutiry (unemployment compensation, compensation for short-time work, early retirement, re-training programs) works to counteract the negative social consequences of crisis and rationalization, those directly affected are not compelled to seek radical solutions to their problems. This is reinforced by the fact that at present no acceptable social and political alternative to the existing social system of the Federal Republic is in sight.

In the 1920s, the idea of socialism, the conviction that society was developing in that direction, still represented such an alternative conception. That which currently presents itself as "real socialism", especially the social system of the German Democratic Republic, does not have this appeal; on the contrary: it is, by and large, rejected. The results of recent studies conducted by the Institute for Sociological Research (*Soziologisches Forschungsinstitut*) in Göttingen indicated that almost all of the workers surveyed rejected the socialism of the GDR — and this not only because of the higher standard of living in the Federal Republic. Many of those surveyed referred explicitly to the "greater freedom enjoyed by workers" in the Federal Republic. Even the "idea of socialism" was either rejected outright or regarded with scepticism. It would probably be a mistake to infer from this a positive identification on the part of workers with the capitalist social system of the Federal Republic. The current crisis situation is probably making workers more conscious of the structurally-grounded ways in which they are discriminated against. They yield to the economic pressure of the crisis because the only hope they have left is that the previous state of prosperity and full employment will soon return.

120   *Walther Müller-Jentsch*

APPENDIX - Table 3: STRIKES AND LOCK-OUTS IN THE FRG, 1961-1978

Year	Workers taking part	Days lost
1961	21.000	65.000
1962	79.000	451.000
1963	317.000	1.846.000
1964	6.000	17.000
1965	6.000	49.000
1966	196.000	27.000
1967	60.000	389.000
1968	25.000	25.000
1969	90.000	249.000
1970	184.000	93.000
1971	536.000	4.484.000
1972	23.000	66.000
1973	185.000	563.000
1974	250.000	1.051.000
1975	36.000	69.000
1976	169.000	534.000
1977	34.000	24.000
1978	488.000	4.290.000
Annual average 1961-1970	98.000	321.000
1971-1978	215.000	1.385.000

Source: Statistisches Bundesamt,Fachserie 1, Reihe 4.3.

Table 4: SHARES OF WAGES AND SALARIES IN GNP 1960-1978

Year	Share of wages		Dependent workers as a percentage of total workforce
	effective [1]	adjusted [2]	
1960	60.4	60.4	77.2
1961	62.7	62.1	78.0
1962	64.1	62.8	78.8
1963	65.1	63.2	79.5
1964	64.8	62.3	80.3
1965	65.6	62.6	80.9
1966	66.6	63.3	81.2
1967	66.4	63.2	81.1
1968	64.8	61.3	81.6
1969	66.1	61.8	82.5
1970	67.8	62.7	83.4
1971	69.1	63.6	83.9
1972	69.5	63.8	84.2
1973	70.7	64.6	84.5
1974	72.6	66.3	84.5
1975	72.5	66.3	84.5
1976	71.1	64.7	84.9
1977	71.8	65.0	85.2
1978	71.1	64.1	85.6

[1] Gross income from dependent work as a share of GNP.

[2] Wage share adjusted for changes in the share of dependent workers in the total workforce (base year: 1960).

Source: Sachverständigengutachten 1978/79 (für 1960-1977); Wirtschaft und Statistik 2/1979, own calculations for 1978.

TABLE 5: MACROECONOMIC INDICATORS AND DEVELOPMENT OF WAGES — YEARLY INCREASES 1970-77

Year	Gross national [1] product real	Producti- vity [2] per worker real	Cost-of- living index	Remuneration for occupied worker		
				gross nominal	net nominal	net real
1970	5.9	4.7	3.4	14.7	12.2	8.5
1971	3.3	3.0	5.3	11.8	9.7	4.2
1972	3.6	3.9	5.5	9.0	9.0	3.3
1973	4.9	4.6	6.9	12.0	8.2	1.2
1974	0.4	2.4	7.0	11.4	9.8	2.6
1975	—1.9	1.5	6.0	7.2	7.3	1.2
1976	5.1	6.0	4.5	7.0	4.2	—0.3
1977	2.6	2.9	3.9	6.9	5.8	1.8
1978	3.4	2.8	2.6	5.2	6.0	3.3

[1] Constant prices; base year: 1970.
[2] GDP per worker.

Source: Bretschneider, Husmann, Schnabel, Handbuch einkommens-, vermögens- und sozialpolitischer Daten, E 12, E 13, H 11/1, Wirtschaft und Statistik 2/1979.

LABOUR MARKETS AND INDUSTRIAL RELATIONS IN THE RECESSION IN GERMANY, 1973-1978

by

JÜRGEN KÜHL

1. INTRODUCTION

This paper concentrates on the basic question of why high and persistent unemployment and other consequences of labour market slack did not change the climate of relative social and political calm fundamentally. This was unexpected for many reasons, mainly because the number of persons hit by unemployment during the recession is estimated to range from 2.5 to 4.6 million people. As far as I remember, this crucial question was raised first at the OECD experts' meeting on structural determinants of employment and unemployment in 1977.

The main thesis of this paper is that the dynamic and structural functioning of the labour market assisted by manpower policy and manifold counter-measures undertaken by unions and employers' organizations was farily successful in preventing the unemployed from taking massive political action. As far as the unemployed are concerned, many of them have a marginal status in society — shown by low attachment to the labour market, high turnover rates, numerous risks of becoming and staying jobless, low income and qualifications, weak organisation — especially in unions, political parties and other pressure groups — and finally by low levels of actual and potential political power and/or cooperation. The traditional system of industrial relations was not therefore basically questioned. Many potential conflicts were overcome or displaced by the processes mentioned above before the labour market pressure groups could — or had to — enter the scene.

Furthermore, the relationship between the dynamic and structural behaviour of the labour market and the system and functioning of industrial relations is still to be explored. But, if sufficient answers could be found to the broader question, the relative importance of that relationship could be determined more easily. Hitherto there has been no satisfactory theory of the interaction between the labour market performance and industrial relations, although promising approaches were offered during our conference deliberations.

Since this paper emphasises the labour market issues, many problems are excluded:[1]

i) The influence of the relatively centralised organisation and action of the German unions as compared to other countries. Problems emerging from the increasing competition between works councils, or even rank and file membership, and union leadership following the steady increase in unionization;

ii) The consequences of the chilly climate resulting from the employers' legal proceedings against the law of co-determination and workers' participation, which led to a temporary halt in the usual top-level meetings between unions, employers and government officials;[2]

iii) The negligible influence of strikes — in 1974 for example 250,000 workers were on strike against 890 enterprises causing a loss of 8.4 million hours of work, i.e. less than one thousandth of

---

[2] During the closing session of the conference, Prof. Halberstadt drew attention to many other aspects of the problem which have not been dealt with, or only touched upon, in this paper. These aspects include:
— the weakening of parliamentary and governmental power;
— the increasing activity of rank and file and unions;
— the lack of internationalization of the unions, except for some DGB-sponsored attempts;
— the growing importance of non-wage and non-monetary matters in industrial relations;
— the weak performance of the traditional methods of conducting industrial relations;
— the relationship between industrial relations and the calming influence of the social security system and the availability of public funds;
— the different mechanisms of industrial relations in the private and in the public sectors — the largest employer.
[2] This case has been decided upon in the meantime by the Bundesverfassungsgericht (the German Supreme Court). The Law of Co-Determination has been declared constitutional.

total working hours — is not dealt with, although strikes were used to enforce special forms of job protection;

iv) Some joint attempts to prevent the closing down of factories and a few successful experiments concerning worker-owned firms; and finally

v) the relatively smooth change to modest wage increases and the break in collective bargaining aimed at flat-rate wage increases in favour of the lower-paid.

This paper proposes eleven hypotheses which are tested in turn with the available knowledge about labour markets and the behaviour of the unemployed. The short-comings of this approach are obvious. Some of the hypotheses are incomplete, some are inconsistent, some overlap. There has been little research done in this field and our statistical surveys, and methods are unsatisfactory. I have laid greater stress on the labour market dimensions of the problem, since Dr. Müller-Jentsch's paper concentrates on industrial relations. The central question posed here is why the FRG did not lose the climate of relative social and political calm which was established during the golden 1960s.

2. ELEVEN THESES

Thesis 1: The dynamics of the labour market

Because of the large and rapid labour turn-over both within and between employment and unemployment during 1973-1978, the majority of the 2 million people who became unemployed each year were hired or re-hired within three to four months on average. Nevertheless, unemployment cannot be explained predominantly by job search/labour turnover theories, because aggregate employment decreased by 1.7 million to about 25 million people and remains at this low level. However, despite the overall deficit of demand for labour, the dynamic flexibility of the labour market confined persistent unemployment to small, specific and therefore so called "hard to employ" groups, having little political and bargaining power and low rates of unionization.

Table 1 shows that there are about five to six million hires and five to six million dismissals a year; the aggregate turnover rate

TABLE 1: LABOUR TURNOVER 1961-1970, 1973-1978.

Year	Dismissals (1000) 1	Inflow of unemployment (1000) 2	% of (1) 3	Hires (1000) 4	Inflow of job vacancies (1000) 5	% of (4) 6	Wage and salary workers (1000) 7	Labour turnover rates % $\frac{(1)+(4)}{2 \times (7)} \times 100$ 8	$\frac{(4)}{(7)} \times 100$ 9
1961	7 922.2	2 147.9	27.1	8 484.2	3 360.3	39.6	20 730.0	39.6	40.9
1965	7 325.3	1 422.3	19.4	7 822.6	3 011.8	38.5	21 758.0	34.8	36.0
1967	6 111.7	2 544.4	41.6	5 905.8	2 882.2	48.8	21 054.0	28.5	28.1
1970	6 471.3	1 295.7	20.0	6 956.3	3 037.7	43.7	22 246.0	30.2	31.3
9173	7 443.2	1 877.1	25.2	7 694.4 a	2 695.3	35.0	22 564.0 b	(33.5)	(34.1)
1974	7 018.1	2 795.3	39.8	5 922.5	2 255.2	38.1	20 790.0	31.1	28.5
1975	6 023.2	3 450.3	57.3	5 435.0	2 188.5	40.3	20 139.6	28.4	27.0
1976	6 119.5	3 255.5	53.2	5 972.7	2 312.0	38.7	19 956.4	30.3	29.9
1977	5 949.6	3 315.0	55.7	5 913.0	2 187.3	36.9	19 963.9	29.8	29.7
1977 I+II	2 806.8	1 637.5	58.3	2 960.9	1 159.2	39.1	19 879.9	29.0	29.8
1978 I+II	2 723.0	1 545.1	56.7	2 905.0	1 131.2	38.9	19 972.2 c	28.2	29.1

a New method leads to double counting.
b 1961-1973, all dependent workers, 1974 et seq., wage and salary workers having social security rights.
c End of first quarter 1978.
SOURCE: *Federal Employment Institute.*

moves around 30 per cent. Internal company turnover adds another five to six million transfers a year. The decrease in total employment was caused mainly by dismissals in 1973-74, leading to an inflow of unemployment of 2.8 million in 1974. Dismissals decreased by one million to six million in 1975.[3] The decline, in many cases even a halt in recruitment, especially in large firms, became the main reason for high levels of unemployment. The inflow of vacancies and the number of hires decreased by about 500,000. Thus the newcomers to the labour market — young female and unskilled people lacking stable work careers — were suffering from unemployment. Primary wokers remained employed or regained jobs quickly.

The immense labour turnover led to a two-fold process of selection. First, workers with low productivity, little education, high rates of absenteeism or "double work roles" like women, pre-retirement workers and foreigners, were *sorted out* in the beginning of the recession. Secondly, newcomers, semi-skilled, unskilled and handicapped workers were refused entry to the employment system. Both groups were marginal to mainstream public opinion. Either one of the potential alternatives of staying at home, entering the educational system, earlier retirement or return migration were held to be acceptable. Or, the reasons for unemployment were attributed to a personal lack of skill, low morale or other deficiencies. Taking both processes of selection and displacement together, the resistance to unemployment was *fragmented* among many groups or even individuals with low status in society having little power to enforce their interests. Dismissals cut the most important organisational and institutional relationships of workers with their firms which are in most cases the only institutions to look after their individual and collective interest. The unemployed are divided and separated from the usual means of protecting their interests. Often they cannot establish alternative relationships within reasonable time.

The distribution of the decrease of employment illustrates both processes. About 70 per cent of the fall in employment was among wage earners and salaried employees, equal to a decline of 1.23 million in the labour force between 1973 and 1977. While employ-

---

[3] It would at this point be very interesting to see whether this decline in dismissals in Germany is also, as in the case of Italy, due to a (relative) decline in layoffs (in addition to the decline in quits) However, data in these two different kinds of employment separation do not exist for Germany.

ment of German workers decreased by 0.6 million (— 3 per cent) among foreign workers it fell by 0.63 million (— 25 per cent), to 1.848 million in the first quarter of 1978 — more than half of the total. The "export" of unemployment thus explains to some extent why there was so little opposition to the slack in the labour market.

Thesis 2: The components of unemployment

The dynamics of the labour market divide total unemployment into two broad categories: i) persons with a high risk of remaining unemployed and ii) workers with a high risk of becoming unemployed, because they are affected by lay-offs above the average level or they become repeatedly unemployed. The result can be described as "quasi-fixed" unemployment on one hand and " moving unemployment" on the other. But only the first category might be inclined to take or demand public counter-measures against persistent unemployment. The second group moves between employment and joblessness without any chance for its members to organinse and change their marginal status.

While the stock of registered unemployment remained constant during 1974-1978 at about one million, nearly 15 million registrations and about as many terminations of unemployment were counted at employment offices. At the moment, unemployment ends after three or four months on average. (At the end of September 1976 more than 40 per cent of the unemployed leaving the registers had been without jobs for less than one month). On the other hand the stock of unemployed now includes more than twenty per cent out of work for more than twelve months.

In Table 2 the unemployment rate is split up into three component types: different categories of the unemployed, the frequency of and the duration of unemployment. The total inflow of unemployment in 1977 was 3.3 million registrations. About 2 million people with a duration of about forty weeks. Women (12.7 per cent), young people (19.2 per cent), unqualified workers (15 per cent), foreign workers (13.1 per cent), and part-time employees (16.5 per cent) were most affected by unemployment.[4]

---

[4] Egle (1977) p. 224 ff.

Table 2: COMPONENTS OF UNEMPLOYMENT - SEPTEMBER 1976

Subgroups	Unemployment rate	Unemployed persons (a)	Frequency (b) of Unemployment	Duration (c) of Unemployment
	%		times a year	weeks
Total	3.9	9.8	1.54	13.5
Male workers	3.0	7.8	1.60	12.5
Female workers	5.5	12.7	1.47	15.0
Under 25 years	5.4	19.2	1.49	9.8
25 — 55 years old	3.4	7.5	1.59	14.9
55 + » »	5.2	6.3	1.48	29.2
Unskilled	6.3	15.0	1.66	13.2
Industrial education	2.8	7.4	1.45	13.6
University degree	2.4	6.0	1.25	16.7
German workers	4.0	9.6	1.52	14.3
Foreign workers	3.8	13.1	1.74	8.7
Salaried workers	3.5	7.9	1.37	16.8
Wage earners	4.3	11.0	1.66	12.3
Seeking full-time work	3.6	9.4	1.56	12.8
Seeking part-time work	9.8	16.5	1.42	21.7

(a) Numbers of persons who became unemployed during preceding year as percentage of all workers.
(b) Spells of unemployment during preceding year.
(c) Average duration of unemployment ending previous year.
Source: Institut für Arbeitsmarkt- und Berufsforschung.

The highest frequencies can be found for unskilled and foreign workers. Lengthy periods of unemployment appear for older workers (over 55 years of age: 29.2 weeks), part-time employees (21.7 weeks), salaried workers (16.8 weeks) and highly qualified manpower (16.7 weeks). Since the last two groups show the smallest figures for all other components of unemployment, there might be an influence due to voluntary job search.

Because of flexible retirement possibilities, seniority rights and special protection against dismissal, older workers are affected by unemployment to an unexpectedly small degree. Those of them who become unemployed show the highest rates for duration.

As a result, quasi-fixed unemployment is concentrated among male and female workers aged 55 and above, personally handicapped and disabled persons, and those seeking part-time work, mainly women. The "moving" type of unemployment is found for young, unqualified and all foreign workers. The rate of multiple unemployment per year is increasing (22 per cent of total unemployment in September 1977, 23.5 per cent in May 1978). The periods of employment between those without work are increasingly short.

Two thirds of those leaving the unemployed registers go into employment. The re-employment rate is (1976-77) 71.3 per cent for male and 61.6 per cent female wage and salary earners. The rate decreases by increasing age of the unemployed and by duration of unemployment. The dynamics of unemployment lead to a process of "structuralization" — i.e. quasi-fixed unemployment — and another process of "marginalization" — multiple changes between employment and unemployment and low attachment to the labour market. Again, both processes diminish the inclination to mobilize public opinion and the mass-media. But "silent" job seekers do not intervene in the industrial disputes.

Thesis 3: The buffer action of working hours

The unemployment effects of labour market slack were less severe than expected, because about a third of the fall in aggregate demand for labour in terms of hours was taken up by a reduction of hours worked instead of lay-offs.[5]

The main components were reduced overtime work, the extension of short-time work (0.77 million workers in 1975), and only a slight fall in part-time employment in view of the massive decrease of aggregate employment. Thus many redundancies could be avoided by measures which distributed work more equally. This effect

---

[5] Bundesanstalt für Arbeit (1978) p. 25.

explains another factor in the climate of relative social and political calm.

Table 3 shows that the potential supply of hours was 50,566 million in 1975 while only 45,942 million hours were actually worked. The utilization rate of potential hours was 90.6 per cent in 1975, remaining fairly constant at that low level until 1978. At the beginning of the 1970s, the rate was above 97 per cent, reaching its maximum of 98.3 per cent in 1970. The number of employed persons ran at up to about 94 per cent of potential labour force during 1975-78. The difference compared with the total under-utilization of potential hours shows that the adjustment of hours worked diminished the number of people who would otherwise have become unemployed. As the development of productivity during the recession indicates, there was additional support by labour hoarding.

The relative success of adjustment in working time instead of redundancy led to an extension of part-time work, above all in government and service sectors. The unions started to believe in reductions of working hours as a means of employment policy. Table 4 summarizes the employment effects of all measures aimed at all forms of reduced hours of work.

Thesis 4: Different patterns of labour market developments for males and females

The fall in aggregate employment was concentrated among male workers. But the corresponding labour market showed a large reduction int he overall labour supply due to a fall in potential male labour force (— 235,000, 1973-77), a decrease in the number of male foreign workers (— 344,000 i.e. the most important element in the total fall of employment), a widespread use of earlier retirement (in 1978 for example 120,000 - 130,000 male workers took up flexible retirement possibilities). There was also an above average participation of male workers in most of the policy measures to reduce unemployment (i.e. job creation, promotion of vocational training and retraining, short-time work). As a result, unemployment of male German workers was relieved as male employment and labour supply fell at the same time. In addition, male German heads of household got special protection against dismissal (social selection). The exchange of male jobs between the generations helped to diminish potential political pressure.

Table 3: LABOUR FORCE, UNEMPLOYMENT, AND THE RATE OF UTILIZATION OF POTENTIAL HOURS OF WORK 1960-1978

Year	Potential labour force			Unemployment		Yearly working hours per worker			Total hours		
	Potential labour force	Actual employment	Rate of utilization	Registered	Unregistered	Potential	Actual	Rate of utilization	Potential (1) (6)	Actual (2) (7)	Rate of utilizat.
	'000s		%	'000s		Hours		%	million hours		%
	1	2	3	4	5	6	7	8	9	10	11
1960	26,398	26,080	98,8	271	47	2,214	2,154	97,3	58,445	56,170	96,1
1961	26,622	26,441	99,3	181	—	2,196	2,126	96,8	58,462	56,214	96,2
1962	26,689	26,534	99,4	155	—	2,196	2,098	96,7	57,888	55,680	96,2
1963	26,782	26,596	99,3	186	—	2,130	2,057	96,6	57,046	54,701	95,9
1964	26,787	26,618	99,4	169	—	2,123	2,078	97,9	56,863	55,317	97,3
1965	26,916	26,769	99,5	147	—	2,101	2,061	98,1	56,551	55,184	97,6
1966	26,890	26,686	99,2	161	43	2,087	2,040	97,8	56,119	54,449	97,0
1967	26,539	25,817	97,3	459	263	2,052	2,005	97,7	54,458	51,761	95,1
1968	26,300	25,839	98,3	323	138	2,041	1,999	98,0	53,678	51,648	96,2
1969	26,419	26,240	99,3	179	—	2,004	1,983	98,9	52,944	52,011	98,3
1970	26,719	26,570	99,4	149	—	1,992	1,969	98,9	53,224	52,224	98,3
1971	26,910	26,639	99,0	185	92	1,984	1,954	98,5	53,401	52,051	97,5
1972	26,973	26,580	98,6	246	142	1,954	19,20	98,3	52,705	51,036	96,8
1973	27,077	26,648	98,5	273	156	1,934	1,887	97,5	52,367	50,275	96,0
1974	26,943	26,155	97,1	582	206	1,911	1,853	97,0	51,488	48,466	94,1
1975	26,820	25,266	94,2	1.074	480	1,885	1,818	96,4	50,566	45,942	90,6
1976	26,654	25,033	93,9	1.060	511	1,915	1,854	96,8	51,272	46,411	90,9
1977	26,609	24,970	93,8	1.030	609	1,888	1,826	96,7	50,230	45,595	90,8
1978	26,655	25,060	93,9	993	642	1,867	1,804	96,6	49,765	45,136	90,7

Source: Institut für Arbeitsmarkt- und Berufsforschung

On the other hand employment of male wage and salary earners fell in 1975 by just 0.16 million; female employment reached its pre-recession level again in 1977, and there are now more women workers than ever before. Neverthless, female registered unemployment increased continuosly after 1970 and reached male unemployment levels in 1977 (0.512 million men — 0.518 million women). The main explanation is the continuing increase in the female potential labour force since 1970 — by 0.336 million German and 0,186 million foreign workers up to 1978. Since there was no corresponding increase in female employment, high and persistent unemployment followed, namely for young or poorly educated women seeking part-time work and those re-entering the labour market. In addition, many women are in unregistered unemployment, which has totalled about 0.6 million males and females each year since 1976 (see Table 3).

Although the rates of female labour force participation increased for many groups during the recession, the attachment of women to the labour market is weaker than that of men. Accordingly, there is a widely accepted view that women have different alternatives to employment, that the discouragement of women in the labour market is not unusual, and that their potential resistance to discrimination in employment can be ignored. Although women were better off in employment, their unemployment rate of 5.5 per cent in September 1978 as against 2.7 per cent for men shows that the unequal distributin of joblessness between the sexes confirmed the widespread expectation that women would abstain from political action.

Thesis 5: The influence of structural unemployment

The development of the labour market since 1973 provides evidence that the main cause of unemployment is the aggregate deficit of demand for labour due to the business cycle and slower growth.[6] There are only a few indications that a minority of the unemployed is unwilling or unable to work or does not immediately find the jobs offered. If there are only some "hard-to-employ" workers and only a few "hard-to-fill" vacancies, the structural flexibility of the labour market implies that the FRG has little structural unemployment. Thus the existing persistent, hard-core unemployment within specific

[6] Autorengemeinschaft des IAB (1978) pp. 62-67.

Table 4 - EMPLOYMENT EFFECTS AND DIMINUITION OF UNEMPLOYME

	1977 (1)		
	Take Up	Effect on la-bour volume	Emplo effe
	Persons/Days/Hours	million	1000 p
1. Extension of vocational education			
1.1 10th year of education	55,000 Persons	100.4	2
1.2 Full-time vocational education/training and retraining	69,000 Persons	126.0	6
2. Reduction of pre-retirement work			
2.1 Take up of flexible retirement schemes	115,000 Persons	210,0	6
2.2 Earlier retirement of 60 - year - old workers after one year of employment	50,000 Persons	91.3	3
2.3 Earlier retirement of disabled workers being 61 years old	—	—	—
3. Prolonged vocations			
3.1 More holidays per employee	0.4 working days	68.4	1
3.2 Paid educational leave	—	—	—
3.3 Maternity leave	—	—	—
4. Reduction of standard working-hours per week and per employee	0.03 hours per week	27.3	1
5. Increase of part-time employment	92,000 Persons	63.0	3
6. Short-time working	231,000 Persons	100.4	
TOTAL (1-6)	—	786.8	3
Diminution of unemployment registered	—	—	2

(1) Preliminary   (2) Estimate.
Source: Mitteilungen aus der Arbeitsmarkt- und Berufsforschung 1 (1979) (*Institute of Emf Research*).

	1978 (2)			1979 (2)	
Take Up	Effect on labour volume	Employment effect	Take Up	Effect on labour volume	Employment effect
s/Days/Hours	million hours	1000 persons	Persons/Days/Hours	million hours	1000 persons
000 Persons	54.1	15	30,000 Persons	53.5	51
000 Persons	124.5	69	87,000 Persons	155.1	87
000 Persons	216.5	72	120,000 Persons	213.9	72
000 Persons	90.2	30	50,000 Persons	89.1	30
—	—	—	20,000 Persons	35.7	12
working days	137.4	38	1.0 working days	173.2	49
—	—	—	—	—	—
—	—	—	38,000 Persons	62.9	19
ours per week	45.3	25	0.05 hours per week	45.2	25
000 Persons	59.0	33	98,000 Persons	65.7	37
000 Persons	90.2	50	250,000 Persons	110.5	62
—	817.2	332	—	1,004.8	408
—	—	219	—	—	269

groups, regions, occupations or industries is insufficient to mobilize and organize collective action. But the FRG may approach structural unemployment, if the demand for labour does not keep up with prevailing unemployment and if it does not absorb the increase in potential labour force of one million within ten years. That is a common problem of all three countries under consideration in this volume.

Table 5 shows that recent unemployment rates (May 1978) in all branches are above the corresponding vacancy rates, except the small "energy, water and mining industries". A comparison of both rates by occupation gives the same picture: in all occupational groups there are more unemployed jobseekers than jobs offered, except for some workers for construction industries. If we compare supply and demand for skilled workers — i.e. those who finished vocational or industrial training — the sum of "excess demand" in all occupations amounts to 36,700 job vacancies and 23,100 unemployed persons.

Another sign that there is only a minor shortage of qualified manpower is given by the fact that just 4 to 5 per cent of all industrial firms report constraints on production due to a shortage of labour. Lack of orders is reported as the main reason for low employment and production.

In addition the regional and/or occupational mobility of the unemployed is an important part of the structural flexibility of the labour market. About 16 per cent of all re-employed persons changed their local residence; 28 per cent of the unemployed, jobless for more than one year, were not opposed to regional mobility. The comparable rate for the whole population is only 5 per cent a year. Half (48 per cent) of the re-employed workers changed their occupational group and/or their branch of economic activity; 31 per cent worked at an unchanged level and degree of qualification; 7 per cent got a new job with the help of retraining and educational measures.[7]

On the demand side, about 200,0000 — 250,00 job vacancies were registered at any time during 1977. If we assume a logging rate of 40 per cent at the employment offices, there are about 600,000 vacancies in the aggregate labour market. But that part of demand for labour is to be compared to total labour turnover and about 8

[7] Sörgel (1978).

Table 5: EMPLOYMENT, UNEMPLOYMENT AND VACANCIES BY ECONOMIC BRANCHES

(May 1978)

	Employment [1] June 1977		Unemployment May 1978		Vacancies May 1978		Unemployment rate May 1978	Vacancy rate May 1978
	1000	%	1000	%	1000	%	%	%
Agriculture	208.0	1.0	10.5	1.2	5.0	2.0	4.8	2.4
Energy, Water, Mining	489.8	2.5	8.9	1.0	1.3	0.5	1.8	2.6
Manufacturing Ind.	8,454.6	42.5	292.2	32.0	83.2	32.6	3.3	1.0
Construction	1,581.8	8.0	69.9	7.7	31.9	12.5	4.2	2.0
Total services	9,133.2	45.9	370.8	40.6	133.0	52.0	3.9	1.4
Distribution	2,762.1	13.9	144.6	15.8	37.9	14.8	5.0	1.4
Traffic, Communication	944.4	4.8	23.0	2.5	9.2	3.6	2.4	1.0
Finance, Insurance	711.0	3.6	16.9	1.8	5.7	2.2	2.3	0.8
Services	3,085.4	15.5	135.0	14.8	61.0	23.9	4.2	1.9
Non-profit institutions	323.5	1.6	12.5	1.4	8.9	3.5	3.7	2.7
Government, public sector	1,306.7	6.6	38.8	4.3	10.3	4.0	2.9	0.8
Other branches, n.a.	12.5	0.1	160.7 [2]	17.6	1.1	0.4	—	—
Total	19,879.9	100	913.0	100	255.5	100	4.4	1.3

[1] Wage and salary earners with social security rights.
[2] Unemployed persons without any employment, interruption of employment and data not available.

Source: Institut für Arbeits-uyprkt- und Berufsforschung

million proposals for placements leading to 2.3 million successful placements.

The average duration of job vacancies registered in 1977 was 32 days. Half of the jobs offered were filled within a fortnight, 75 per cent of them after 37 days. Merely 11 per cent of all job vacancies stayed on the records for more than 5 months, because of restrictive age, qualification and skill limits. Job vacancies in agriculture, construction industries, government, many occupations in manufacturing industries, and jobs demanding low qualifications are filled easily and soon after registration. A relatively long time-lag is found in the service occupations, in the insurance and banking sectors and in jobs demanding high qualifications and skills.

Thus job vacancies are an integral part of the dynamic flexibility of the market described above. Their number and structure does not indicate that there are severe discrepancies between the profiles of demand and supply nor that there are major frictions in the functioning of the placement process.

In we take into account the idea that active manpower policy means spreading the negative consequences of structural change over all members of the labour force and all firms, the mobility of the unemployed and their readiness to accept less attractive jobs seem sufficient for their re-employment if demand for labour increases. The majority of the unemployed were employed just before registration (83.1 per cent in May 1978); 10 per cent had remained out of work for more than six months. Only 5.4 per cent of all unemployed had never worked before.

Finally, there is little evidence indicating "voluntary" unemployment. A representative survey recently found that in 1977/8 about 11 per cent of all unemployed (sample 1,636) did not look for work actively. Half of them were in a transitional status between different functions, e.g. further education, retirement or military service. The other half were mainly women willing to work, but who abstained from active job search because of child care and personal reasons.

One preliminary conclusion is that at least 80 per cent of the unemployed would be hired if aggregate demand for labour increased because of further growth of final demand and/or as a result of forms of reduced hours of work and additional jobs in public and private services. But more than half of all unemployed persons are occupationally unqualified, a quarter are personally handicapped, nearly 20 per cent have now been jobless for more than one year.

Unfortunately, this hard-core of unemployment is increasing. So even if there were sufficient demand for labour, it would be more and more difficult to re-integrate these groups of unemployed into the employment system. Thus unemployment, which at the beginning of the recession had been predominantly caused by a general lack of demand, is changing by itself into a structural phenomenon. It is not known whether widespread structural unemployment would change the individual and political reactions of workers affected and their families.

Thesis 6: The concept of employment and manpower policy

At the beginning of the recession, labour market and employment policies were being concentrated on specific objectives and targets in order to improve the process of matching labour supply and demand and the dynamics of unemployment. Selective policies were fairly successful, especially in some regions, occupational groups, so-called problem groups and economic sectors. This partly offset the short-comings of aggregate employment policies, which included: too little expenditure, deviation from mid-term fiscal plans, change of planned outlays on programmed budgets without net increases in total expenditure, and widespread anti-Keynesianism although total demand fell short of potential supply of labour and existing capacity. The growth in selectivity of policy helped to manage the continuing fragmentation of labour market problems. The gaps left by insufficient dynamic and structural flexibility were filled more and more as different policy measures and increasing expenditure proved to be fairly effective. Specific labour market problems thus provided little spur to public and political action by people who feared or suffered from unemployment.

The system of selective policies includes:

— policies for hard-to-employ people or so-called problem groups;

— policies for improving the match between labour demand and supply;

— policies for stabilizing employment or preserving jobs;

— policies to induce regional or sectoral mobility;

— policies for improving work conditions or increasing earnings for specific groups;

— policies to reduce the overall labour supply by keeping specific groups out of the labour market or by inducing people to leave the labour market;

— policies to reduce the overall labour supply by keeping specific groups out of the labour market or by inducing people to leave

— policies to increase the social acceptability of partial downgrading.[8]

The employment effect of aggregate policies to combat unemployment was an annual average of about 235,000 jobs created or preserved during 1974-78. A programme to promote investment until 1980 has a yearly impact of 70,000 jobs. The "Seventh Plan to improve regional structures" is aimed at creating 75,000 jobs a year until 1981 and is intended to preserve another 42,000 jobs a year.

Direct and selective employment policies are developed, implemented and financed by the Federal Employment Institute (Bundesanstalt für Arbeit). Table 6 shows the impact of these policies on employment and unemployment during 1973-78. On average, the employment effect was more than 230,000 jobs a year. The greatest effect was in 1975 with 394,000 jobs — equal to 2 per cent of all wage and salary earners. The impact on registered unemployment is smaller than the employment effect because additional demand for labour is satisfied partly out of unregistered unemployment — an increase in the potential labour force — and to some extent by workers from outside the EEC.

Table 7 demonstrates that at the beginning of the recession there was a change of emphasis: measures taken to stabilize employment in the seasonally-affected construction industries became less important as compared with general support for training and retraining, short-time work, and recently job creation (1978 and 1979: planned take-up 50,000 jobs for unemployed persons per year).

Short-time work clearly functions as a counter-cyclical policy, showing relatively the highest take-up and expenditure in 1975/76 at the trough of the recession: markedly more than in 1967.

[8] Schmid (1978) p. 1.

The second shift of emphasis was more severe because the most important policy for overcoming shortages in qualified manpower and the lack of skill of workers during structural change was cut and restricted to the unemployed.

After the peak of take-up had been reached in 1975 — 130,000 participants in full time training — the employment period needed before help with training could be claimed was raised from three to six years, unemployed people und workers without any training became the most important target groups, and maintenance grants for all other participants were cut from 80 per cent of last net wage to only 58 per cent. As a result the take-up of training measures for upward mobility declined as expected — but the participation of the unemployed and other target groups did not increase accordingly. During the first half of 1978 the take-up of all training measures increased by about 42 per cent, and 44 per cent of all participants had previously been unemployed.

As already mentioned, job creation increased its take-up and expenditure year by year having almost a double impact on employment because of multiplier effects. The emphasis was changed from the construction industries to social services, and part-time jobs, especially for women. (A tentative figure for the multiplier is between 2.2 and 1.2.)

Finally it is worth noting that the share of "active" expenditure was 72 per cent of total outlay in 1973. It decreased to about 38 per cent in 1976 because the majority of spending was on unemployment insurance/income compensation (see thesis 8).

In recent years the promotion of first-time employment has become an increasingly important aspect of placement activities. In 1973, 33.4 million DM were spent in supporting 0.5 per cent of all placements leading to contracts of employment of more than three months. In 1977, 355 million DM were spent in extending 8.6 per cent of placements into jobs of more than three months' duration. Experiments in combining the promotion of first-time employment with special training measures were less successful (1.4 per cent of corresponding placements in 1977).

Special federal labour market programmes were aimed at regional and local centres of unemployment; young, old, handicapped workers, wamen and part-time workers. A special wage subsidy programme provided 600 million DM in 1974/75 — two-thirds were spent, mainly employing men (83.6 per cent of all participants),

Table 6: The impact of different measures on employment and unemployment in the Federal Republic of Germany 1973-1978

| | Take up | | | | | | Employment impact | | | | | | Unemployment impact (diminuition of unemployment) | | | | | |
| | | | | | | | Persons per thousand | | | | | | | | | | | |
	1973	1974	1975	1976	1977	1978	1973	1974	1975	1976	1977	1978	1973	1974	1975	1976	1977	1978
1. Short-time work	44	292	773	277	231	161	11	73	223	96	55	50	7	48	147	63	36	33
2. Job creation	2	3	16	29	38	50	4	8	41	75	72	90	3	6	30	58	61	77
3. Training and Retraining	100	115	130	101	69	69	100	115	130	101	69	69	68	81	96	78	57	57
Total	146	410	919	407	338	310	115	196	394	272	196	209	78	135	273	199	145	167

For comparison:

Total change in employment in '000s: +68, −493, −899, −233, −63, +50

Total unemployment in '000s: 273, 582, 1,074, 1,060, 1,030, 993

Source: Mitteilungen des Instituts für Arbeitsmarkt- und Berufsforschung, H. 1/1979.

Table 7: Expenditures on manpower policies by the Federal Employment Institute during 1973-1988

Measures of manpower policy	million DM			expenditure in %				index: 1973=100				
	1973	1976	1977	1970	1973	1976	1977	1970	1972	1974	1976	1977
(1)	(2)	(3)	(4)	(5)	(6)	(7)	(8)	(9)	(10)	(11)	(12)	(13)
Promotion of vocational training	1,819	2,178	1,491	25.9	34.4	15.8	11.7	43	99	117	120	82
Vocational education	238	260	303	24.5	13.1	11.9	20.3	81	118	89	109	127
Further training	233	288	217	16.0	12.8	13.2	14.6	54	128	114	124	93
Retraining	67	160	169	9.8	3.7	7.3	11.3	115	121	130	239	252
Maintenance grants	1,233	1,427	771	47.4	67.8	65.5	51.7	30	90	121	116	63
Institutional promoting of training	48	43	31	2.3	2.6	2.0	2.1	37	83	148	90	65
Vocational rehabilitation	315	453	479	2.6	6.0	3.3	3.8	24	63	125	144	152
Promotion of work start	142	273	355	4.2	2.6	2.0	2.8	89	80	87	192	250
Support for construction industry	1,420	1,262	1,371	43.2	26.8	9.1	10.7	92	70	99	89	96
Bad weather support	511	678	576	93.8	36.0	53.7	42.0	239	123	104	133	113
Winter-work	778	514	702	—	54.8	407	51.2	—	—	102	66	90
Additional expenses	48	50	67	2.8	3.4	4.0	4.9	77	31	135	104	14
Other support	84	20	26	3.4	5.9	1.6	1.9	52	89	26	24	31
Job creation	20	170	579	0.5	0.4	1.2	4.5	70	85	160	860	2,895
Short-time work	74	990	594	0.4	1.4	7.2	4.7	16	377	915	1.338	803
Total active expenditures	2,791	5,326	4,869	76.7	71.6	38.6	38.2	61	83	123	140	128
Unemployment pay and other compensation	1,503	8,473	7,891	23.3	28.4	61.4	61.8	47	91	256	564	525
Unemployment benefit	1,395	6,906	6,283	92.6	92.8	81.5	79.6	47	92	255	495	450
Welfare payments to the unemployed	108	1,299	1,332	7.4	7.2	15.3	16.9	48	78	206	1,203	1,233
Wage compensation at bankruptcy	—	268	276	—	—	3.2	3.5	—	—	100	377	389

Source: Bundesanstalt für Arbeit (Federal Employment Institute).

young workers up to 25 years old (31.8 per cent) in place of workers
over 60 years old (4 per cent). About 25 per cent of 78,900
subsidised jobs were newly created. The result leads to the concluion
that wage cost subsidies are not a decisive instrument of aggregate
employment policy.

It is apparent from this short overview of concepts, different
measures of manpower policy and their impact, that a selective policy
approach was necessary and effective in improving the regional,
occupational and group-specific distribution of unemployment. Those
groups that were hard to employ were helped as aggregate demand
for labour fell short of potential labour force.

Thesis 7: Public policy and industrial relations

Looking at the relationship between public policy during the
recession and the system of industrial relations, a major conflict — at
least with the unions — was to be expected, since the effect of anti-
inflationary policies and the severe measures taken to stabilize the
budget worked pro-cyclically ono the labour market. But as soon as
expansionist measures of aggregate and specific policies led to unemployment peaking and then falling slightly in the following years, the
conflict lost its original threatening character and the climate of
relative political and social calm was preserved.

During the recession, the public sector — Federal State, Länder
and Local Governments — played a crucial part in combating
unemployment and skill shortages through public expenditure, investment, employment and vocational education. In view of the
persistent employment crisis, some critics of the activities undertaken
by the state point out that the public sector not only did not act
anti-cyclically, but partly even pro-cyclically, leading to a delay — or
even the end — of the small economic recovery during 1976 (GNP
growth: 1975: — 2.1 per cent, 1976: + 5.6 per cent, 1977:
+ 2.8 per cent). The arguments are based on the following indicators:

i) Public demand for goods and services during the recession fell
short of medium-term fiscal planning, (*mittelfristige Finanzplanung*),
causing a loss of 200,000 jobs in 1976. If these fiscal plans had been
pursued, the unemployment rate would have been one percentage
point lower than it actually was.

ii) At the end of 1975 it was decided to reach a better budgetary balance by cutting public expendiure and net new credits. As a consequence, the overall effect was estimated to be contractive (— 10 billion DM in 1986 and — 16 billion DM in 1977). Net new credits decreased by 12.1 per cent in 1976 and by 31.3 per cent in 1977.

iii) Public investment in 1975 remained constant at the 1974 level of 46 billion DM. In 1976, it decreased by 4.4 per cent; in 1977, public investment increased by just 0.9 per cent. There was a decisive change in public policy in 1978 with a 10.5 per cent increase in public investment. In addition, a special investment programme of 16 billion DM was enacted in March 1977.

iv) Public Sector employment — which increased by 1.36 million jobs to 4.37 million in the period 1960-74 (2.7 per cent on an annual average during 1960-74) — grew by 1.1 in 1975 and just 0.4 per cent in 1976. A slight decrease of — 0.2 per cent followed in 1977. Thus the public sector reduced its employment — contrary to its special responsibility for full employment — and ceased taking on those who were made redundant in industrial sectors, a process exactly opposite to the structural change in employment in pre-recession years.

v) Public vocational education increased at a below-average rate, and the rate of participation was the lowest of all economic branches.

All in all, the contribution of the public sector to the increasing demand for jobs and vocational education was too small compared to the severity and duration of the employment crisis. In particular, the change of policy in 1975/76 worked out pro-cyclically on the labour market. The Keynesian policies pursued were effective, but too limited and interrupted too early to overcome the crisis. The partial return to expansionist public sector budgets and politicies in in 1977/78 led to a process of recovery showing some improvements in the labour market in 1978 and 1979.

The crucial question whether public policy as described above was intended cannot be answered. Some elements of planned action are indicated by the deviation from medium term fiscal plans; the change of planned outlays into programmes to stimulate growth and investment without major net increases in total expenditure; the savings-philosophy of the Law concerning the Consolidation of

Public Households (*Haushaltsstrukturgesetz*) and the unsolved conflict between Federal State, Länder, and Local governments, which diminished outlays and/or net new credits while the federal authorities increased their expenditure. But there was no explicitly declared strategy of state action. On the contrary, there was a discrepancy between declared policies and actual outcome of the political, economic and labour market processes. As a result, the marginalization of problem groups, the increased selectivity of firms hiring labour and the crowding-out of large groups of workers minimized the potential political power of the unemployed and kept it at a low level.

Thesis 8: The importance of unemployment pay

Another part of the explanation for social and political calm stems from the fact that 70-90 per cent of the unemployed, (the actual rate depends on the method of measurement) received unemployment insurance payments.[9] Most get it very soon after losing their job, and payments are transferred to bank accounts, like wages and salaries. During the first half of 1978, for example, unemployment pay (*Arbeitslosengeld*) for a month was 1,089 DM, and unemployment welfare payment 877 DM as compared to 1,548 DM net income on average.

If we take the stock of unemployed, the proportion of unemployed persons eligible for some type of payment was 80 per cent in September 1977. The corresponding proportion of all persons hit by unemployment during 1977 was 71 per cent (males: 69 per cent, females: 74 per cent). The rate fell after May 1975 (90 per cent), because payments generally end after one year when the duration of unemployment increases. The second reason for this fall was that an increasing group of the unemployed were new-comers to the labour force without UI-rights. Also of increasing importance was the fact that many people interrupted employment and did not gain new UI-rights thereafter. If we combine all unemployed persons who received payment at a certain date and those who had payment rights either then or previously we may roughly reach a 90 per cent level of unemployed persons eligible for benefits. Though unemployment pay is earnings-related, as are other social security benefits, the average sum per head per month in 1977 was a little less than in

[9] Karr (1978) pp. 1-6.

1976, indicating the stagnation of UI-reference earnings. UI-payments are income related — 68 per cent of previous pay — and limited to one year. These high proportions and the unbureaucratic payment methods may explain how the social security system worked to the advantage of political and social calm. Nevertheless, according to a recent survey 82 per cent of all unemployed reported financial difficulties; 73 per cent reduced expenditure on consumption or savings. The most severe problems were experienced by men, single people, the long-term unemployed and those losing jobs several times. The average loss of net income of the long-term unemployed was about 45 per cent — thus making them eligible for special welfare payments. Thus we cannot agree with claims that living on UI-payments is — or might become — a widespread phenomenon, though there is some abuse as is the case for any welfare payment. In general, UI-recipients have a shorter total duration of unemployment than non-recipients.

To sum up, political unrest and action can be expected only if unemployment is accompanied by an absolute deprivation in terms of family income; but the net of social security prevented poverty — even though relative incomes declined.

Thesis 9: Employment policy at company level

Small and medium-sized firms employing between 10-49 workers took a less than proportional share of all dismissals during the recession. The capability of resisting cyclical and other falls in employment seems to decrease by size of enterprise. However, although large-scale firms with a work force of 1,000 workers and more were responsible for the majority of total lay-offs, they developed and implemented a wide range of policies and sometimes even new measures to relieve the individual and social consequences of the decline in labour demand. This process of varying and attenuated responses may be a further explanation of the relatively quiescent political and social scene despite the employment impact of the recession.

Table 8 gives the structure of different employment policies at company level during 1973-75. The earlier thesis that working hours became an important part of the adjustment to lower levels of economic activity is confirmed. Enterprises with sophisticated personnel planning reported the smallest proportion of redundancies.

148   *Jürgen Kühl*

Table 8: STRUCTURE OF EMPLOYMENT POLICIES AT COMPANY LEVEL DURING THE
RECESSION 1973-75

Measures	Enterprises without any personnel planning (385) %	Enterprises with good personnel planning (27) %	All other enterprises (921) %
Reduction of overtime work	78.7	77.8	84.6
Reduction of additional shifts	13.2	11.1	14.1
Short-time work	33.8	31.8	36.9
Dismissals	62.3	55.6	60.4
Redundancy plans and payments	2.9	25.9	5.4
Reduction of temporary work	11.4	18.5	14.2
Earlier retirement	7.8	33.3	12.3
Freeze of recruitment	35.8	63.0	44.7
Further education at company level	0.3	7.4	3.7
Reduction of external orders	6.8	14.8	13.6
" Social plans "	2.6	11.1	5.4
None of these measures	(27.8)	(18.5)	(18.9)

Source: Institute for Social Research, Munich.

Along with the freeze on recruitment they offered earlier retirement (44 per cent), special redundancy plans and payments (26 per cent), the reduction of temporary work (19 per cent), and internal further education and retraining (7 per cent). One in seven firms passed on their employment problems to smaller firms. Special schemes with a strong emphasis on the social and financial interests of redundant workers ("Social plans") were devised by 11 per cent of all large firms.[10]

[10] Schultz-Wild (1978).

Enterprises without any personnel planning and all other enterprises used to a large extent the well-known and traditional measures of employment policy at company level. It is unfortunately not known how many workers were affected by different measures and how much money was spent per redundant worker.

Although the occasionally costly mix of measures involved a lot of time in negotiations between management and works councils, it proved fairly successful in stabilizing the primary work force and securing the necessary jobs around it. Firms went on to pursue a medium-term strategy of stable employment which offered additional security to their workers and which became an alternative to a process of continued hiring and firing. However, severe conflict could emerge if the amounts by which production and thus employment need to adjust in response to changing orders increase, while at the same time labour becomes a quasi-fixed factor limiting adjustments to fluctuations of employment by the company. There is growing evidence that firms try to increase their ability to adjust flexibly to changing demand by offering shorter-term, fixed-term and "lump-style" employment.

As mentioned in thesis 1, the most important change in the status of the unemployed is the separation from the organizational and institutional framework within firms. It is not known whether firms try to break these relationships systematically as far as specific groups of workers are concerned.

Thesis 10: The contribution of the unions

The union movement and the representatives of the workers at company level offered a lot of possible solutions and solved many of the conflicts which emerged during the crisis of employment. The issue of unemployment gained importance compared with questions of wages, pay structure, and income distribution. The unions enforced, and keep demanding, reductions in daily, weekly and yearly working hours as well as career lengths; they cut overtime and increased flexibility and options in working hours; to a certain degree, they obtained agreements against downgrading and de-skilling. They began to preserve available jobs and the hiring of older workers, and they negotiated for protection against rationalization and for optional earlier retirement. They started to offer more choice between income and leisure in the case of overtime work and for older workers.

All forms of reduced hours, more freedom of choice, increased flexibility of hours, and better protection against down-grading and unfair dismissal are in line with the basic aspirations of the majority of workers. Although the reduction of standard working time slowed down during the recession to 0.6 per cent per year — from the long-term trend of nearly 1 per cent per year, and at a stage when 92.6 per cent of all employed workers reached the 40-hour week — the 1979 target is more than 1 per cent. Since half of that reduction is removed by a once and for all jump in productivity, as recent surveys in industry show, the employment effect of bargaining over cuts in hours might increase the number of jobs by 100,000-150,000 in 1979. The unions are therefore making major contribution to overcoming unemployment. Unions are now aiming for the 35-hour week; the steel industry has made the first test. At a top EEC meeting, DGB leader Oscar Vetter recently proposed reduccing working hours by 10 per cent over the next four years.

A survey comprising 8,963 individuals over the age of 15 in all EEC countries indicated that in November 1977 the highest proportion of all employed persons had a preference for a reduction in weekly hours over other options:[11]

Table 9: PREFERENCES CONCERNING REDUCTIONS OF WORKING TIME

Preferences in percentage of	Total population	Working population
Reduction in weekly hours	33	37
Longer vacations	23	25
Earlier retirement	38	33
No answer	6	5

Some 71 per cent of the total population, and 72 per cent of the working population, favour a flexible retirement scheme allowing continued work for shorter hours. At around 50 years of age, workers prefer early retirement; at 60 years and over they look for flexible retirement with reduced hours.

[11] Kommission (1978), pp. 34-41.

In Germany the experience of the cigarette industry showed that 80 per cent of workers over 60 years old decided to opt to work only 20 weeks at unchanged pay; 10 per cent retired earlier on 75 per cent of their final wage.

A slight majority (51 per cent) of the EEC's 100 million working population prefers a reduction of hours to increased income (42 per cent). This holds true for all income groups. There is a strong relationship between the standard of living (national income) and the proportion of the working population prefering reduced hours of work. For Ireland, Italy and Luxemburg a clear majority in favour of wage increases was reported by the EEC survey.

As a consequence of the labour market slack, the German unions started to use collective bargaining as a means of employment policy, to protect workers and to humanize work. The yearly growth of productivity of about 4-5 per cent per hour will therefore be distributed between wages and leisure in a different manner. In the coming 10 years of growing labour supply the job element of collective bargaining — job creation and protection of workers, skill and jobs — might have priority over wages and incomes policies. This marked change in union policy has been supported by the fact that real wages continued to rise during the recession, although at a lower pace. The employment effect of restraint in wage demands is either uncertain or indecisive in most economic branches and segments of the labour market; but the reduction of hours leads to additional recruitment and keeps the unions in line with basic desires of their membership. The shift of emphasis towards manpower and employment policies by union action thus seems both reasonable and encouraging.

Moreover, these new strategies should be pursued soon and on some scale, largely because the climate of relative calm might disappear if economic growth sinply absorbs productivity gains and unemployment stagnates with a stock of around one million and a flow of two million unemployed.[12]

Thesis 11: The potential and the actual degree of organization

The prevailing political and social calm might be lost if the unemployed united, entered the unions and political parties and if

[12] Kühl (1977).

they mobilized mass-media, political leaders and unions in order to get jobs or even to try to change governments. However, if an average duration of unemployment of 3-6 months is expected, it does not seem worthwhile to organize and join the pressure groups. On the other hand, those unemployed who suffer from long-term unemployment, and who should organize themselves, have to a large extent the lowest political potential, with mininmal abilities to look after their interests and join active groups.

Although our knowledge about political aspects of unemployment is very poor, a survey in autumn 1975 allows the tentative conclusion that the unemployed are not a source of potential radical rejection of our Western capitalist/pluralist/bureaucratic system of society. Only 4 per cent of the unemployed surveyed were reported to be critics of that system. Just 9 per cent of them recommended uniting in order to increase political power although at that time almost nobody was a member of an "association of unemployed persons" (0.2 per cent). One in six unemployed German adults was a union member (16 per cent.)

Asked for the main reasons behind persistent unemployment, 20 per cent cited economic problems, (e.g. the worldwide recession, currency problems, inflation, exports, shortage of investment, rationalization etc.). Another 30 per cent pointed out that political causes might be most important (e.g. the ruling government, economic policy etc.). A third of the unemployed did not answer. There are no discernible differences of opinion between the unemployed and the total population as far as their opinions on the main causes of the employment crisis are concerned.

The low degree of organization and/or unionization shows that the unemployed might not become inclined to collective action against the political system and its institutions. Instead, there is a fall in self-confidence and morale leading to pessimism and fatalism as joblessness continues. There are some indications that unemployed worked workers turn to the social democratic party at election day because they believe that party to be most vigorously combating unemployment.

On the other hand, the rate of unionization of all wage and salary earners moves between 38 and 40 per cent — DGB 33 per cent — indicating that the unemployed may be of minor interest to the unions as a recruitment target because of their much smaller rate of unionization. Nevertheless, as thesis 10 showed, the unions look to the interests and priorities of their members as well as pursuing general strategies to regain full employment in order to strengthen their bargaining power and to offer jobs to everybody able and willing to work.

3. CONCLUDING REMARKS

As far as the labour market issues of the recession are concerned, until now there have been no major disturbances in industrial relations. By and large collective bargaining has still concentrated on the interests of those in work, namely organized labour. The unemployed have got little help, because the dynamic and structural flexibility of the labour market — assisted by an increasing selectivity in manpower policy — was believed, and proved, to be sufficient to prevent a process of destruction of social calm and industrial relations.

Employers' organizations and the unions agreed to hold down wage increases to small gains in real terms. Since unemployment proved to remain persistently high in the mid-term, a substantial shift of emphasis in the aims of collective bargaining towards the employment issue was demanded by the unions. Agreements reached which secured existing jobs and work-places by means of variations in working hours — i.e. reductions and flexibility. Workers made vulnerable by technical progress, rationalization investments, disability and old age received additional protection against redundancy and occupational or financial downgrading. Thus collective bargaining diminished the inflow of new unemployment and restricted downward mobility.

Although some of these agreements were settled after strikes and other forms of workers' "participation", there was a considerable degree of consensus in industrial negotiations which enabled some important contributions to the fight against unemployment. There were only minor attempts at action through publicity and demonstrations. Although some factory closures were stopped and although some redundancies were delayed, the employment effect of this strategy was small —but greater than if there had been no public action at all.

It is, however, at this point that possible deficiencies of the approach taken in this paper become clear. There are more than 30,000 different collective bargaining agreements and even more supplementary agreements at company level. Even if the majority of these regulations were known sufficiently, it would be very difficult to calculate the aggregate employment effect of all micro-level measures. Although the different aims of employment-oriented policies to be pursued during the next round of bargaining are well known, it is still very uncertain whether the new emphasis given to a policy on hours of work adds up to even a 1 per cent reduction of hours. The well-known problem of the relationship between micro-and macro-level effects intervenes.

The FRG may move towards severe industrial conflict if two developments occur:

(i) If the recently emphasised attempts of the unions to combat unemployment by means of a policy on working hours coupled with the various measures of job protection fail, their mid-range bargaining power on wages might be weakened for years. In addition, there is some evidence that the unions and the works councils might change their aims and actions from consensus-prone to conflict-prone policies in order to meet the increasing demands of workers for extensive protection. If these processes proved to function counter-productively, the employers will certainly put up more resistance than before.

(ii) The main groups of immediate concern to the unions might become affected by persisten unemployment if the dynamic and structural flexibility of the labour market supported by selective manpower becomes ineffective in producing a segmentation of unemployment into marginal, secondary workers with low unionization on the one hand, and primary workers — i.e. skilled wage and salary earners — with high rates of unionization and/or a strong backing from works councils at the firm level, on the other. The shift of emphasis towards employment oriented aspects of collective bargaining may have been influenced by the fact that the recession had been hitting skilled wage and salary earners for some time.

At the moment, these tendencies cannot beexcluded from consideration, but the mid-term trends seemto be moving towards an active use of collective bargaining and other means to resolve industrial conflicts. Inaddition to the existing institutions, a reactivation of the tripartite self-administration system at the local level of the employment office is a common theme. Some experts and politicians emphasise the apprenticeship system of industrial education, arguing that on the whole, except for some minor regional and occupational discrepancies, it coped with the increasing demand for the relevant types of qualifications. The consequences of the baby-boom from the early 1960s were a central issue in industrial relations. Meanwhile, another attempt is being made to find new procedures to manage industrial conflict — i.e. consultation arrangements, special conferences dealing with sectoral, regional or local labour market problems to find common solutions. Following the Swedish experience, special systems of negotiations are discussed instead of legal and/or fiscal interventions in industrial disputes.

Some of the empirical data seem to support a model of the "divide and rule" type as a possible explanation for the climate of relative politic and social calm during the recession. The operation of the labour market, both employers and unions, used the dynamics of employment and unemployment so that the risk of becoming and staying jobless varied inversely to thepotentia l political power of the corresponding group. There were some public counter-measures against this process. In 1966/67, a small increase in unemployment, accompanied by a surge in nationalistic policies and the student movement, was sufficient for active manpower and employment policies to be implemented. There is little to back the view that there might be a deliberate public policy of fragmentation of political protest. Nevertheless, the state acted to some extent pro-cyclically in terms of the labour market during the recession.

But these findings are insufficient to link segmentation of the labour market, the role of the state, the rate of unionization and the phenomenon of under-representation with each other. Moreover the interaction between the labour market and industrial relations is still to be explored.

As can be seen from the very simple approach of this paper as well as from its limited conclusions, it is self-evident that more research work necessary in this field. Perhaps future research would be most promising in those fields which were excluded at the start.

BIBLIOGRAPHY

Autorengemeinschaft (1978): "Der Arbeitsmarkt in der Bundesrepublik Deutschland 1978 (insgesamt und regional). Entwicklung, Strukturprobleme, arbeitsmarkpolitische Maßnahmen", *Mitteilungen aus der Arbeitsmarkt-und Berufsforschung*, 1, 1978.

Bundesanstalt für Arbeit (J. Kühl, A. G. Paul, D. Blunk) (1978): *Überlegungen II zu einer Vorausschauenden Arbeitsmarktpolitik*, Nürnberg 1978. (To be translated into English and French).

F. Egle (1977): "Zusammenhang zwischen Arbeitslosenquote, Dauer der Arbeitslosigkeit und Betroffenheit von Arbeitslosigkeit". *Mitteilungen aus der Arbeitsmarkt- und Berufsforschung*, 2, 1977.

W. Karr (1978): "Die Leistungsberechtigten in der Arbeitslosenstatistik", *Mitteilungen aus der Arbeitsmarkt- und Berufsforschung*, 1, 1978.

Kommission der Europäischen Gemeinschaften (1978): *Die Erwerbspersonen und die Perspektiven des Ruhestandes*. Brüssel, Mai 1978.

J. Kühl (1977): "Expansion of Demand or Reduction of Labour Offered — the Real Alternative". Paper presented at the Colloque on Unemployment of the European University Institute, Nov./Dec. 1977.

G. Schmid (1978): *Selective Employment Policy in West Germany: Some Evidence of Its Development and Impact*. International Institute of Management, Berlin 1978.

R. Schultz-Wild (1978): *Betriebliche Beschäftigungspolitik in der Krise*, Campus Verlag, Frankfurt/New York 1978.

N. Sörgel (1978): *Arbeitssuche, berufliche Mobilität, Arbeitsvermittlung und Beratung*, München 1978.

CHAPTER III

THE ITALIAN CASE

LABOUR MARKETS AND INDUSTRIAL RELATIONS IN THE 1970s: THE ITALIAN EXPERIENCE *

by

GIANCARLO MAZZOCCHI

1. INTRODUCTION

It is very hard to talk about management of industrial conflict in the Italian case, not because the institutional framework for resolving industrial conflict is very extensive, but for precisely the opposite reason. That is, apart from the important role of collective bargaining, there exist in Italy very few instruments such as have been adopted in other countries for resolving industrial conflict. Moreover, the philosophy of the trade unions, which are very jealous of their autonomy and independence of political power, is more favourable to self-regulation and self-discipline (albeit sometimes only on paper) than to the creation of machinery for the resolution of industrial conflict. In these conditions the speaker has had to use some imagination to be able to produce the paper. I should like finally to point out that this paper intends to furnish only a few interpretative 'notes' on the Italian case, which I have taken from a wider and more complex research that we are endeavouring to develop at the Economics Institute of the Catholic University of Milan.

2. SOME REMARKS ON THE EVOLUTION OF CONTRACTUAL STRUCTURES IN ITALY

I think that, to be able to give an adequate evolution, even if

* Translated from Italian by Ian Fraser

briefly, of the evolution of the labour market and of the management
of industrial conflict in Italy it is useful to illustrate the evolution of
the collective bargaining structure and the reasons for that evolution.
It is well known that in the immediate post-war period Italy was
characterized by a very centralized collective bargaining process. This
collective bargaining process, because of high unemployment and the
unions' great fear of increasing that unemployment, aimed at fixing
contractual wages on the basis of the 'capacity to pay' of marginal
firms. Edelmann and Fleming have discussed this phenomenon very
acutely. They state:

> "For small firms and marginal ones, whose product markets are
> local or limited, it is important that labour costs be kept to a
> minimum level consistent with public order; and for these
> national contracts establishing wage minima are highly suitable.
> For the most advanced sectors of the economy, however, low
> labour costs are less important than some other objectives: above
> all labour peace and an adequate supply so as to gain marimum
> advantage regarding product mix, markets, wages and prices. It
> is evident that as production becomes more capital intensive,
> labour costs become less important to management, and the
> efficient employment of capital, the acquisition of new markets
> and the avoidance of work stoppages become more important.
> This is essentially the calculus that has faced the more efficient
> and expanding Italian firms in this period. For them the national
> bargains and the general rules are of little use except as they
> help to maintain stability and quiescence in the less advanced
> sector of the economy. For them an additional set of institutions
> are being developed: more flexible and so fashioned that they
> can be tailored by each large company to its oxn require-
> ments.
> In this period the basic industrial relations device in the arsenal
> of the advanced sector is planned wage drift. Using this tactic
> and some related ones, the large companies have been able to use
> wage policy not only to maintain a high measure of control over
> their labour costs but also to maximize labour docility, minimize
> strikes and even exert considerable control over the development
> and political complexion of the labour movement".[1]

I feel that the use of 'wage drift' may be regarded as the
principal instrument used in Italy, obviously after collective, bargaining, for the management of industrial conflict. It is easy to see that
this is an extremely dangerous instrument for the unions, since if the

[1] Edelman, Fleming (1965) p. 35.

union proves incapable of controlling 'wage drift' and working conditions and rules within a firm, it is destined to lose credibility with its membership and to facilitate the rise of autonomous trade unionism, as in fact happened in 1952 at Fiat.

This is in my opinion the main reason why, from the mid-fifties, the CISL, in Italy opposed by the CGIL, began to think about a decentralized structure of collective bargaining so as to give more room to 'industry bargaining' than to 'company bargaining'. The aims of this decentralization of the collective bargaining structure were, in the opinion of the union leaders, a greater control over the growth of earnings and over working rules, which the high rate of technical progress was continually modifying, and greater participation by the workers. It is interesting to point out that after the initial opposition, in fact fifteen years after, the General Secretary of the CGIL, Luciano Lama, stated that the decentralizing tendency sowed the seed, through greater worker participation, for a rise in class consciousness and therefore for greater unity of the labour movement.[2] In my opinion, this fact is important for understanding the evolution of industrial conflict in Italy and the scarce viability of an incomes policy.

With the 1960s, after the difficulties of and with considerable resistance from the employer associations, there came the decline of the centralized collective bargaining structure and the rise of an articulated and decentralized collective bargaining system based mainly on industry bargaining, and, though to a lesser extent, company bargaining. This change allowed a renewed control over earnings growth, over work rules and over working conditions inside an industry and inside firms, but obviously also tends to produce a phenomenon which is somewhat disturbing for the trade unions, namely the creation, this time not through wage drift but trough the direct action of the union, of considerable wage differentials, based on the differing ability to pay different industries and firms. In other words, even though the trade union resumes control over the growth of earnings and over work rules, it essentially ratifies, through wage increases and labour cost structures that differ between industries and firms, the creation of considerable differences in labour costs. But this development, even if controlled by the trade union, is very damaging to it since it means, in the opinion of some union leaders,

[2] Lama (1973).

a greater spread in wages and therefore less solidarity and unity within the labour movement.[3] This is in my opinion a fairly relevant point, since it allows one to understand the growth of the strongly solidaristic and egalitarian policy that the Italian trade unions introduced at the beginning of the 1970s.

3. THE SEVENTIES

After this brief section on the evolution of the collective bargaining system in Italy, I should now like to look at Italian experience as regards wage policy and industrial conflicto in the 1970s, since, as in other European countries, it was precisely in the 1970s that Italy experienced what Crouch and Pizzorno have baptized *The Resurgence of Class Conflict.*[4] The first big Italian wage explosion in 1963, which for the first time since the war brought wage increases that considerably exceeded the increases in labour productivity and thereby brought about increases in the general level of prices and deficits on the balance of payments, was absorbed by using the well known remedy of a "Phillips curve menu". The reduction of aggregate demand, through a strict monetary policy, increased the unemployment rate, which in 1963 had reached a historical minimum for Italy (2.5 per cent), and consequently the 1966 wage agreements seemed very "responsible" and compatibel with price stability. At that period the fear of a new recession was much in the forefront of the union leaders' minds, so that the 1966 wage increases were perfectly in line with increases in labour productivity. Previously, as we have seen, *planned wage drift* had been the instrument for absorbing industrial conflict; now the remedy used was the control of aggregate demand based on the "Phillips curve" hypothesis.

While this remedy worked in the 1960s, it seems to have lost much of its power in the 1970s. The wage agreements of 1969 show a considerable "wage push" by contrast with those of 1963 where there was a high "wage pull".[5] At this point I should like to present some data, accompanied by some simple reflections, on the growth of wages in monetary and real terms, of labour productivity, of unit labour costs and of prices, without going into the internation-

[3] Foa (1961).
[4] Crouch, Pizzorno (1978).
[5] Tarantelli (1973).

al comparisons which have already been dealt with in Prof. Saunders' papers. The first two very simple, and by no means original, observations I should like to make are the following: 1) from the beginning of the 1970s the movement of labour costs, of unit labour costs and of prices have undergone very considerable accelerations. (Table 1).

2) Real wages ave also experienced considerable increases (Table 2). It is, however, necessary to devote more attention to analysing the trends in external and internal wage structures, since this allows an evaluation of the impact of the egalitarian philosophy adopted by the trade unions at the beginning of the 1970s, not only on wage structures but also on the inflationary process of the economy. As already said, at the beginning of the 1970s, the Italian trade unions tried to restrain the growth of the internal and external wage differentials that were threatening to fragment the labour movement and

Table 1: PRODUCTIVITY, COSTS AND PRICES FOR MANUFACTURING INDUSTRIES: 1970-1977
(Annual percentage rate of change)

Years	(1) Production	(2) Productivity	(3) Labour cost	(4) Unit labour cost	(5) Prices
1971/70	0.3	0.3	10.9	10.5	6.7
1972/71	4.1	5.2	11.1	5.7	7.0
1973/72	10.8	9.1	22.5	12.3	15.8
1974/73	6.7	4.3	23.2	18.1	22.5
1975/74	— 9.5	— 9.3	22.2	35.0	21.4
1976/75	12.4	12.1	24.0	10.6	17.8
1977/76	1.9	1.8	19.0	16.8	14.0
Total period 1970/1977	28.0	24.3	235.2	169.8	164.1

Notes: (1) Production: Value added at factor cost (at 1970 prices).

(2) Productivity: Value added (at 1970 prices) per employed.

(3) Labour cost: Compensation of employees per employed.

(4) Unit labour cost: Ratio between labour cost and productivity: (3)/(2).

(5) Implicit prices for the value added at factor cost.

Source: ISTAT.

Giancarlo Mazzocchi

Table 2: COST OF LIVING AND EARNINGS FOR MANUFACTURING INDUSTRY

(Annual percentage rate of change)

Years	Cost of living	Earnings	Real earnings
1971	5.0	12.2	7.2
1971	5.0	12.2	7.2
1972	5.6	10.7	5.1
1973	10.4	24.2	13.8
1974	19.4	22.3	2.9
1975	17.2	21.4	4.2
1976	16.5	23,8	7.3
1977	18.1	26,3	8.2

Source: ISTAT.

to reduce that class consciousness and unity that the unions (and the left-wing parties) needed to propose and achieve the so-called structural reform of the Italian economy. The egalitarian philosophy was the necessary economic and social complement of the unitary process that the unions began to pursue from the end of the 1960s, which had begun in the firms when the collective bargaining structure had been decentralized. This egalitarian policy began to be realized firstly through 1) greater coordination between the various industry agreements, 2) flat rate wage increases, 3) as regards internal wage structures, also through automatic progressions from one grade to another and, in some cases, the abolition of the lowest grades, and subsequently, i.e. as from 1975, 4) the sliding scale (scala mobile), the great Automatic Equalizer.

The effects of this egalitarian policy are summarized in the following tables (Tables 3 and 4). The conclusions are very clear: the egalitarian policy seems to have functioned very well in closing the external differentials between sectors and especially the internal ones between job positions. At the Catholic University of Milan, a large-scale investigation into internal differentials is being undertaken. The first results of the investigation indicate that the narrowing of

Table 3: ANNUAL GROSS AVERAGE EARNINGS BY SECTORS

(Industry = 100)

Sectors	1970	1974	1977
Agriculture	65	71	78
Industry	*100*	*100*	*100*
— Energy industry	226	195	174
— Manufacturing industry	106	105	105
— Minerals, iron and non-iron ore and metals	142	133	126
— Minerals and products based on non metall. minerals	100	103	103
— Chemical and pharmaceuticals products	169	156	152
— Metallurgical products	99	96	88
— Agricultural and industrial machinery	133	117	144
— Office machinery	135	128	131
— Electrical machinery	135	122	118
— Motor vehicles and related engines	159	130	122
— Other vehicles	143	127	122
— Foods and tobacco	117	115	126
— Textiles and clothing products	64	72	75
— Leather and footwear products	66	76	82
— Timber and related furniture	61	70	71
— Paper, printing and publishing	125	120	116
— Rubber and plastics prod.	106	112	115
— Other manufactured prod.	94	86	86
— Construction	71	74	73
Tradable services	135	125	114
— Distribution, hotels, shops	72	73	75
— Repairs	61	61	62
— Wholesale and retail distribution	80	78	81
— Hotels and shops	61	68	72
— Transport and communication	182	156	138
— Home transports	167	154	138
— Sea and air transports	330	267	223
— Related transport services	136	121	118
— Communications	193	149	127
— Banking and Insurance	328	285	234
— Miscellaneous services	144	131	116
— Services provided to firms	149	146	135

Cont. Table 3: ANNUAL GROSS AVERAGE EARNINGS BY SECTORS
(Industry = 100)

Sectors	1970	1974	1977
— Teaching and research	91	79	80
— Health services	193	165	134
— Cultural and recreation services	90	78	74
Non-tradeable services	147	125	106
— Public administration serv.	168	142	120
— Other services	60	44	36
TOTAL ECONOMY	*114*	*109*	*103*
Coefficient of variation (× 100)			
— for 18 industrial sectors	34,5	27,5	24,5
— for 14 services sectors	57,4	53,7	47,0
— for 33 sectors of the whole economy	51,0	44.2	37,0

Table 4: ANNUAL PAY BY JOB POSITION MANUAL AND NON-MANUAL WORKERS
(Manufacturing industry: 1972-74)
(Thousands of liras)

	1972	1974	Rate of change (1974/1972) %
Manual workers			
— Job position with the lowest pay	1,940	2,883	+ 45.5
— Job position with the highest pay	3,417	4,594	+ 34.4
— Coefficient of variation (%) for 37 job positions	15.4	13.3	
Non-manual workers			
— Job position with the lowest pay	2,378	3,377	+ 42,0
— Job position with the highest pay	6,520	8,021	+ 23.0
— Coefficient of variation (%) for 52 job positions	26.6	23.8	
Manual + Non-manual workers			
— Coefficient of variation (%) for 89 job positions (%) for 37 job positions	36.0	31.8	

the differentials has in fact been very drastic, not only because of the effects of the sliding scale and the flat rate increases but also because of those of a large number of other factors, such as various bonuses (incentive bonus, Christmas bonus, etc., educational allowances, union meeting hours, etc.) that act side by side with other less important factors of differentiation such as seniority payments, reserve payment, personal merit awards.

The labour cost structure in Italy is terribly confused, and only the most patient specialists can manage to follow it! [6]

Two questions seem to me important for discussion. Why has the compression of the internal and external wage structures in Italy not led to the re-establishment of traditional diffrentials? Can the situation last for long? To answer the first question I would distinguish two periods: the period *without* the sliding scale (1969-1975) and the period *with* the sliding scale. In the first period the re-establishment of traditional differentials could be realized in the manner well described for other countries by Weber:

> "The usual mechanism for adjustment to institutional modifications of wage structures is wage drift, controlled or no by the trade unions. But when wage drift is superimposed on institutional determination, the average effect is to raise the entire level of national wage structures in order to preserve the internal relationships among different industrial and occupational groups. Clearly this sequence of events has taken place, at least in the past, in Denmark, England and to some extent, the Netherlands and Australia".[7]

On this reasoning, to bring about a significant reduction in external and internal differentials it was necessary to reduce the space for wage drift, — which in turn required a big wage push based on "the capacity to pay" of the industries and firms with the greatest "capacity to pay", i.e. the most advanced industries and firms. This big wage push was achieved in the major "wage rounds" of 1969-70 and 1972-73. It hindered the restoration of traditional differentials but also violently accelerated Italian inflation. I should like to stress that this interpretation has been accepted by the most recent Italian studies on the evolution of wage structures.[8]

---

[6] One of these patient specialists is E. Pontarollo who has recently published an excellent work on labour cost structure and wage bargaining. See Pontarollo (1978).
[7] Weber (1963) p. 146.
[8] Dell'Aringa (1977).

The restoration of traditional wage differentials became still more difficult when, besides the flat rate wage increases, that great automatic equalizer, the sliding scale, came into operation in 1975. With this not only does the reduction of wage differentials become automatic, i.e. without trade union intervention, but the very attemtps at restoring the differenials paradoxically lead to their reduction. This is because the attempt to restore the traditional differentials leads to an increase in the level of wages and of prices. The price increase "leads, through the sliding scale, to the reduction of wage differentials. This may give rise to demands to restore the traditional differentials. If this happens, and wages and prices increase, the sliding scale leads to a reduction in wage differentials which leads to a demand to restore the wage differentials which leads, through the sliding scale, to a reduction of the wage differentials, and so on *ad infinitum*.

The second question is whether this situation can last for long. I think that this is one of the greatest problems for the Italian trade unions, which is causing considerable difficulty in their ranks. The reduction of wage differentials is today causing tension not only between non-manual and manual workers but also among the manual workers themselves, namely between skilled and unskilled workers. This has been recognized by the unions themselves. In his report to th IXth Congress of the CGIL, the General Secretary, Luciano Lama, stated:

> "One point the Congress has to take its stand on is the character which the philosophy of egalitarianism ought to have in present conditions. In this connection we must recognise that in the last ten years there has been a definite tendency to erode wage differentials inside one and the same contract, and that this reduction has maybe gone a bit too far. Workers' real skills ought to be recognised through the wage packet, since otherwise any increase in work capacity is discouraged, with negative effects on the growth of productivity. Undoubtedly in the past there were excessive wage differentials between various grades in the same category, but today we've gone over to the opposite extreme. The internal wage structures need to be balanced through a fairer recognition of the value of skill".[9]

This approach can also be seen in the proposals for the next collective agreement of the most militant Italian union: the engineer-

[9] Lama (1977) p. 35.

ing workers. These proposals represent an attempt to restructure the wage structure and to reopen, to a certain extent, the wage differentials (*riparametrazione*). However, the union also insisted on flat rate increases, which, together with the sliding scale, tend to reduce wage differentials. A widening of differentials could be brought about only through a large increase in monetary wages, which, however, the unions themselves rule out because of the not exactly brilliant economic condition of the country. This is the reasonwhy the widening of wage differentials envisaged by the engineering workers' proposal is in my opinion destined (unless there are vast wage increases) to remain on paper. This is the real dilemma facing the Italian trade unions, particularly in manufacturing industry.

This obviously does not mean that all Italian wage differentials are "just". We have many privileges linked to educational levels except for many university workers, rightly termed *precari* (shaky), which penalize manual labour. This also produces grave distortions in the labour supply, with an excess of supply (and consequent unemployment) among non-manual workers. Furthermore, there is a serious situation in the public sector characterized by the so-called "pay jungle". In this sector a partial sliding scale is in function, that is, a sliding scale that covers price increases only partially, and there are large wage differences even for "equal work" because of the big differences between contracts in the various subsectors. In public employment the rule of equal pay for equal work is systematically violated, also compared to the private sector. These are the reasons why autonomous trade unions flourish in the public sector.

I am very much aware that it is very hard to describe the Italian situation to foreign observers. Seeking to summarize the situation briefly, I can say that it is characterized by an apparently inextricable mix, made up of a narrowing of traditional differentials, especially internal ones and especially in manufacturing industry, with a continuation of large "unjust" differentials especially in the public sector. This is why the Italian situation is so complicated. This situation contains two grave dangers: that of provoking uncontrolled wage driftin the private sector of the economy and that of stimulating the rise of autonomous trade unionism, especially in the less favoured sectors of public employment.

In this situation it is rather hard to think of a possible solution. I feel that a solution would call for a re-thinking of the Italian collective bargaining structure.

1) I think the first stage should be a return to greater wage uniformity between industries. It should definitely be recognised that if a greater wage uniformity between industries, private and public, is wanted, greater importance should be given to the central level of collective bargaining. 2) Bargaining by trade and by firm ought to aim in the first place at the construction of rational, just and accepted wage structures and also to agreed wage increases that to some extent follow the capacity to pay of individual industries and firms, so as to control the phenomenon of wage drift. 3) Finally, company bargaining should be reserved principally for the definition of work rules and the cotnrol of conditions and of work organisation in the company. The role of the various levels of the collective bargaining structure changes with the changing condition of the economy. While in the past Italy perhaps needed more decentralised collective bargaining, today I feel there is a need to retrace steps at least as far as the determination of wages is concerned. Whether it will be easy to get the unions to accept this is quite another matter.

4. THE MANAGEMENT OF INDUSTRIAL CONFLICT: THE STRANGE ADVENTURE AND EXPERIENCE OF THE CASSA INTEGRAZIONE GUADAGNI (C.I.G.) (WAGE SUPPLEMENT FUND)

During the 1970s, and particularly after its reform in 1975, an important role was played in Italy by the *Cassa Integrazione Guadagni*, a fund for the payment of wages (93 per cent of the wage previously received) to workers on short time. This instrument differs from unemployment benefits since the workers is not dismissed but remains linked to the firm. This is in my opinion a brilliant example of an attempt to manage industrial conflict, which instead provoked certain conflicts through the effects exercised on the economy and on the labour market. It would seem in fact that the progressively increased use of the C.I.G. reduced turnover in manufacturing industry and thereby contributed to the creation of a secondary labour market and of youth unemployment, which are today causing considerable conflict. At this point I should like to go further into the question of labour turnover in the 1970s, even though in a fairly crude manner, given the present state of research.

To calculate the labour turnover (in manufacturing industry) the data supplied by the Ministry of Labour on the entry and departure of workers in the establishments surveyed were used. From 1975 on, the data on entries are divided into the following categories: 1) transfer from other establishments of the same firms 2) new intake another establishment of the same firm 2) dismissals 3) resignations 4) departures because of death, retirement and other reasons. Refer- 3) re-hirings. The data on departures are divided into 1) transfer to ring to the most recent period, the measure of labour turnover has been taken as half the sum of the entry and departure movements. The course of this index is shown in Figure 1, which also shows the trend in employment.

As can be seen, from 1965-69 turnover grows by 7 percentage points (from 33.3 to 40.3 per cent). Except for 1965, entries exceed

Figure 1: Turnover Rates and Employment in Manufacturing Industry

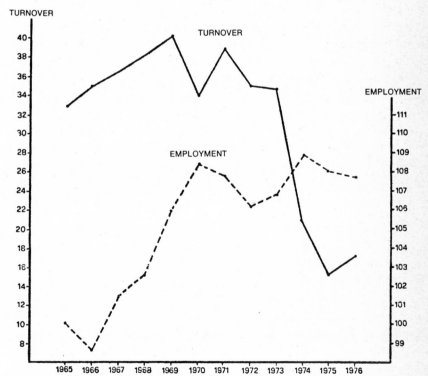

NOTES: TURNOVER: SEMI ADDITION OF ENTRY AND EXIT TOTAL FLOWS, AS
   PERCENTAGE OF EMPLOYMENT
SOURCE: *ISTAT e Ministero del Lavoro [Ministry of Labour].*

departures. The increase in turnover during an expansion phase [10] was also observed in the period 1959-63. In these two periods (1959-63 and 1966-69) one notes an increase in resignations, or of voluntary mobility, and a reduction in dismissals (involuntary mobility). Tese phenomena are perfectly comprehensible not only theoretically but also by considering the experience of other countries.

Between 1969 and 1970 and in subsequent years these trends become less clear. During 1970 — a year of growth in employment — dismissals continued to declined, contrarily to what had taken place previously. In subsequent years dismissals and resignations no longer moved in a countercyclical direction. Moreover, both variables show a tendency to fall, resulting in a collapse of the average turnover (Figure 2).

The clearest and most interesting conclusions can be derived from an examination of dismissals. After a continuous fall until 1970 there is a perceptible increase in both 1971 and 1972. Contrary to what happened previously (1964), the reduction in the volume of employment took place through dismissals more than through a reduction in intake. From 1974 the picture changes radically. Employment begins to decline (in manufacturing industry). In these conditions an increase in d. could be expected, but instead they fall drastically, as obviously do resignations. In 1975 — a year of deep economic crisis — the rate of d. reached the lowest value ever, namely 5 per cent, whereas in 1965, also a year of severe economic crisis, it reached 20 per cent. The average turnover rate, which towards the end of the 1960s was close to 40 per cent, falls to little more than 17 per cent in 1976. We do not yet have the figures for 1977. However, some analyses from ISTAT, for establishments of more than 500 employees, show that this trend towards lower labour mobility is still continuing.

On the other hand, the seriousness of this problem for Italy is shown from the data given in Table 5. In this connection I should, however, like to make an observation. It is very probable that the high mobility that we find in other countries concerns not only indigenous workers but also the "others", namely the foreign workers, of whom there are less in Italy than in other countries.

It has not been possible to carry out more refined analyses of these figures for this Colloquium. However, it is hard to resist the

---

[10] Modigliani, Tarantelli (1979).

Figure   2: Lay-offs   and   quits   in   manufacturing   industry   1965-1976
(As Percentage of Employment)

———————   LAY-OFFS

— — — — —   QUITS

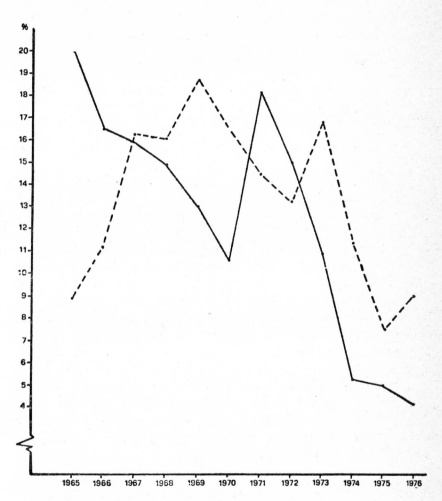

SOURCE: *Ministero del Lavoro [Ministry of Labour]*.

hypothesis that the changed economic and union context, the growing internationalisation of the labour market and the massive use in
these recent years of the C.I.G .as an instrument of industrial

Table 5: Reasons for Unemployment in some European Countries - April 1974 (%)

	Italy	W. Germany	France	Belgium	Netherlands	G. B.
Job losers	23.1	62.3	43.2	69.4	65.5	34.9
Job leavers	4.6	9.0	19.1	6.7	16.1	22.2
Seeking first job	61.8	12.9	14.3	21.8	11.1	6.4
Other reasons	10.5	15.8	23.4	2.1	7.3	36.5
TOTAL	100.0	100.0	100.0	100.0	100.0	100.0

Source: EEC, Labour Force Sample Survey, 1975.

conflict management are responsible for this drastic fall in labour mobility.

In this work we have not been able to do a complete analysis of the consequences of this phenomenon. However, it seems to me that fall in labour mobility is a hindrance to structural changes in the economy, but especially tends to progressively develop a secondary labour market, and therefore unstable employment and unemployment. This development of the secondary labour market is particularly serious because the personal and professional characteristics of those who enter the secondary labour market are reinforced by "the process of working in secondary jobs and living among others whose life-style is accomodated to that type of employment".[1]

Naturally, the growth of the secondary labour market and of youth unemployment provoked violent union opposition which raised industrial conflict. This is the reason why I said previously that an instrument designed to reduce industrial conflict had tended to intensify it. Employers complain that labour mobility is low. The unions reply that mobility can increase only when new jobs are created. And the circle is closed.

5. The growth of the left in the latest elections and industrial conflict

Finally, I should like to investigate whether the growth of the left (particularly the Communist Party) in the latest elections (1976)

[11] Piore (1970) p. 56.

has affected industrial conflict, as measured by the strike activity. Naturally, I have in mind the well-known anlysis of Hibbs, who looked at the relations between the variation of the (average) strike activity before and after the Second World War and the variation in the share of ministerial posts held in the cabinets of a number of countries by the left (Socialists, Labour, Communists) and found a "close association between the evolution of strike activity and the shift of political power between the social groups and classes".[12] In other words, the greater the political power of the political forces that are supposed to represent, in the words of Samuel Beer, the organised working class, the less the strike activity.

To apply this type of analysis to Italy for the most recent period is a rather difficult exercise, to put it mildly, not to say schizophrenic, since while in the past we have had centre-left govenments, with some cabinet posts occupied by the Socialists, since the great growth of the lift in the 1976 elections we have had only Christian-democratic governments! However, it is also true that today the left and especially the Communist Party have greater influence on government decision-making, and furthermore, they are in power in important Italian regions. This is the reason why I have attempted an analysis along the lines of Hibbs, to enable us to evaluate, if nothing else, the *announcement effect* of the greater influence of the left on the government and, to a certain extent, on the prospects for entry into the government.

The strike activity, measured by the total hours lost for the whole economy, is illustrated in graphs 3 and 4. Figure 3 shows strike activity from 1969. Figure 4 looks at a more recent period (1976-78), particularly the period following the general elections on 20 June 1976. It should be recalled that Figure 4 shows data on strike activity as a whole, and strikes for the "structural reforms". In Table 6, I have summarized the average figures for man-hours lost through strikes for the whole economy.

The second part of the table shows the average figures for strike activity for governments of various types. For reasons of comparability, the five months with the highest strike activity are excluded, since they involve the renewal of collective agreements. In other words, only those months outside the influence of the renewal of agreements are considered.

[12] Hibbs (1976).

Figure 3: Index of total strikes (Man-Hours) July 1969 - June 1978
(Mean Value - 100)

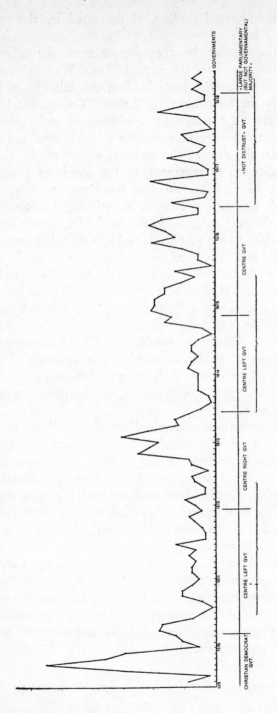

Figure 4: Index of total strikes and strikes for structural reforms
(Man-Hours) January 1976 - June 1978)
[1969 1978 Mean Value = 100]

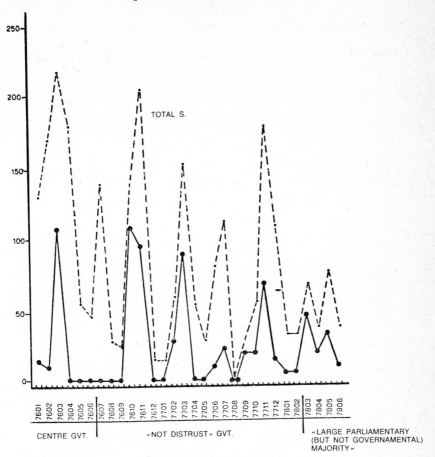

It is quite clear that these data can say little on the effect of the left and the changes in governing coalitions on strike activity, especially in view of the limited number of observations available.

Total strike activity or that for structural reform seems to show a declining trend. This is an incorrect impression in my opinion for total strike activity, since the data do not take account of the massive strikes for the renewal of major agreements in the transport, hospital and school sectors that took place in these latest months.

There does instead seem actually to be a declining trend for strikes for structural reforms. This is easy to understand, since these

Giancarlo Mazzocchi

Table 6 : Total man-hours lost for strikes in Italy, 1970-1978.

(monthly data)
PART ONE

Subperiod	Dates	Mean values (man-hours × × 1,000)
1	July 1970 — June 1972	8,223.5
2	July 1973 — June 1975	11,708.9
3	July 1976 — June 1978	9,413.7

PART TWO
Different government coalition mean values
(monthly data) *

Coalition	Dates		Mean values (man-hours × × 1,000)
Centre-right	Feb. 72/Oct. 72	(9 months)	7,746.6
Centre	Dec. 74/Nov. 75 May/June 76	(14 months)	14,529.8
Centre-left	Apr. 70/Jan. 72 July 73/Nov. 74	(39 months)	9,103.3
« Not distrust » gov.nt	July 76/Feb. 78	(20 months)	9,824.8
« Large parliamentary (not governmental) majority »	Mar. 78/June 78	(4 months)	7,358.5

* Five top months of job contract renewals excluded.

strikes are controlled by the central trade union organizations, which have shown more readiness to cooperate with the government, at least recently. The more marked falling trend in strikes for structural reform by comparison with total strikes seems therefore to show a reduced capacity of the central organizations to control the actions and obtain the consent of the rank-and-file.

6. In place of a conclusion

I fully realise that it is not easy to draw a conclusion, as would be usual, from this work, which comes out as rather fragmented. In fact, I shall not give a proper conclusion, but confine myself to some statements that I hope will serve for discussion.

a) One of the central ideas of the social sciences in this post-war period, namely that of "pluralist industrialism", maintains that the evolution of industrial societies will lead to a reduction of industrial conflict as a result of the growth of institutions for resolving conflict and of the separation of political conflict from economic conflict. This may be true for some countries in the Western world (I am thinking in particular of the Federal Republic of Germany) but does not seem to be true for the Italian case. As we have tried to show for the Italian case, some instruments for absorbing industrial conflict (like the *sliding scale* and the *Wage Supplement Fund* (C.I.G.) have diverted but not reduced industrial conflict, and it would therefore not seem that there has been that separation of political conflict from economic conflict that "pluralist industrialism" had foreseen.

b) This observation leads us to the second point. For many countries the decline in industrial conflict has been seen as the result of the change in the power structure of society resulting from the coming to power of the labour movement and the parties allied with it. In Italy it is certainly true that today the left and the unions have greater influence over government decisions. But it is also true that there continues to exist, to use Tarantelli's words, an "unsatisfied political demand" [13] that affects industrial conflict.

This also allows one to understand why it is so difficult in Italy to administer an incomes policy, not to speak of a *wage freeze*, as proposed in the recent three-year plan. The pioneering study of Bruce W. Headey on experience with incomes policies in the post-war period shows that there are two essential conditions for the cooperation of the labour movement with such policies. The first is that the government be trusted by the unions. In practice that means that the political parties linked with the unions (socialist, labour, communist) must be in government or share in it. The second

[13] Tarantelli (1978).
[14] Heady (1970), p. 407.

condition is that the degree of centralization of the trade union movement must be such that the central bodies can exercise sufficient control over wage demand and over strike decisions of the major categories of workers.[14]

If we consider these two conditions as essential conditions for an incomes policy, it is easy to understand why in Italy it is very hard to administer such a policy. On the one hand, the collective bargaining process is very articulated and decentralized, and furthermore, we have today strong competition between the various trade unions, that is, between the C.G.I.L., C.I.S.L. and U.I.L. On the other hand, even though, as we have said, the left parties and the unions today exert considerable influence on government decisions, the government does not seem to receive unconditional trust from the unions and the parties that support the large parliamentary (but not government) majority.

c) In reality the attempt to establish greater cooperation between the unions and the left parties with the forces in government seems to cause some division among the unions and the left parties themselves. There is a very interesting analysis by Walter Korpi of the Swedish trade union political and trade union situation, which I feel is very useful for interpreting the possible future developments of the Italian situation. Walter Korpi says:

> "The interpretation suggested here is thus that electoral difficulties of the Social Democrats have arisen largely from the continued superiority of the power resources of the capitalistic class, which has constrained Social Democratic policies, necessitating compromises with dualistic consequences for potential supporters. The traditional view with its stress on changes in class and community structures underestimates the importance of popular movements and the role of political action and political goals for the mobilization of people".[15]

But this is a problem that would call for another meeting of the European University Institute.

[15] Korpi (1978), p. 322.

BIBLIOGRAPHY

C. Crouch and A. Pizzorno (1978): *The Resurgence of Class Conflict in Western Europe since 1968*, London 1978.
C. Dell'Aringa (1977): *Egualitarismo e sindacato*, Milano, Vita e Pensiero 1977.
M. Edelman and R. W. Fleming (1965): *The Politics of Wage-Price Decisions*, Urbana 1965.
V. Foa (1961): "Politica salariale e sviluppo economico", in: *Economia e sindacato*, Sept. 1961.
B. W. Headey (1970): "Trade Unions and National Wage Policies", in: *The Journal of Politics*, May 1970.
D. A. Hibbs, Jr. (1976): *Long-run Trends in Strike Activity in Comparative Perspective*. Center for International Studies, MIT, Cambridge, Mass. 1976.
W. Korpi (1978): *The Working Class in Welfare Capitalism*, London 1978.
L. Lama (1973): "Il sindacato di classe, ieri e oggi", in: *Quaderni di Rassegna Sindacale* 1973.
L. Lama (1977): *Relazione e conclusioni al IX Congresso CGIL*, Roma 1977.
F. Modigliani and E. Tarantelli (1979): "Structural and Transitory Determinants of Labour Mobility: Holt's conjecture and the Italian experience", in: *Banca Nazionale del Lavoro Quarterly Review*, Sept. 1979.
M. J. Piore (1970): "Jobs and Training" in S. H. Beer and R. E. Barringer: *The State and the Poor*, Cambridge, Mass. 1970.
E. Pontarollo (1978): *Struttura dei costi del lavoro e contrattazione*, Milano, Vita e Pensiero 1978.
E. Tarantelli (1973): "Distribuzione del reddito e rinnovi contrattuali nell'esperienza italiana", in: *Rivista Internazionale di Scienze Sociali* 1973.
E. Tarantelli (1978): *Il ruolo economico del sindacato: il caso italiano*, Bari, Laterza 1978.
A. R. Weber (1963): "The Structure of Collective Bargaining and Collective Bargaining Power, Foreign Experiences", in: *The Journal of Law and Economics* 1963.

INDUSTRIAL CONFLICT AND TRADE UNIONS IN THE 1970s: THE ITALIAN CASE

by

VITTORIO VALLI

1. The crisis in the system of industrial relations

As the events of the last decade in several industrialized countries have demonstrated, economic evolution, the industrial relations system and the policy of the State are closely interrelated.[1]

At the end of the sixties and at the beginning of the seventies the industrial relations system collapsed in several countries: its relatively smooth functioning has been superseded by a situation of conflict and instability which State policy has failed to keep under control in a non-inflationary context. This has led to a number of important effects on economic evolution; but even the mass-unemployment reached in several economic systems after the great economic crisis of 1974-75, although it reduced the unions' pressure on wages in some countries, could not restore the less conflictual situation of the fifties and part of the sixties.

Against this general background the Italian events are not at all unique, but they nevertheless present some interesting features.

2. Changes in the Italian system of industrial relations (1969-1978)

Since the end of the sixties the system of industrial relations has

---

[1] See Tarantelli (1978; 1979).

gone through several very important changes with respect to the previous two decades.

a) From 1968 to the mid-seventies Italy has experienced an extraordinarily rapid increase in unionisation (see Chart I and Table 1), even in a period of high unemployment (Table 2). CGIL, for example, increased its membership by 66 per cent in the period 1968-1975, while the membership of CISL rose about 60 per cent.

More recently, however, there have been growing symptoms of a reversal of this trend and a creeping discontent among some members of the trade unions.

The growth of unionisation was partly due to a sharp rise in the unionisation rate of already highly unionised sectors of industry, such as the metallurgical and mechanical sector; but was also to a very large extent due to a greater diffusion of union membership among white-collar workers in industry and in the tertiary sector.[2] There was also a considerable rise in the unionsation rate in Public Administration (among civil servants, teachers, etc.). In the tertiary sector, moreover, several workers left the so-called "sindacati autonomi" (autonomous unions), i.e. the unions which are not associated to the three big confederations (CGIL, CISL, UIL) "and became members of one of the three confederations.

However, there has recently been some discontent among some of the workers about the strategic lines of the three confederations; some workers have left the unions, and there has also been a recovery in the influence of the autonomous unions, but these phenomena are relatively limited.   ;

[2] The unionisation rates (members of the three big confederations as percentage of the total employees) in the metallurgical-mechanical sector grew from 28.9 in 1968 to 46.3 in 1972 while the union membership in Public Administration in the period 1968-73 rose by 15 per cent for CGIL, by 8 per cent for CISL and by 18 per cent for UIL (see Regalia, Regini, Reyneri, "Conflitti di lavoro e relazioni industriali in Italia", in: Crouch, Pizzorno (1977).

[3] CGIL (Confederazione generale italiana del lavoro) is mainly linked with the Communist and the Socialist Party, while CISL (Confederazione itaiana sindacati lavoratori) has connections with the Christian Democratic Party, although it also includes some members of the left-wing minority groups, and UIL (Unione italiana del lavoro) is linked to the Socialist Party, the Social Democratic Party and the Republican Party. However, in the sixties and at the beginning of the seventies there was a strong tendency towards a greater autonomy on the part of the unions from political parties, but since 1973 this trend has tended to be reversed.

We may finally recall that there is also a fourth confederation (CISNAL) linked to the right-wing parties, but whose importance is very limited; and there are also several "sindacati autonomi" whose importance is considerable among white-collar workers in the public sector.

Table 1: MEMBERS OF CGIL AND CISL AND UNIONISATION RATEO IN ITALY: 1960-1977

Years	CGIL (a) (thousands)	CISL (thousands)	Total (thousands)	Unionisation (b) rates (%)
1960	2,584	1,327	3,911	33.2
1961	2,531	1,402	3,933	32.5
1962	2,605	1,444	4,049	32.5
1963	2,616	1,505	4,121	32.5
1964	2,701	1,516	4,217	33.5
1965	2,540	1,469	4,009	32.8
1966	2,453	1,484	3,937	32.6
1967	2,420	1,515	3,935	31.9
1968	2,461	1,622	4,083	32.8
1969	2,625	1,642	4,267	33.7
1970	2,943	1,809	4,752	36.8
1971	3,136	1,973	5,110	39.1
1972	3,214	2,184	5,399	41.2
1973	3,435	2,214	5,649	42.3
1974	3,827	2,473	6,299	45.8
1975	4,081	2,594	6,675	47.9
1976	4,321	2,833	7,154	50.7
1977	4,482	2,810	7,292	50.8

Notes: (a) The data of CGIL for the last two years are not strictly comparable with the ones of the preceding period;
(b) CGIL + CISL members as percentage of dependent employment.
Sources: For unionisation in the years 1961-1975 see Regalia, Regini, Reyneri, op. cit., p. 71; for the other years see Pettine, Papan (1978), p. 50 and Acocella (1978), p. 78. For dependent employment ISTAT: new series on labour force (Roma, 1978).

Table 2: INDICATORS OF THE ITALIAN LABOUR MARKET (*a*)

Years	Labour force (thousands) (1)	Employment (thousands) (2)	Labour force in search of employment. (thousands) (3)	Labour force as % of population (4)	Employment as % of population (5)
1960	21,544	20,329	1,215	44.0	41.5
1961	21,536	20,428	1,108	43.8	41.6
1962	21,306	20,337	969	43.0	41.0
1963	20,852	20,045	807	41.8	40.1
1964	20,870	19,996	904	41.4	39.6
1965	20,611	19,501	1,110	40.5	38.4
1966	20,369	19,176	1,193	39.8	37.4
1967	20,506	19,401	1,105	39.7	37.6
1968	20,556	19,384	1,172	39.5	37.2
1969	20,369	19,209	1,160	38.9	36.7
1970	20,436	19,325	1,111	38.7	36.6
1971	20,405	19,296	1,110	38.4	36.3
1972	20,293	19,996	1,297	37.9	35.5
1973	20,491	19,185	1,305	38.0	35.9
1974	20,714	19,601	1,113	38.0	35.9
1975	20,946	19,716	1,230	38.1	35.9
1976	21,284	19,858	1,426	38.5	35.9
1977	21,607	20,062	1,545	38.9	36.1
1978	21,730	20,159	1,571	39.6	36.6

(*a*) Unpublished new series on labour force and employment (ISTAT). Since 1977 they result from the new ISTAT survey on the labour force. For the preceding years the data are unofficial rough estimates not strictly comparable with the data for 1977 and 1978. The figures for employment, unemployment and labour force are considerably higher than the ones given by the old official series but probably they are more realistic.

b) Since 1969 there has also been *rapid growth in conflictuality*, as is shown by the figures for hours lost because of labour conflicts (see Chart I and Table 3 in Appendix). Not only in the 1969 "autunno caldo" ("hot autumn"), but also on average throughout the period, the level of conflictuality increased substantially compared with the fifties and a part of the sixties. The high unemployment level hardly reduced unions' conflcituality, though the rise in unemployment and the economic crisis of 1974-76 led to some weakening of the unions' pressure.

The rise of conflictuality was associated with a greater wage push from the rank and file, a much larger diffusion of bargaining and conflicts in individual firms and a widening of the set of objectives which union policy aims to achieve.

The pressure from rank and file workers on the unions was very important. The process of concentration, reconversion and rationalisation of the productive system carried out by companies in the period 1964-1968 had led to a very rapid increase in labour productivity, but also to cuts in working time, increases in the intensity of work, etc. At the same time, the almost complete failure of the "Programma economico nazionale" (National Economic Plan) for the years 1966-1970 as regards its social objectives (full employment, North-South income and employment differentials, social investments, etc.) [4] increased the unsatisfied demand of the workers for public goods and services. Thus, in 1969, there was a strong reaction from the working class directed both at companies, in claims for higher wages and better working conditions, and at the Government for the social reforms that it had promised, but not carried out. The labour unions became the main catalyst of the increasing social unrest and they included in their vindications a long list of social reforms, significantly widening the range of their objectives.

They asked for, and obtained, through strikes and demonstrations, a reform of the social security system, a law protecting the rights of workers and unions (Statuto dei lavoratori - 1970) and a new and more complete system of wage indexation (1975),[5] but they failed almost completely to achieve results as regards the North-South problem, housing, and health.

---

[4] See, for example, Ruffolo (1973); Valli (1977), pp. 111-116.
[5] Since 1973 the unions also obtained in some collective agreements the "150 ore" (150 hours), i.e. the possibility to attend some educational courses during the working time for not more than 150 hours in three years.

188   *Vittorio Valli*

Table 3: CONFLICTUALITY, WAGES AND PRODUCTIVITY IN ITALY: 1960-1977

| Years | Labour conflicts | | | | Wage and salary income per capita at constant prices (% rates of change) (6) | G.D.P. at constant prices employee (% rates of change) (5) |
	Total number (1)	Conflicts in the firms (2)	Workers involved (thousands) (3)	Hours lost (millions) (4)		
1960	2471	1707	2338	46	—	—
1961	3502	2478	2698	79	5.9	9.8
1962	4562	2536	2910	182	7.5	7.3
1963	4145	3413	3694	91	11.5	7.3
1964	3841	3128	3245	105	6.1	2.9
1965	3191	2675	2310	56	4.1	5.0
1966	2387	1953	1887	116	5.0	7.6
1967	2658	2251	2243	69	5.4	5.8
1968	3377	2860	4862	74	6.0	6.4
1969	3788	3219	7507	303	4.6	5.3
1970	4162	3537	3722	146	10.0	4.4
1971	5598	4831	3891	104	7.2	1.9
1972	4765	4099	4405	136	3.8	4.2
1973	3769	3225	6133	164	6.5	6.2
1974	5174	4465	7824	136	1.2	2.3
1975	3568	2997	10717	181	2.8	— 3.6
1976	2667	2264	6974	132	3.1	4.8
1977	3259	2558	6434	79	3.3	1.3

Source: ISTAT, Ministero del Lavoro.

c) As is argued by Tarantelli in his model which is summarised in the Introduction, the rise in conflictuality was also due to *important changes in the composition of the unionised labour force.* These changes had started at the beginning of the sixties, but accelerated at the end of the decade and at the beginning of the seventies. Young and more educated workers entered the unions in this period. Having not suffered from the unions' defeats and frustratios of the fifties, they gave a strong impulse to conflictuality. Moreover, the growth of industrial concentration in the period 1964-1968; the rising importance of modern sectors compared with the traditional ones, and the exclusion of part of the weaker labour force (women, young and old people) from the "regular" labour market, led to a greater homogeneity of the labour force employed in the regular labour market and to a larger concentration in the big factories. These trends contributed to the upsurge of conflictuality at the end of the sixties and thus induced the enterprises to decentralise production more and more in the following years.

d) Finally, the rise in conflictuality was also due to the growing expansion of the so-called "contrattazione articolata", i.e. decentralised forms of negotiations at company level. While at the beginning of the sixties the collective agreements were mainly held at industry or sectoral level, during the decade there was a gradual diffusion of additional negotiations at company level especially among the big corporation.[6] There were 2860 of these company agreements in 1968, and the figure rose to 4831 in 1971 (see Table 3). The diffusion of the more decentralised forms of negotiations caused a greater spreading of conflictuality in area and in time. While in the fifties conflictuality was highly concentrated in the periods of the main national collective agreements at industrial level, which in Italy are held every three years, in the late sixties and in the seventies they were more equally distributed over time.

e) Since the end of the sixties there had also been *fundamental changes in labour institutions and laws.*
The "Statuto dei lavoratori", which was approved in 1970 and which recognised the basic rights of workers and unions in the factory, contributed powerfully to strengthen and secure their position, but, since it made it very difficult for companies to fire workers,

---

[6] See also the paper by Mazzocchi in this volume, paragraph 2.

it tended to reduce the mobility of labour and discipline in the factories.

Moreover, since 1970 there was a growing tendency to decentralise the unions' structure through the institution of the so-called "Consigli di fabbrica" ("factory councils"), which are composed of representatives ("delegati") directly elected by each group of workers. The "Consigli di fabbrica" gradually replaced the preceding structures ("Commissioni interne" and "sezioni sindacali") in most enterprises, although their penetration was much more difficult in the public sector. Whereas in 1972 there were only 8,101 "consigli di fabbrica" with 82,923 delegates, they had already reached 16,000 with 150,000 delegates in 1974.[7]

As we already know, important changes in the social security system and in the indexation of wages were also achieved in the first half of the seventies; however, a bill which attempted to regulate work done at home (1973), and another which tried to increase youth employment (1977) almost completely failed in their objectives.

The process towards a greater unity of the three big confederations started at the beginning of the sirties, accelerated after 1969. Finally, in 1972, it led to the "Federazione sindacale unitaria", i.e. the federation of the three main confederations CGIL, CISL, UIL; but in the following years the process towards a more complete unity was effectively halted because of the increasing divisions between the Confederations and within them.

3. The increasing segmentation of the Italian labour market

These developments in the system of industrial relations were closely interrelated with the main trends in the Italian labour market since 1969:[8]

a) a tendential stagnation in employment (if measured as % of the population) after the reductions registered in the sixties, but a substantial increase in unemployment after 1974, due to a slight rise in the labour force.

---

[7] See Regalia, Regini, Reyneri, op. cit., p. 72.
[8] See, for a more detailed analysis, the paper by Mazzocchi, see also Table 2, Table 4 and Chart 2

Figure 1: Unemployment rate; annual rates of change of G.D.P. (a) at constant prices, unionisation rate (b) and conflictuality rate (c) in Italy

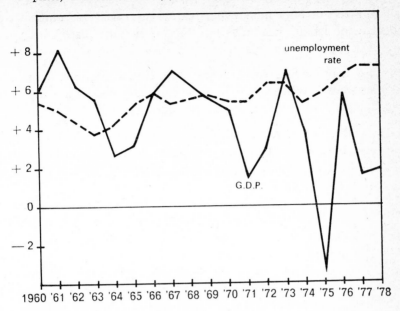

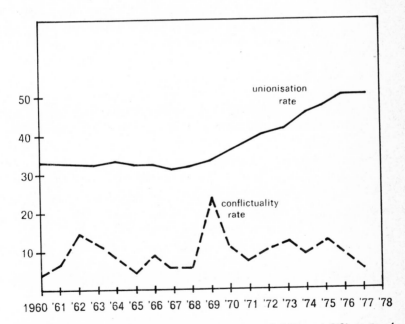

Notes: (a) Gross domestic product; (b) members of CGIL and CISL in % of dependent employed labour force; (c) hours lost for labour conflicts divided by dependent employed labour force.

Sources: Istat; Tables I and 4.

b) a rise of both money and real wages, on average higher than the rise of labour productivity, with at first decreasing and then relatively stable profit margins.[9]

c) a considerable reduction in differentials between wages and salaries since 1969 (we must remember that in the sixties they were much higher than in other industrialized countries).

d) a sharp increase in the decentralisation of production owing to a larger recourse to "black labour" or other forms of precarious or irregular labour on the part of companies.

This last phenomenon deserves some further comments because of its great importance in the Italian case.

In an effort to limit increases in labour costs, to respond to increasing rigidity of the labour force, and also to limit the growing power of the unions — which is largely dependent on large scale concentrations of workers in the big factories — companies in sectors such as clothing, electronics, etc. have tended more and more to decentralise a part of their production or some phases of their productive process (assembling, etc.). They have, therefore, made increasing use of the output of small enterprises or of people working at home.

The productivity of this labour force is probably low (because of its limited technical equipment), but its labour cost is even lower, because of the low wages and of the massive evasion of social security contributions and taxes in this section of the labour market.

The existence and the expansion of these forms of irregular labour have had two important consequences. First of all, it is very difficult to measure the size of this phenomenon, so that official ISTAT statistics give severely underestimated figures of labour force and employment, though the new survey on the labour force has provided higher and much improved figures (Table 2).[10]

Secondly, the expansion of this *economia sommersa* ("submerged economy"), though it has contributed in a considerable way to sustain production, employment and international competitiveness of

[9] See Ferri (1978).
[10] The statistical series also gave underestimated figures for unemployment, because of the difficulty of measuring how much labour would have been offered if the demand for labour had been higher; so, the new statistical series on labour force gives higher values for employment, labour force *and unemployment* than the old one. As regards the labour force participation rate, we may recall that some unofficial local

Figure 2: Output, employment and hourly labour productivity in the Italian industry (a)

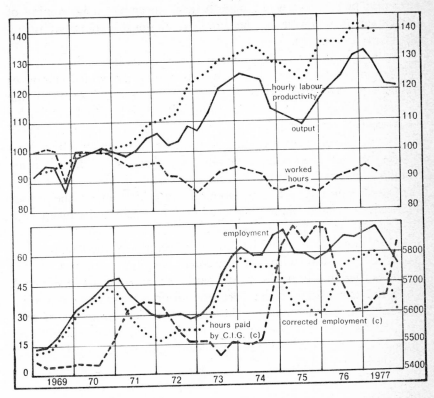

Notes: (a) constructions excluded; (b) « Cassa Integrazione Guadagni »; (c) employment corrected taking into account the hours conceded by the « Cassa Integrazione Guadagni ».

Source: Banca d'Italia, *Relazione annuale* (1977), Roma, 1978, p. 113.

the Italian economy, is nevertheless based upon very precarious foundations. Moreover, since te "submerged economy" is essentially non-unionised, its expansion has tended to weaken unions and to increase the segmentation of the labour market. The growing segmentation has, for its part, helped to loosen the linkage between the purely economic sphere and the industrial relations system, emphasizing the role of the State and of political parties. From the analytical point of view we have had, for example, a weakening of the explanatory power of the Phillips relationship between unemployment and wages.

In a very stylized way we can describe these trends using the distinction between sector A of the labour market (which comprises the labour force employed with a regular contract) and sector B (the "submerged" labour market) including all other labour force.[11] Also because of a semi-stagnation in employment in sector A, the demand for labour in this sector is mainly addressed to workers who have already had some working experience, so that they primarily come from other firms of sector A or from sector B.

On the contrary the new labour force which enters the labour market is to a large extent composed of young men and women with high school or university degrees.

This labour force would like to enter Sector A of the labour market directly, possibly with a white-collar position. However, in the seventies there has been a semi-stagnation of employment in Sector A while the expansion of the decentralisation of production has increased the demand for labour in Sector B which for technical reasons, such as the small size of its economic activities, mainly requires bluecollar workers. There has, therefore, been a growing imbalance in the labour market.

surveys found that it was much higher (from 19 per cent to more than 100 per cent more) than appeared from the official data (original series on labour force or population census). Some interesting local surveys were carried out in Modena, in sixteen "comuni" (local government areas) in Emilia-Romagna, in a "comune" near Cuneo, in some "comuni" of Marche, etc.

(See Fuà (1976). See also CENSIS (1976) and the numerous contributions by Frey in the period 1970-1978).

[11] The division of the labour market in only two sectors probably gives an oversimplified picture of the Italian situation. It would be possible to distinguish Sector A in two segments (big and small enterprises); or to distinguish both sector A and B, from the labour supply side, according to sex, age, educational level, etc. Finally the territorial characteristics of the demand and supply of labour are very important in a country in which regional imbalances are so great. But the dual division presented in the text has the great advantage of simplicity, and nevertheless provides some interesting insights.

In other words, labour demand is different *in quality* from labour supply. Moreover while the former is mainly concentrated in the Centre-North, the latter is very large in the South. These trends have changed very rapidly the composition of unemployment, and have also influenced both the overall dynamics of wages and the differentials between wages and salaries.

While in the fifties and in the sixties the unemployment rate was much higher for workers with primary and junior high school degrees than for workers with university degrees, in the seventies the situation has changed greatly. In 1977 the unemployment rate was 4.6 for the labour force with a primary school diploma; 9.3 for workers with junior high school diplomas; 13.8 and 6.7 for, respectively, high school and university graduates.

Tis helps explain, together with demographic factors [12] and the consequences of the economic crisis, the abnormally high unemployment rate of young men and women. It also provides an economic basis for the sharp reduction of the differentials between wages and salaries experienced in Italy since 1969 (which is, however, also due to the egalitarian policy of trade unions and the different indexation of wages and salaries in the public sector).[13]

Finally, since labour unions derive their power principally from the blue-collar workers of sector A, and these workers were relatively scarce in the labour market and less mobile because of the greater rigidity introduced by the "Statuto dei lavoratiri", it is possible to understand the remarkable levels of conflictuality and wage increases eperienced even in a period of very high overall unemployment.

4. THE TWO PHASES IN LABOUR CONFLICTS

Up to now we have discussed the period 1969-1978 as if it were basically homogeneous over time. We can, on the contrary, distinguish two phases for the industrial relations system in the last decade: a) the period 1969-1973; b) the period 1974-1978.

The first phase was a period of very severe labour conflicts, increasing decentralization of wage negotiations and conflicts and a substantial rise in the unions' bargaining power.

---

[12] See the paper by Tarantelli.
[13] See the paper by Mazzocchi.

The second phase registered a slight but continuous decrease of conflictuality and the unions' pressure upon wages; an increasing effort by political parties and the leadership of the unions to control the tendency toward excessive decentralization; a reduction of the autonomy of unions from political parties and of the cohesion among the confederations. Several analyses have already been devoted to the first phase.[14] We shall, therefore, from now on concentrate our attention upon the second period which has been explored much less.[15]

5. THE ECONOMIC CRISIS AND THE UNIONS' POSITION

Since 1969 the Italian economy has passed through two recessions: in 1971-72 and from the end of 1973 up to now. The length and intensity of the two crises have been, however, very different, as the macro-economic indicators of Table 4 clearly show. The second one has been by far the longest and most severe crisis of the entire post-war period and we shall focus our attention especially upon it and upon its impact on the Italian system of industrial relations.

As we have already remarked, the period 1974-78 registered a gradual weakening of the pressure of unions on the enterprises. This phenomenon is basically due to two main factors:

a) the evolution of the political situation;

b) the impact of the economic crisis.

From the political point of view we can stress the fact that the policy of the "compromesso storico " ("historic compromise") between communist and catholic groups formulated by the leader of the Communist Party, Berlinguer, in September 1973, led to an acceleration of the "long march" of the Italian Communist Party towards power in the central government. Thus the Communist Party tried to reduce the pressure of the CGIL on the industrial system in order to legitimatize its aspiration to enter the central government together with the Christian Democratic Party, and in order of try to solve the severe employment problems of the Italian

[14] See, for example, AA.VV. (1976), (1977); Regalia et al. (cit.); Pizzorno (1968-1972); Fuà (1976).
[15] Some interesting considerations are however expressed in Manghi (1977).

Table 4: SELECTED MACROECONOMIC INDICATORS IN ITALY: 1960-1978*(b)*

Years	GDP at constant prices (% rates of change) (1)	Gross fixed investment at constant prices (% rates of change) (2)	Unemployment rate (%) (3)	Balance of payments (billions of lire) (4)	Implicit GDP price deflators (% rates of change) (5)
1960	6.3	12.3	5.6	274	2.0
1961	8.2	11.4	5.1	359	3.0
1962	6.2	9.5	4.5	31	5.8
1963	5.6	8.0	3.9	— 783	8.4
1964	2.6	— 5.9	4.3	483	6.5
1965	3.2	— 8.4	5.4	996	4.3
1966	5.8	4.3	5.9	435	2.3
1967	7.0	11.7	5.4	203	2.9
1968	6.3	10.9	5.7	392	1.5
1969	5.7	7.4	5.7	— 869	4.2
1970	5.0	2.7	5.4	223	6.8
1971	1.6	— 3.1	5.4	489	7.1
1972	3.1	1.0	6.4	— 747	6.3
1973	6.9	7.7	6.4	— 208	11.7
1974	3.9	3.5	5.4	— 3588	17.7
1975	— 3.5	— 13.0	5.9	— 1324	17.2
1976	5.7	1.9	6.7	— 1028	18.3
1977	1.7	0.1	7.2	2129	18.3
1978*(a)*	2.0	— 1.8	7.2	4400	13.9

(*a*) Preliminary estimates.

(*b*) New not-official statistical series.

Source: ISTAT.

economic system. This strategy seemed to be politically successful as long as it was associated with considerable electoral gains such as in the regional election on June 15, 1975 and in the political election on June 20, 1976 and with some small "step by step" changes of line by the Christian Democratic Party such as the acceptance of the "not distrust" (1976-77) and of the "large parliamentary but not governmental" (1978) formulas.[16] However, at the end of 1978 and at the beginning of 1979 this policy met with increasing difficulties under the double pressure of the growing dissatisfaction of rank and file workers and the continuous refusal of the Christian Democratic Party to allow the Communist Party to enter central government. These difficulties contributed to cause the Communist Party small losses in local elections in 1978.

From the economic point of view (but the political and economic spheres are closely interrelated) the trade unions were little by little, *though with a substantial lag*, influenced by the consequences of the economic crisis. The rise of unemployment and of the recourse to the "Cassa integrazione guadagni",[17] the increasing gap between sector A and sector B of the labour market, the worsening of problems such as juvenile unemployment, the South, etc., tended to weaken the position of trade unions.

The impact of political events and of the economic crisis on the unions was partly hindered by the workers' resistance to changes in the strategic line of the Confederations; by the effects of a greater indexation of wages [18] (through the agreement of January 25, 1975), and by the persistence of a great gap between the political demand of the collectivity and State response (Tarantelli, 1978: pp. 69-80).

A gradual change in the attitude of trade unions is, however,

---

[16] Since July 1976 to January 1978 there was a Christian Deomcratic government externally supported by the other major parties (including the Communist Party). Since March 1978 to the end of January 1979 the Communist Party had entered the majority which prepared the programme of the government, but the government itself remained with the Christian Democratic Party.
For the impact of these political changes on conflictuality see the paper by Mazzocchi.

[17] The "Cassa integrazione guadagni" is a public institution which pays a high percentage of the wages of the workera of enterprises which are suffering a severe temporary crisis. These workers maintain their job at the enterprise, but are paid mainly through public funds.

[18] In Italy there is a mechanism (known as the 'scala mobile') by which there is an automatic but delayed increase in wages as the cost of living rises. In January 1975 this mechanism was reformed and improved.

evident if we analyze their documents, the collective agreements and the papers of declarations of their leaders.[19] The round of major collective agreements in 1975-76 led to lower increases in wages and less innovations in the normative rules than the two preceding rounds in 1969-70 and in 1973 (we must, however, remember that the reform of the mechanism of indexation of wages on the basis of price increases in January 1975 had given wages a substantial, though not complete, protection against inflation).

In the ensuing period the union leaders tried to limit the rise in wages and to reduce the rigidity in the labour market in order to stimulate a recovery of accumulation, increase in employment especially in southern regions and among young people, and to obtain a large influence in the control of investment decisions. This was the strategic line which prevailed at the EUR meeting of trade unions "cadres" in February 1978. In an outspoken way the general secretary of CGIL, Luciano Lama, in an interview given to the daily newspaper "Repubblica" (Jan. 24, 1978), maintained that "wages were not any longer to be considered as an independent variable".

Lower increases in wages, a greater mobility of the labour force and "the end of the system of labour permanently assisted by the government" were, according to him, necessary to bring about a recovery of accumulation and employment, but the accumulation process had to be accompanied by more effective industrial planning on the part of the government.

It is rather surprising that, from the purely analytical point of view, the EUR line was in some degree similar to the position held by the Bank of Italy in the sixties: wages and productivity determine the profit margins; the profit margins influence investments; investments influence the level of income, which determines employment. In the EUR document, more through a responsible policy of the unions than through the functioning of the Phillips curve, unemployment can, in its turn, exert some influence on the dynamics of both wages and productivity. Naturally, though the similarities with the Bank of Italy documents are rather striking from the analytical point of view, the policy concolusions are different. The unions wanted in fact to achieve more effective forms of economic planning, a

---

[19] See Trentin (1977); Lama (1976), (1977); Manghi (1977).

greater "industrial democracy" and the participation of left-wing parties in the government.

Moreover, the above-mentioned relationships are not always valid. High profit margins do not in fact necessarily lead to high levels of investment and employment.

In any case the EUR line has been endangered by three facts. First of all, it became evident that the recovery in profit margins since 1975 (Ferri, 1978: pp. 4 and 7) has not led to a meaningful rise of investment and employment. Secondly, the slow and in some years negative, dynamics of real wages in the public sector, partly due to less favourable indexation of wages compared with the private sector, led to a growing discontent in the public administration, and thus to a recovery of the power of autonomous unions and to the explosion of some wild-cat strikes (as happened in hospitals in autumn 1978).

Thirdly, no real industrial planning has been carried out by the government, and the unions have not yet achieved a more effective influence in the investment decisions.

Finally, the autonomy of the three main confederations from the political parties has diminished, and this has contributed to halt the process of unification among them.

There have been, therefore, some tensions within each Confederation and among them as regards important matters such as the proposals of a reduction of working time "and the preparation of a unified platform for the main collective agreements to be discussed in 1979.

During the second half of 1978 and at the beginning of 1979 there have, however, been increasing symptoms of a marked change of the EUR line, partly emerged in the debate of the second EUR meeting of trade unions" "cadres" in February 1979. This process has probably been accelerated by the discontinuance of the support given by the Communist Party to the Government and by the governmental crisis of February 1979. The Italian industrial relations system might therefore be on the brink of a new phase of bursting conflictuality, but the overall economic background is now less favourable to its expanding process.

---

[20] A part of CISL has insisted on a rapid and generalized reduction of the working time from 40 to 38 hours a week in order to increase the level of employment, while the position of CGIL and UIL has been favourable to a more gradual and flexible approach. On this theme see, for example, Frey (1978).

6. CONCLUDING REMARKS

The economic crisis of 1974-75 has to some extent weakened union power and decreased the rate of conflict; but as our analysis has shown, this trend is not clear-cut and depends on both economic and political factors. Political factors may offset the impact of the economic crisis. The state will play a crucial role: its continual failure to satisfy basic social needs will contribute to foster industrial conflict.

Meanwhile, however, the increase in size of the "irregular" labour masrket and of the "submerged economy" is undermining the possibilities for successful state intervention in the economy. And these factors have a further impact — through the evasion of tax and insurance contributions, they contribute to the very financial crisis of the state itself.

202   *Vittorio Valli*

BIBLIOGRAPHY

AA.V.V (1976), *Problemi del movimento sindacale in Italia, 1943-73,* "Annali Feltrinelli" (1974-75), Milano 1976. Essay partly reprinted in: AA.VV (1977), *Movimento sindacale e società italiana,* Milano, Feltrinelli 1977.
AA.VV. (1978), *Conflittualità e aspetti normativi del lavoro,* Bologna, Il Mulino 1978.
G. Acocella (1978): "La Cisl nel Mezzogiorno: sviluppo e fisionomia di un'organizzazione (1950-1977)", in: *Quaderni di Rassegna sindacale,* marzo-aprile 1978, pp. 65-86.
CENSIS (1976): *L'occupazione occulta,* Roma 1976.
C. Crouch, A. Pizzorno (1977): *Conflitti in Europa,* Milano, Etas Libri 1977.
P. Ferri (1978): *Distribuzione del reddito, stagnazione e processo inflazionistico,* riunione scientifica della Società Italiana degli Economisti, Roma, November 6-7, 1978.
L. Frey, *Il potenziale di lavoro in Italia,* ISVET, Roma (various volumes).
L. Frey (ed.) (1975), *Lavoro a domicilio e decentramento dell'attività produttiva nei settori tessile e dell'abbigliamento,* Milano, F. Angeli 1975.
L. Frey (1978), "Prospettive dell'occupazione e gestione del tempo di lavoro", in: *Tendenze dell'occupazione,* Nov., Dic. 1978.
G. Fuà (1976), *Occupazione e capacità produttiva: la realtà italiana,* Bologna, Il Mulino 1976.
L. Lama (1977), *Il sindacato nella crisi italiana,* Roma, Editori Riuniti 1977.
L. Lama (1976), *Intervista sul sindacato,* Bari, Laterza 1976.
B. Manghi (1977), *Declinare crescendo,* Bologna, Il Mulino 1977.
F. Modigliani, E. Tarantelli (1977), "Market Forces, Trade Union Action, and the Phillips Curve in Italy", in: Banca Nazionale del Lavoro, *Quarterly Review,* vol. XXX, 1977, p. 3.
B. Pettine, T. Pipan (1978), "La sindacalizzazione nella CGIL meridionale, 1968-77: considerazioni e dati", in: *Quaderni di Rassegna sindacale,* marzo-aprile 1978, pp. 40-64.
A. Pizzorno (ed.): *Lotte operaie e sindacato in Italia (1968-1972),* Bologna, Il Mulino (various volumes).
I. Regaia, M. Regini, E. Reyneri (1977): "Conflitti di lavoro e relazioni industriali in Italia", in C. Crouch e A. Pizzorno, *Conflitti in Europa,* Milano, Etas Libri 1977.
G R.uffolo (1973): *Rapporto sulla programmazione,* Bari, Laterza 1973.
P. Sylos Labini (1977): *Sindacati, inflazione e produttività,* Bari, Laterza 1977.
E. Tarantelli (ed.) (1976): *Salario e crisi economica,* Roma, Savelli 1976.
E. Tarantelli (1978): *Il ruolo economico del sindacato,* Bari, Laterza 1978.
E. Tarantelli (1979): *Industrial conflict in the '60's and in the '70's, Introduction and Overview* (in this volume).
B. Trentin (1977): *Da sfruttati a produttori,* Bari, De Donato 1977.
V. Valli (1977): *L'economia e la politica economica italiana (1945-1975),* Milano, Etas Libri 1977.

CONCLUSION

THE IMPACT OF THE LABOUR MARKET CRISIS ON THE CONDUCT OF INDUSTRIAL RELATIONS: SOME OBSERVATIONS ON THE CONCLUDING DISCUSSION

by

GERHARD WILLKE

It seems appropriate to introduce these reflections on the concluding general discussion by restating briefly the intentions of the
organizers of the colloquium, particularly with regard to the final
session. These intentions reached beyond the themes and main arguments of the six papers, aiming, even if tentatively, at comparison
and synthesis. Following the introduction, therefore, the papers'
findings about the impact of the crisis on the conduct of industrial
relations are summarized and commented upon. These observations
are then linked to selected arguments of the concluding discussion
which, naturally, touched upon many more topics than can be recorded here. Finally, some personal conclusions are drawn.

1. THE INTENTION FOR THE CONCLUDING SESSION

The emergence of a puzzle

A notable feature in our preparatory conversations in 1978 was
the general astonishment about the obvious lack of disruptive action
of organized labour in response to the most severe labour market
crisis in the post-war period.

The apparent inability of governments to stabilize their shaky
economies and of private enterprise to secure the jobs of millions of
people failed to provoke violent attacks from organized labour on the
established prerogatives of economic and political decision-making. In
1974/75, when in most countries industrial production was not only

not growing but rapidly declining, and unemployment rates were driven up to a multiple of previous levels, many economists and politicians were deeply worried about the potential economic and political consequences of a depressive world economy. What haunted them were not merely the recent anti-capitalist and anti-democratic slogans of the 1968/69 revolts but the recollection of the destructive effects of the Great Depression.[1]

The worldwide recession of the 1970s, however, was managed — or endured — in a climate of relative social and political calm. Contrary to expectations, this critical period witnessed a stabilizing role of the unions. Even if disenchanted, they did not jeopardize the political-economic system but kept relations with management and government that helped to manage the crisis.

Why would the boom-years of 1968 and 1969 witness widespread social revolt and industrial action, whereas the crisis-ridden years of the mid-seventies would feature a "non-barking dog" (the pet-animal of the colloquium), i.e. acquiescent unions?

It was not only the conventional belief [2] that unions would not tolerate serious failures in securing high levels of employment that had been proven wrong. It was a deeper belief nurtured over two decades of extraordinary growth and prosperity that the stability of western advanced societies depended on an incessant expansion of welfare, consumption and opportunities. Weren't these allegedly the pacifiers of the capitalist economies, the illusory foundations of the working class' loyalty and, therefore, of the system's legitimacy? *Edelman* and *Fleming's* hypothesis, concerning the 1950s in Italy and Germany, that "planned wage drift was management's basic industrial-relations device to deliberately maximize labour docility" [3] is a pertinent reflection of these conventional beliefs.

---

[1] Rightly or wrongly, the perception is widespread that "it was unemployment between 1930 and 1933 that was to a large extent responsible for bringing Hitler to power, and hence for the Second World War". Hutchison (1977) p. 7.

[2] Note the parallel between the beliefs of the post-war and the interwar periods: "In the 1930s, public debate was divided between those who predicted that mass unemployment would lead to organized revolution, and those who foresaw apathy and disintegration". Jahoda (1979) p. 492.

On the increased political acceptability of unemployment today see Ashenfelter, in: OECD (1977 c). But note also the view expressed in the discussion of this OECD conference, that the greater tolerance may be due to continued assurances from governments that high unemployment was only temporary. However, if "unemployment is truly structural in nature and does not fall significantly, tolerance of high unemployment may wear thin". OECD (1977b) p. 35f.

[3] Edelman, Fleming (1967) pp. 95f.

It seemed necessary to ask the question whether industrial relations and, more specifically, the role of the labour unions had changed. Have the 'tripartite' arrangements — incorporation of the unions into policy making, whether formal or not, and attemtps at a 'joint regulation' of the economies — have these previous concessions changed organized labour's response to critical economic performances? Has the 'stake' of labour in the mixed economies, i.e. their "sunken, irretrievable membership costs"[4] accumulated to such an extent that they have become defenders of the system and "agents of social control" (*Thomson*)?

Labour market performance and industrial relations

Answers to the above questions require some clarifications of the ties between economic performance and political action, specifically between labour market developments and the conduct of industrial relations in the comprehensive sense of tripartite relationships between unions, management and government.

In that respect, the analysis of a crisis not only sheds light on the particular historical event under consideration but — maybe more importantly — it reveals changes in the functioning of economic institutions and group relationsships which remain unnoticeable in 'normal' times whereas they become salient in critical circumstances.[5] One such change seems to be the increasingly selective and segmented functioning of the labour market turn-over because of the various protective measures that have accumulated over time to make the group of core workers (i.e. the core of the unions) quasi immune to layoffs. This has produced a particular composition of the stock of unemployed, fragmenting the impact of the crisis among the weaker groups of the labour force and thereby allaying the strain on the system.

Another such change may be that the unions and the bulk of the working class — provided such a class still exists — become grad-

---

[4] Schmitter (1979) p. 3. I should mention that Schmitter, in the quoted paper, is not dealing with the unions' integration into the present systems but with international regional integration. Still, I submit, the thrust of his argument is pertaining to our issues, i.e. the integration of infra-national units. Take his definition of interdependence as a state where "all are reciprocally indebted" (p. 6).

[5] Cf. Luhman (1970) p. 25.

ually integrated into the mixed economies to such an extent that their membership turns 'crisis-proof' and even stabilizing in periods of genuine challenge.[6]

Two approaches

The issue of the links between labour market performance and the conduct of industrial relations has been rather neglected by the profession in the last ten years.[7] One is therefore left without much help in analysing the topical question. What we are looking for is a hypothesis about the transformation of perceived actual and expected strain (with regard to pay, working conditions, job security, and, more generally, political discontent) into action by organized workers and/or unions, seeking redress. In general terms, and without reference to unions and labour markets, *Hirschman*[8] and *Schmitter*[9] have analysed modes of action in response to discontent and strain. Following these lines, we can distinguish three types of response: exit, voice, and suffrance. Exit, in our case, means withdrawal from the labour market and cessation of job search. This response, even if

---

[6] It appears to be open whether this amazing fact is attributable to the population's and unions' fundamenal aversion to radical alternatives of socio-economic organization or whether they are so constrained in their volitions that certain issues are not even seriously considered. The first alternative seems to be suggested by Willey (1974) who says that the hard core of the unions has always "consisted of middle-aged family men ... interested in bread-and-butter issues and ... adopting new-middle-class attitudes and life-styles" (p. 56). The other alternative is pointed out by Lindblom (1977):

> "An additional fragment of evidence is the continued stability of volitions on the fundamentals of politico-economic organization in the face of remarkable recent instability of opinion on such once deep-seated beliefs as sexual behavior, marriage, dress, and polite speech. Clearly in some circumstances people break out of old patterns of thought, even abruptly. Yet neither war, nor weapons or rivalry among nations, nor inflation, nor unemployment, nor threat of nuclear destruction has opened up a greatly broader range of volitions on the grand issues of politico-economic organization" (p. 209).

It is not obvious, however, that Western unions would, in the final analysis, defend the market economy. In a 1976 OECD conference, the point was put forward that in France, Belgium and the UK "basic disagreements by significant sections of union leadership as to the necessity for the preservation of the market system could cause major difficulties". OECD (1977c) p. 17.

[7] Exception should be made for the Symposium on "European Labor and Politics", reported in Industrial & Labor Relations Review Oct. 1974 and Jan. 1975. This symposium covered union-party relationships pre-1973.

[8] Cf. Hirschman (1970).

[9] Cf. Schmitter (1979).

it does not soothe individual frustration, still relieves the system. Those who withdraw are usually cut off from their webs of working group affiliations; part of the strain ceases to feed into organizations to induce collective action.

The remaining responses for groups and individuals are voice and suffrance. To the extent that during the crisis voice of individual workers, but also of unions, is subdued at workplace and enterprise levels, this type of response is likely to shift to the political arena. Parallel to that shift one would expect the degree of suffrance to rise.[10] The use of voice is generally encumbered by the uncertainties and lags of the political process. In a more fundamental sense, it is definitely limited by the degree of structural power imbalances. Given the entrepreneurial prerogatives of decision-making in the market economies — private business cannot be forced to invest but requires inducements to do so — economic policy must be careful not to create additional disincentives for entrepreneurs in a recession.

Dismissals and the more pervasive threat of working place insecurity, as well as the definite limits of unions' voice in politics — given the categorical imperative of favourable conditions for private sector investment — these elements together operate as periodical reminders to workers and their organisations of that basic structural power imbalance which seems to be part of the membership costs of unions in mixed economic systems. This statement is not meant to imply that organized labour's actions and voice have no effect, on the contrary. Usually, in a recession, politicians in order to allay restive unions and to reduce losses in mass support accept bargains which may be symbolic *prima facie* but which imply obligations in the future. Extending, e.g., tripartite arrangements to ever more issue areas including legislation, is intangible at the moment but will have its quite tangible effects over time.

These arrangements may limit the potential of the private sector to cope with future challenges, and may constitute elements of a vicious circle that has been analysed under different aspects by *Bacon/Eltis* [11], the German Sachverständigenrat [12] and others.

The propensity of industrial conflict to extend into the political arena is enhanced in times of recession when the limits of distribu-

[10] Cf. Rehn, in: OECD (1977 c).
[11] Bacon/Etis (1978).
[12] Sachverständigenrat zur Begutachtung der gesamtwirtschaftlichen Lage. Jahresgutachten 1974/75 ff.

tional battles at firm and industry level become obvious, and political
conflicts over the rules of future distribution seem more promising.
Over and above the merely defensive battles, unions can then point
at positive achievements in the political field. Still, this may not be
sufficient for the degree of suffrance not to rise in a crisis. It will
seek relief in recovery and boom years when the going is better. Not
surprisingly, a cyclical pattern in the conduct of industrial relations
emerges from these arguments. Not only do labour's demands expand-
and contract with the business cycle, but also the locus of impact
shifts from the business to the political arena — with partly irreversible results.

This reasoning links up with one strand of analysis concerning
the conduct of industrial relations and labour markets, namely the
relation between strike activity and business cycles.[13] The hypothesis seems to be well established that strike activities generally
vary according to the business cycle. The 'propensity to strike' (*Rees*)
is said to be related to the divergence of expectations between employers and unions which reaches a maximum in the boom of a cycle.
More specifically, as *Ashenfelter* and *Johnson* have shown, it is a
mismatch of expectations between employers and union *members*,
leaving union leadership in the awkward position of having to
support strikes, often against their better knowledge, for the
'political' reason of maintaining or recovering control over the rank
and file.[14]

What emerges from this reasoning is a periodic shift in the
requirements for internal consensus *within* unions and external consensus *between* unions and the other actors in the tripartite system.
Internal consensus between members and leadership becomes a pre-
dominant goal for unions in the peak phase of an upswing when
expectations between employers and union members diverge most.
Industrial strife and work stoppages tend to dampen union members'
expectations as well as fostering internal coherence. Union leadership
need not worry about the consensus with management and with
government suffering in such a situation; these are not running any
immediate risks. On the other hand, in a recession, the reduced
expectations of union members secure internal consensus, whereas

---

[13] See e.g. Rees (1952), O'Brian (1965), Hibbs (1976). A rather complete
bibliography on this issue is given by Stern (1978) p. 32, footnote 1.
[14] Ashenfelter, Johnson (1969).

unions must now take care not to jeopardize external relations with management and government because this may inflict on them avoidable losses in growth and real income, and prolonged unemployment. Unions will normally, therefore, seek external consensus in recession, and be less outspoken about it in boom phases.

If this recurring pattern of pressures and responses constitutes the rules of the game, acknowledged by the participants in conditions of *normal* cyclical swings, it is, however, quite open whether the same rules also apply to exceptional situations when the system breaks out of the 'corridor' of acceptable levels of unemployment and inflation rates. In fact, there would have been nothing particularly surprising about a moderated conduct of industrial relations in the 1974-78 period had it only been a matter of a normal growth cycle downturn. But it wasn't. What is validly called the 'crisis of the 1970s' was the most severe post-war recession, as all participants in the Colloquium acknowledged. It actually pushed most Western economies out of the corridor of hitherto experienced inflation-unemployment compounds, and reactivated a widespread anxiety with regard to the security of working places and the value of money. Therefore, the fear was not unfounded that such a crisis might lead to a break-down of the external consensus between the major societal groups, to political turmoil, and to a revival of trade union militancy, which had proved to be dangerous for several systems only a few years ago.

Now, given the fact that the labour market crisis of the 1970s put exceptional strain on labour and on the conduct of industrial relations, how can it be explained that the crisis was managed with relative social and political calm? Certainly, the 'common external enemy', i.e. the OPEC cartel, could not be ignored. But that's only part of the story. More important seems to be the fact that the unions, as organisations with an interest in their future viability, were disinclined to opt for exit. To terminate the basic consensus on which the mixed economies are based could have meant to destroy the established webs of inter-organisational relations and interests, and would in fact have meant risking uncontrollable upheavals. The unions' revealed preference was to utilise their voice and extend their role in the tripartite networks, pursuing the road towards corporatism and towards gradualistic changes of the existing systems.

Having mentioned earlier the 'prosperity hypothesis' to explain the socio-political stability of the mixed economies in the 1950s and

1960s, we should now remark on a competing hypothesis for the system's stability in the less favourable conditions of the 1970s. The stabilization crises observable in many countries in reaction to accelerating inflation rates revived the *Kaleckian* idea of a 'broken-back economy' as a means to control the potentially destabilizing claims of the working class. What may be surprising with the conduct of industrial relations during the crisis in the light of the "prosperity hypothesis" is readily explained by *Kalecki's* idea that the threat of unemployment and deprivation imposed upon the working class by a deliberately instigated slump keeps voice down effectively. But what do these two sweeping hypotheses explain? In prosperous times it is prosperity and in depressed times it is depression which allegedly guarantee the working classes' acquiescence in the capitalist system. These somewhat simpleminded approaches appear inadequate as mutually exclusive 'explanations'. A different story may, however, come out of a combination of these two hypotheses for an explanation of the cyclical pattern in the conduct of industrial relations. Then, it cannot be discarded off-hand that the carrot of prosperity periodically requires the complementary stick of a recession to 'drive home the facts of life'.

The more fundamental problem with the depression hypothesis is that *Kalecki's* world is not our world of today. Despite the basic power imbalance mentioned earlier, unions today are not defencelessly complying with the strategic decisions of a political elite. Unions are themselves firmly entrenched in present political-economic systems, and major actors in economic government. This is in fact seen, by the present writer, as the crucial precondition for the unions' prolonged acceptance of self-denying restraint and for their role as stabilizers in the crisis of the 1970s: Had they not perceived themselves, even if to different degrees, as parts of the various political-economic systems in which they had a considerable stake, and had they not been convinced of a fair chance in achieving some of their wider goals in the political arena, the unions might in fact have terminated the basic consensus on which the relatively successful management of the crisis depended. Unions who had nothing to lose in the early thirties reacted differently.

The notion of the 'relative' success needs to be stressed, however. There is no such thing as a free sharing of responsibilities in a crisis. The heavy reliance on corporatist structures and channels during these critical years has brought about their confirmation and extension. *Thomson* has elsewhere [15] given an impressive table demonstrating the expansion of the corporatist state in Britain. Similar tables could be constructed for other countries. To me, this suggests that *Flanders'* often-quoted dictum of governments having shared control in order to regain it needs amending: in order to *regain it for a short run.* In the longer run, we will live to see that after any such burden-sharing for crisis management the system will not be the same again.

2. INDUSTRIAL RELATIONS IN THE CRISIS: SOME COMPARATIVE EVIDENCE

In order to elucidate the particular patterns of pressures and responses within the tripartite networks of unions, employers, and governments under the impact of a prolonged labour market crisis, it seems appropriate now to identify those elements in the papers presented which touch specifically on this aspect of the colloquium's topical problem.

The Case of Britain: Attempts at a Social Contract

The British case shows a rise in the overall rate of unemployment, attributable to a fall in industrial production comparable to that of Germany (see Tables 1 and 2, and Figures 1 and 2). An important difference, however, is that the UK experienced *the* crisis as yet *another* crisis rather than as a major break, as *Thomson* points out.

The 'labour market' paper on the British experience in the crisis therefore focuses on the development of the pay structure. *Christopher Saunders* traces the evolution of wage dispersions and differentials under the influence of incomes policies which were largely designed as voluntary 'crisis-agreements' between the Government and the TUC, who accepted pay moderation in return for government-backed, centrally bargained pay policies (and some more fundamental changes in the operation of the political economy, to which they had aspired). As regards the labour market, Table 6 of *Saunders'* paper on the composition of unemployment shows a fragmentation

[15] Thomson (1979).

Table 1: INDUSTRIAL PRODUCTION [a] 1973-79
(Volume; percentage changes)

	73	74	75	76	77	78	79
FRG	3,4	—1.1	—6.2	7.4	2.8	2.0	5.6
I	9.7	3.9	—8.8	11.6	0.0	2.1	6.5
UK	8.2	—1.8	—4.9	2.9	4.7	3.0	3.7
EC	7.4	0,6	—6.6	7.3	2.2	2.4	4.4

[a] Without construction.

Source: European Economy Nov. 1979 and March 1980, Annex.

Table 2: UNEMPLOYMENT RATES 1973-79
(Registered unemployed as percentage of civilian active population)

	73	74	75	76	77	78	79
FRG	1.0	2.2	4.2	4.1	4.0	3.9	3.4
I	4.9	4.8	5.2	5.6	6.4	7.1	7.6
UK	2.0	2.4	3.8	5.3	5.7	5.7	5.3
EC	2.5	2.9	4.4	4.9	5.3	5.5	5.6

Source: European Economy Nov. 1978, Table 7, p. 33; March 1980, annex, Table 7.

of the impact within the sharply rising numbers of unemployed similar to that of Germany and Italy.

The most vulnerable groups of the labour force, such as general (unskilled) labourers, juveniles, women, and people over 60 years of age, were most notably affected.

It is worth noting that *Saunders* — much like *Mazzocchi* — puts the topical problem of the colloquium in a broader perspective: The crisis of the 1970s is seen in the light of the foregoing inflationary

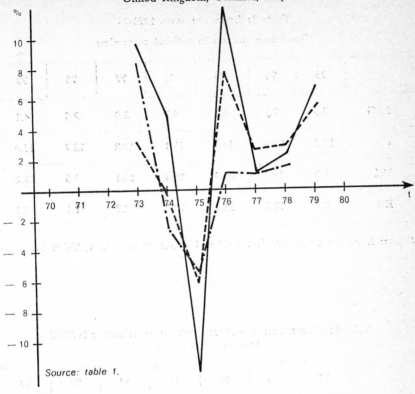

Figure 1: Industrial Production 1973-79
United Kingdom, Germani, Italy

Source: table 1.

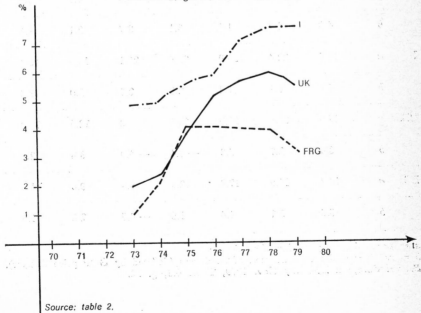

Figure 2: Unemployment Rates 1973-79
United Kingdom, Germany, Italy

Source: table 2.

Table 3: INFLATION RATES 1973-79

(Percentage changes in national currencies)

	73	74	75	76	77	78	79
FRG	7.6	7.1	6.1	4.5	3.9	2.5	4.1
I	12.2	20.8	17.6	18.1	18.2	12.7	15.0
UK	8.2	17.2	23.9	15.4	15.1	8.6	13.2
EC	8.7	12.8	12.9	10.1	9.7	7.1	9.0

Source: European Economy Nov. 1979 and March 1980, Annex, Table 18.

Table 4: NOMINAL AND REAL COMPENSATION OF EMPLOYEES 1973-79
(Percentage changes)

		73	74	75	76	77	78	79
FRG	a	12.9	12.1	7.8	7.8	6.6	4.8	6.0
	b	4.9	4.7	1.6	3.1	2.7	2.1	1.6
I	a	19.6	22.4	30.9	20.9	21.1	15.0	18.4
	b	6.6	1.1	11.2	2.3	2.5	2.0	2.8
UK	a	12.3	20.6	29.9	15.5	9.2	12.6	15.2
	b	3.4	2.7	5.3	−0.4	−4.9	3.8	2.1
EC	a	14.4	16.9	17.8	12.9	9.9	9.8	11.0
	b	5.5	3.1	4.4	1.6	−0.5	2.8	1.9

a = per capita compensation of employees
b = *real* per capita compensation of employees (deflated by GDP price deflator).
Source: European Economy Nov. 1979, Table 4.3, p. 52.

crisis and both are related to persistent industrial conflicts and relative uncompetitiveness in Britain, which are in turn linked to severely deficient organizational structures of collective bargaining. Excessive inflationary pressures are said to stem from structures which favour continuous leapfrogging and subsequent restoration of 'just proportions', not only between and within sectors and industries but even within firms (*Thomson*). Exactly the same type of 'tortoise and hare race' between eroding and restoring of pay differentials is observed in Italy (*Mazzocchi*).

It could be said that the crisis set the stage for a reactivated 'Social Contract' in the classical mode of the trilateralism of a 'bargained economy': compensation for what the opposite-number-party cannot or does not want to deliver is claimed from a third party. Some of the shock of the crisis was absorbed by the unions' (TUC) accepting restraint in pay increases and even cuts in real wages over an extended period — in order to ease inflationary pressure and allow profitability to be restored or improved — on the understanding that they might trade this acquiescence for some substantial "shifts in the operation, in the power balance, in the priorities of the mixed economy" (H.D. *Hughes*). For a period, the TUC managed to substitute the "anarchy of procedures" for centralized pay arrangements which were linked to the government's incomes policy. This may be interpreted as a success on the part of the TUC, to replace fragmentation and short-term-mindedness for more centrally coordinated and longer-term wage policies following the impact of the crisis.

However, it must also be seen that the well-intended redistributional 'flat-rate' increases and the special provisions for low-pay groups pushed through by the TUC in much the same way as by the Italian unions tilted wage relativities in the wrong direction when seen from the vantage point of market-clearing wages: the apparent improvements in the juvenile-adult, the unskilled-skilled, or the female-male relativities produced more than average unemployment rates for exactly those 'target groups'.[16]

As the crisis persisted, however, sectional interests and short-term considerations proved to be preponderant again. When the TUC's more fundamental political claims ran up against strong resistance, and the distributional problem of 'just proportions' became

[16] Gruen (1978) p. 72.

virulent again with the slight recovery of 1978, the strategy to contain inflation by way of more centralized bargaining, and to improve economic conditions, began to falter. The intrinsic dilemma of centrally organized pay restraint and re-distribution, even if modest, became obvious: from within the unions and from the shop floor a counter-movement to restore 'eroded' differentials and 'comparability' is triggered off. This underlines Saunders' point that the essential difficulty for the TUC in securing acceptance of pay restraint is the tension created by the distributional distortions of that policy.

As *Thomson* explains in great detail in his paper, labour market developments did not really have a decisive influence on the conduct of industrial relations in the UK. Although the rate of unemployment had doubled between 1974 and 1976 (and almost trebled since, rising from 2.4% in 1974 to clearly over 6% in 1979, — the highest level for forty years), pay issues remained dominant for the union and for the TUC-government relations. The attention of both sides was directed at the joint determination of the provisions of various "phases" of incomes policies,[17] and the TUC had to invest efforts in persuading its member unions to observe the agreements. It was the control of inflation that was considered the most urgent problem, and incomes and price restraints were held to be the right instruments for bringing down inflation. Clearly, the unions requested political concessions in return for their 'favourable' attitudes: e.g. the strengthening of price control powers, the reinforcement of the closed shop, and the setting up of new wages machinery like the 'Statutory Joint Industrial Councils' to conduct collective bargaining in places with low unionization. Thomson does point at a series of measures that were taken by government, to ease the impact of the recession through the creation of new — mostly public — jobs, and the lowering of effective labour costs. But one significant contrast with respect to Germany remains: British union leadership is hampered on their way into corporatist and "responsible" economic government by the relatively stronger independence and virulence of union members (the shop floor). This explains why their main concern continued to be the struggle for better pay. They cannot risk to lose control of part of the rank and file as did Italian unions with the separation of the 'autonomi'.

---

[17] On details of the history of the 'Social Contract' see Hughes (1979).

The unions, says *Thomson*, "must ultimately respond to the expressed desires and priorities of their present members rather than pursue general social policies, and these desires have generally been very narrow and sectional in orientation". That is the problem. If union leadership find it difficult, as stated in a recent OECD conference,[18] to soothe member unrest by explaining the basic trade-offs between wages, prices, employment and growth, then other mechanisms must necessarily do this job, — even if in a more painful way.

The Case of Germany: Fragmentation of Impact and the Shift to Qualitative Demands

In his paper about labour market developments in Germany, *Kühl* points out that the sudden rise in the number of unemployed — the number of available, i.e. profitable, jobs was reduced by 1.7 million during the crisis — did not lead to an explosion of industrial and social unrest because its impact was highly fragmented among the less protected groups of the labour force: foreign workers, women, young people entering the labour market, people close to retirement age, the handicapped, etc.

With respect to the expected impact of the labour market crisis on the conduct of industrial relations, account should be taken of the fact that the substantial rise in unemployment apparent in present labour market statistics represents something quite different from what it meant a decade or two ago. It may well be considered less meaningful as a reflection of personal or family hardship,[19] which might command conflictual action, because of the increase in the share of families with two or more wage earners, rising levels of unemployment benefits and other forms of social security and, last but not least, a growing relative weight of the 'voluntary' element in involuntary unemployment that could arguably be ascribed to different life styles and changing attitudes towards work. A rising incidence and duration of search may partly be attributed to higher aspirations concerning the characteristics, location, and environment of a job, and the kind of satisfaction any particular work is expected to yield.[20]

---

[18] OECD (1977 c) p. 16.
[19] "The unemployed do feed the economic pinch, of course, but much less so than in the 1930s. Through the provisions of the welfare state, they fortunately no longer suffer acute physical deprivation". Jahoda (1979) p. 439.
[20] Cf. Economic Impact 25 (1979).

Returning to *Kühl*'s argument, the main impact of the prolonged
recession on the labour force seems to have been a filtering and
sorting-out of categories of labour who are characterized by various
— and sometimes cumulative — handicaps like low skill, little
attachment, absenteeism, old age, little work experience, high turnover rates, etc., and who involve excessive overall costs relative to
productivity.

The 'filtering-out' of the relatively better qualified among the
unemployed by way of a competition for a decreasing number of job
vacancies produces a particular composition of the stock of unemployed (*Kühl's* "moving" and "quasi-fixed" types) which goes some way
in explaining the lack of social and political turmoil during the crisis.
Not only do the groups affected by high rates and/or long duration
of unemployment show a low degree of unionization, and are far
from becoming a pressure group with some bargaining power, they
are also basically irrelevant to the unions' overriding goal of survival
and growth as institutions (*Ashenfelter* and *Johnson*). These groups
are in fact most prone to exit and suffrance as modes of response to
unemployment. They are still lacking voice.

Many of these points are underlined by *Müller-Jentsch*. He
stresses that despite the continuous increase in the degree of unionization and a generally higher level of industrial action in the 1970s as
compared to the previous decade,[21] the conduct of industrial relations during the crisis has been surprisingly controlled. At the beginning of the crisis the unions' wage claims practically ignored the
changed conditions, i.e. the substantial cut in disposable national
income due, among other things, to the higher raw materials bill.
This, incidentally, is true for all three countries under consideration,
as is shown in Table 4 where the rates of increase in real compensation of employees do not depict a decline in the crisis years, on the
contrary: in the UK and most notably in Italy, there was a sharp
increase in 1975, and only a moderate reaction in 1976.

When the basic counter-productiveness of high real wage claims
in the crisis became clearer, the strategy of the unions to absorb
discontent and conflict was to substitute to some extent 'qualitative'
claims for 'quantitative' ones, and to shift the locus of conflict from
industry to politics. These qualitative claims concerned job-security

[21] The peak years of industrial action in the 1970s, however, were 1971 and
1978. (See his Table 3).

including the introduction of property rights in jobs (in Germany, 52% of workers older than 55 are now exempt from regular dismissal) as well as claims regarding 'quality of work' and 'humanization of labour'.[22] These demands prevailed over pay claims — with the exception of Britain where unions had to cope with extraordinary inflation rates during that period, but are also said to suffer from a "fixation with pay".

As *Müller-Jentsch* notes, between late 1974 and spring 1978, there was a virtual stop of industrial action for higher wages in Germany. This contrasts with the British unions whose primary concern with pay did not suffer in the crisis.

The Italian Case: Diverting the Conflict and Recovering Control

The British unions instituted the Labour Party as their political arm, and the German *Sozialdemokratie* established the unions to take care of the immediate economic interests of the working class. This common offspring seems to have facilitated the gradual integration of the labour movements into the advanced welfare states. Italy lacks these historical links between party and unions, and the implied division of labour. The Italian labour movement today is divided along party lines, and is still in principle committed to a position of autonomy with regard to government and State. A functional consequence of this peculiarity is the high degree of politicisation of the unions, required to carry on a political struggle alongside the economic one.

In the late 1960s and early 1970s, the unions in Italy, as elsewhere, were taken by surprise when outbursts of shop-floor militancy occurred that were partly even directed against themselves as established institutions. In order to divert part of the conflict from the plant level to an area better under their control, the unions started an offensive of political demands concerning reforms of housing, education, public services etc. The combined occurrence of 'direct actions' on the shop-floor, of far-reaching political demands from the unions, together with some anti-capitalist slogans, has been

[22] It should be noted that these are not new demands. In the last century, too, there were demands and strikes for "better shop conditions". Cf. Edwards (1979) p. 60.

On the intensified trend towards qualitative claims in many European countries see Lecher (1979).

dramatized to mean a "resurgence of class conflict" (*Crouch* and *Pizzorno*). What did, however, most conspicuously emerge in those years, were the conflicts *within* the working class, notably the struggle of mostly non-unionized unskilled and semi-skilled workers, tutored by agile theorists, for some of the privileges which their skilled and unionized colleagues were believed to enjoy.

While many of the economic demands of those restive groups — flat rate increases, generalized upgrading, *inquadramento unico* etc. — were endorsed by the unions and were eventually fulfilled, the offensive for social reforms ended, as did the myth of the resurging class conflict, in failure. Whether deliberately instigated or not, the years of the crisis of the 1970s were convenient for the unions to recover control over their most militant and particularistic groups, and for business and government to recover control over some of the more disruptive claims and activities of the unions. Even if this dismays them, the unions after 1969 share a common interest with the ruling elites in recovering control over what is happening in plants and to enterprises. This is a reflection of the unions' ambiguous position between, on the one hand, their task of organizing and representing their members' claims in terms of pay, working conditions, participation etc., and, on the other hand, their interest in defending the system against potentially destructive demands and activities of groups either within or outside their organization.

This is not the least reasons for the unions' propensity to alternate between challenging the system and defending it, between 'ariding the tiger' of revolt and acting as 'agents of social control' within an institutional setting that, after all, has become what it is thanks to the struggles of these very unions. To this ambiguity, a further level is added in the case of the Italian unions. They have always claimed — and hence their high level of politicisation — to have a say in the decisions determining the political and economic development of the country. On the other hand, their deep-seated disinclination to share responsibility for sustained concerted actions, and to commit themselves to any formal Social Contract, has so far blocked any serious attempt at solving the problem of the apparently permanent crisis of the Italian economy.

As *Mazzocchi* points out in his paper, the unions in Italy succeeded in establishing, in the years following the 'hot autumn' of 1969, a two-pronged protection — at least for those covered by these provisions — against the dismal effects of inflation and recession:

the 'scala mobile' for automatic pay increases, and a number of regulations guaranteeing property rights in jobs held by unions members. Legal and customary obstacles against layoffs — together with the introduction of the *Cassa Integrazione Guadagni* for short-time workers — have led to a drastic fall in the labour turn-over rate during the crisis years, freezing existing job and employment patterns at the expense, mainly, of new-comers to the labour market. One reflection of this is the disproportionately high level of youth and female unemployment rates.

As economies cannot function properly without a certain degree of flexibility, these developments contributed further to a segmentation of the labour market, in particular to the expansion of the unstable secondary labour market and to the growth ot the 'submerged' economy which is largely outside the reach of the unions, much as it is outside the reach of tax authorities and of social security. The size of this submerged sector is now estimated, even if quite tentatively, to have grown from one fifth to one third of 'official' Italian GDP.

Contrary to expectations which widespread revolutionary rhetoric might have nurtured, the crisis of the 1970s did not create the conditions for a social or political revolt.

On the contrary, the severe recession moderated the level of conflictuality. The impact of the crisis seems to have been diverted successfully to the political arena and, as in the other countries, to the secondary labour market, i.e. to the less protected segments of the labour force. It is interesting to note that, even if somewhat late in the day, the leader of the communist labour union, *Lama*, acknowledged some of the basic 'laws' of a market-oriented economy by arguing that wage increases should be in line with productivity increases and with the need for accumulation to provide for new jobs. In a surprisingly corporatist spirit, he proposed a moderation in pay claims in return for political concessions, i.e. for the extension of industrial democracy, for more effective industrial planning in terms of a greater influence of the unions on investment decisions, and a more substantial participation of left-wing parties in government (*Valli*).

While in Britain and in Germany union leaders regularly issue such or similar statements to nobody's surprise, the Lama statement caused an outburst of excitement just because of its exceptional character. As *Valli* states, however, this move didn't lead very far. In recent months, the inflation rate has reached 20%, and the unions are pondering about a general strike to oppose the proposition of a devaluation of the Lira.

3. THE CONCLUDING DISCUSSION IN RETROSPECT

Of the many other issues that were brought up in the concluding discussion, I can only comment upon two which turned out to be rather controversial. The first issue concerned the question to what extent the crisis of the 1970s was cyclical or structural in nature. Now, almost all participants agreed that an either-or approach was unhelpful. But the controversy concerned the relative weights of cyclical and structural elements, and their respective importance for the management of industrial relations. The question was raised whether the participants in the trilateral industrial relations network perceived the crisis as a basic discontinuity in the development of the various socio-economic systems, and whether new attitudes and institutional settings should be expected to emerge as a consequence? Or were the cyclical elements of the recession perceived to be dominant? This would lead one to expect that the conduct of industrial relations would perform its usual pendulum swing.

The idea of a structural change seemed to underly *Hughes'* notion that the economies under consideration represented a type of *Kaleckian* 'semi-slump' or 'broken-back' economy in the sense that over the extended period of prosperity the unions had become too strong for employers and governments to control industrial relations. As a consequence, they instigated a persistent recession to facilitate control over industrial relations — and over inflation. Other speakers challenged this view and referred to the probability of a more conflict-prone conduct of industrial relations in the years to come because the opportunity costs of conflict had been lowered. Tight and comprehensive social security nets were assumed to remove part of the individual strain from unemployment.

The fragmentation of the impact of unemployment among those groups of the labour force on whom "flexibility" was imposed because of their relative weakness, and the fact that the group of unionized core workers remained rather unaffected, appeared to weaken the idea of the recession as a "disciplinary action". In all three countries, a conspicuous rise in the degree of unionization would hint rather at a potentially more conflict-prone attitude on the part of organized labour.

The issue of cyclical vs. structural was, of course, not discussed exhaustively. One difficulty was the acknowledged intermingledness of short-term cyclical phenomena with longer-term structural elements in this severe recession. I should like to observe that there is a further aspect to this issue. The apparently successful application of Keynesian recipes, i.e. of short-term anti-cyclical demand management, has, I submit, produced structural implications which are adverse, in the long run, to the functioning of the mixed economy. This is a variant of the idea which Max *Weber* has called "*die Paradoxie der Folgen*", i.e. the unintended adverse effects of measures intended as short-term remedies. Anti-cyclical policies within a Keynesian approach, designed to attenuate market sanctions in order to secure full employment regardless of the behaviour of the actors in the market, are likely to produce longer-term effects which erode the very basis on which demand management is constructed. For instance, Keynesian policies have been based on the treacherous idea of "money illusion"; that illusion has certainly evaporated. Because of the consequent increase in wage pressure, what are widely believed to be Keynesian policies end in failure because they induce inflationary spirals. In addition, wage differentials are eroded by redistributive policies, and are restored in periods of lax or suspended incomes policies.

These unintended effects add further inflationary pressures. Due to short-term fiscal policies, structural disequilibria between the public and the private sector tend to emerge.

These and other factors have overloaded the cyclical movements — which were once thought to be manageable — with structural problems that are to a considerable extent a result of these well-intended short-term interventions. With respect to Keynesian policies one is tempted to quote *Hutchison's* observation that "nothing fails like success".

If there is any important economic consequence emerging from the crisis of the 1970s, it might be a general re-orientation of economic policies towards medium-term objectives and towards a higher degree of stability. In any case, the use of 'easy money policies' to accomodate wage-cost pushes has been discredited. And the feasibility of carrying through a sustained, if painful, stabilization policy has been shown, at least in principle.

The second issue was introduced by a remark of a French participant (*Salmon*) concerning the fact that his country would have been
particularly interesting for the purposes of this conference because
France apparently was the only country in which an endeavour on
the part of the government to establish a consensus with the labour
organizations could *not* be detected. This might be indicative of a
more general recognition of the limits of tripartite industrial relations, or group bargaining, at the national level. A few years ago, the
idea was fashionable that a consensus between different main categories of organizations, within the neo-corporatist model, had become
indispensable for the management of the mixed economies. But the
limits of this concept are now apparent. The importance of traditional
political responsibilities, and the degree of freedom left to governments, was being re-discovered. Naturally, there were institutional
differences between countries, as the examples of Italy or Germany
easily suggested. But if, as in Germany — and in France since the
Barre government — the trade unions hesitated to go along with
some minimum guide lines, then governments could in fact do without the unions under certain circumstances. For the moment, the
French or *Barre* way of handling the trade unions was, according to
Salmon, not obviously working worse than the consensus alternatives
of, say, Britain.

(Indeed, as *Saunders* indicated in a post-scriptum, the *Thatcher*
government which came into power in Britain in summer 1979,
seemed to be moving towards an approach similar to *Barre's*).

In the vein of analysing the performances of governments in the
crisis, a vivid critique of, and an ensuing controversy about, Germany's economic policies was triggered off. The critique was based
on the view that the German government had actually adopted an
'anti-Keynesian' stand (*Hughes* and *Halberstadt*), aiming at price
stabilisation irrespective of the costs, whether internal or external.
The 'purist' line of the German authorities, it was asserted, not only
aggravated the output and employment problems within the Federal
Republic but, more importantly, had negative repercussions on the
nascent recovery on the partner countries within the European
Community. What's more, it largely ignored the spirit of international agreements to cooperate in difficult times.

Such a critique seemed rather surprising, as the chairman of this
concluding session, Sir Andrew *Shonfield*, remarked. In the light of
what appeared to be mainstream thinking in international economic

relations since the mid-1970s, it were some other European countries which had failed in economic performance because they had not accomplished the German combination of price stability, full employment and balance-of-payments surpluses. It appeared to be a standard recommendation that these countries should correct their bad ways and follow the German lead in achieving economic stability. Now, on the contrary, Germany was considered a non-model. Far from being desirable, it would have been a disaster for each country and for the Community as a whole if the example of the Federal Republic had been followed.

Responding to this challenge, two German participants (*Müller-Jentsch* and *Willke*) presented partially divergent views. Both, incidentally, underlined the implication of the *Hughes-Halberstadt* line: their kind of convergent or coordinated economic policies would have meant the German government's accepting to go along with international inflation, — and thereby worsening it. *Müller-Jentsch* explained that the German unions would have been willing, for the sake of increasing employment, to reflate the economy and accommodate a higher rate of inflation. It was the "very autonomous" Bundesbank policy, however, operating independently of the unions' influence, which imposed restrictive guide-posts for economic policy. The unions, even if unwillingly, had to accept the line of the monetary authorities.

Willke, on the other hand, wished to qualify the charge of an 'anti-Keynesian' economic policy in the crisis. What are the criteria by which to judge performance? If Keynesian policies consist in running public deficits to compensate deficient private demand, then should deficits soaring to DM 60 billion per year (almost 6% of GNP) be called anti-Keynesian? It is true that after this immense thrust of public expenditure in 1975, the size of deficits was cut down in the following years for the sake of consolidating public finance and compressing interest rates to alleviate private investment. But the deficits still ran up to around DM 40 billion. Is it Keynesian always to increase public deficits? There are distinguished students of *Keynes* who deny this.[23] Given the strong stimulation of aggregate demand, the expectation didn't seem to be unfounded that the upswing could become self-sustaining.[24]

[23] Cf. for instance Hutchison (1977).
[24] Cf. OECD (1977 b) p. 37.

Consequently, the stabilization of prices was put first. From an increase of 6% in 1975, consumer prices rose less than 4% in 1977. It is true that from a purely public finance point of view this approach tended to curb the recovery in 1979, and to exert a negative public sector influence on economic activity in 1977. But there is more to a recovery than running public deficits. The business community, particularly in Germant, is sensitive to a weak public sector financial position and, above all, to inflation. Not only a boost of public demand but, more generally, a return to stability was called for.

So, the fact is undisputed that the approach of the German authorities contrasted sharply with the conduct of economic policies in either of the other two countries under consideration. But what have these countries done? Stylizing strongly, one could say that in Italy, the labour force members were kept in their jobs like "Pompeyans" (*Tarantelli*) even if work was wanting, and — apart from the implications for productivity — public finance (*Cassa Integrazione Guadagni*) was charged with a very heavy future burden. In Britain, many workers dismissed in the private sector were absorbed into public employment — or rather, failing firms "collapsed into public ownership" (*Hughes*) — aggravating the well-known problems described by *Bacon* and *Eltis*.[25] In Germany, basically, redundant workers and employees were dismissed, even if in many cases with 'golden handshakes' and/or by discontinuing work permits of foreign workers. What *Hughes* calls the "organization of inefficiency" — keeping redundant workers or shifting them to unprofitable public jobs — was only quite selectively accepted in Germany.

The difference between these approaches is reflected in economic indicators, e.g. in the rates of productivity increases during the 1970s, or in present unemployment and inflation rates. These approaches, I submit, should not be judged on the grounds of whether or not they fit the controversial label "Keynesian'. It is the results, and above all the medium- and longer-term results that count. At some point in time, the question of the re-deployment of the labour force in a changing production structure will come up. Clearly, each country has to find its particular solution for reconciling the basic need for security with the competing need to limit rigidities and preserve adaptability to structural change. But it should also be clear

[25] Bacon, Eltis (1978).

that there are costs involved in some of the well-intended short-term remedies. The drastic fall in the Italian labour turnover rate, just to take this example, is considered by *Mazzocchi* "a hindrance to structural change".

To defend, comparatively speaking, the German approach to crises management and recovery, does not at all imply the notion of Germany serving as a model for the other countries to follow. Apart from its undesirability this would not even be feasible. What it does imply, however, is the notion of a certain degree of competition among national stabilization policies in order to avoid a coordinated but grossly mistaken approach, and to leave room for the "discovery' of efficient alternatives.[26]

A view widely shared by the participants in the Colloquium was that the divergence between the countries under consideration — and more broadly the divergence between the member countries of the European Community — had been accentuated by the crisis. While state power and the authority of government had arguably not been impaired in some 'strong' countries, the weakening of state power in Britain and Italy seemed quite obvious. This change coincided with a situation where the functions assumed by, or imposed upon, the state had largely increased when at the same time the confidence in what the state could do had been disappointed.

Saunders suggested that what really distinguished the various countries was "the balance, or ought one to say perhaps the imbalance of powers between the state level, the union level, and what is loosely called the shop-floor level". If things were to take a turn for the better, a restoration of authority would have to come from somewhere, and it would then be a mixture of state authority and union authority. It was in fact, according to *Saunders*, the loss of union authority over a large part of the unions' very own field, namely industrial relations, which was causing temporary breakdowns. A central problem appeared to be the future location of authority in all aspects of industrial relations, a problem strongly accentuated by the crisis of the 1970s.

[26] Cf. Vaubel (1979) p. 17: "For example if Switzerland and Germany had been prevented from pursuing their disinflationary stabilization policies over the last few years, citizens in Italy, the United Kingdom and elsewhere might not have realized as clearly that inflation in their own countries was and is due to the inappropriate monetary policies conducted by their own governments, and consequently the public pressure on these governments to reduce inflation would have been much weaker".

A final remark

In some respects, the question of the management of industrial relations in the crisis of the 1970s is also a question of which forces are preventing societal systems of today from destabilizing when they have manoeuvred into an upsetting disequilibrium. Can we count on _Durkheim's_ 'organic solidarity' of the ever more specialized and interdependent elements in a complex society to achieve an operational degree of integration and equilibrium? This seems to be quite doubtful. A certain minimum of tutelary or preceptoral authority of the state and of the major groups in relation to their constituencies may be indispensable for a level of performance of modern socio-economic systems that prevents them from being trapped in a destructive dead-lock.[27]

The unions today make up, together with business and the political parties, the most powerful groups in modern societies; they play a crucial role in the pattern of pressures and responses that determines the stability or instability of systems. After having studied _how_ the unions have behaved during the crisis in various countries, we should now, in concluding, address again the questions of _why_ they behaved the way they did. I suggest approaching the question from two extremes. Not even in Britain or Italy, let alone Germany, are the unions _seriously_ entertaining, I submit, a radical alternative to the present mixed economic systems. They are basically aware of the incompatibility of some 'real existing' socialism with free and independent unions. On the other hand, they refuse to accept — even if in different degree — the status quo of the basic structural imbalance in the distribution of power, property rights, and income. Within these two border constraints, the unions are facing a dilemma: on the one hand, they may choose a 'constructive' mode of conduct of industrial relations; this tends to improve the chances of higher real wage increases but may perpetuate the status quo. On the other hand, they might turn to a 'conflictual' mode of conduct which reduces real wage gains through the 'organization of inefficiency' (_Hughes_) but appears to offer some prospects for changing the status quo.

Arguing this way means arguing against highflying critiques and sweeping interpretation of inherent 'capitalistic' contradictions pre-

[27] Cf. Malinvaud, in: OECD (1977b) p. 22.

venting full employment and stability, or of the dominant class instigating a broken-back economy to discipline the working class. These, to my mind, are conspiratorial and obscurantist notions.

If simpler notions have a similar explanatory power, they should be preferred. And it seems simpler to me to assume that unions — like other societal groups and institutions including the government — are facing problems of choice within reasonably well defined constraints under the conditions of risk, uncertainty, and, hence, liability to error.

The consequences of different modes of conduct are arguably too important for society to be left to the discretion of unions. Political authority is required to assume responsibility for how a country is managed. In this sense, "much of politics is economics, and most of economics is also politics".[28] This is in line with *Saunders'* comment that there is — in a precisely circumscribed way — need for the restoration of authority — not because authority in itself is so desirable but because its dilution invites factional interests to predominate at the expense of the society as a whole.

[28] Lindblom (1977) p. 8.

BIBLIOGRAPHY

1. O. Ashenfelter, G. E. Johnson (1969): Bargaining Theory, Trade Unions, and Industrial Strike Activity, in: *American Economic Review* 59 (1969).
2. R. Bacon, W. Eltis (1978): *Britain's Economic Problem: Too Few Producers*, London, Macmillan 1976 (2nd ed. 1978).
3. BfA - Bundesanstalt für Arbeit: *Amtliche Nachrichten* 1978.
4. Commission of the European Communities: *The economic situation of the Community*. Various issues.
5. *Economic Impact* (1979) No. 25: Employment/Unemployment, Washington: ICA.
6. M. Edelman, R. W. Fleming (1967): *Unemployment and Wage-Price Politics*, in: Employment Policy and the Labor Market, ed. A. M. Ross. Berkeley and Los Angeles, UCP 1967, pp. 89-112.
7. R. Edwards (1979): *Contested Terrain. The Transformation of the Workplace in the Twentieth Century*. New York: Basic Books 1979.
8. F. H. G. Gruen (1978): *Structural Unemployment as a Rival Explanation: A Survey of an Inconclusive Argument*, in: Capital Shortage and Unemployment in the World Economy. Symposium 1977. Ed. Herbert Hiersch, Tübingen: Mohr, 1978, pp. 59-83.
9. D. Hibbs (1976): Industrial Conflict in Advanced Industrial Societies, in: *American Political Science Review*, Dec. 1976.
10. A. O. Hirschman (1970): *Exit, Voice and Loyalty*, Cambridge: HUP, 1970.
11. J. Hughes (1979): Die Entwicklung der britischen Gewerkschaften in den Krisen der 70er Jahre, in: *WSI-Mitteilungen* (1979), No. 4, pp. 197-204.
12. T. W. Hutchison (1977): *Keynes v. the 'Keynesians' ...? with Commentaries by Lord Kahn and Sir Austin Robinson*. IEA Hobart Paperback No. 11, London 1977.
13. M. Jahoda (1979): The psychological meanings of unemployment, in: *New Society*, 6 Sept. 1979, pp. 492-495.
14. Jahresgutachten des Sachverständigenrates zur Begutachtung der gesamtwirtschaftlichen Entwicklung 1978/79: *Wachstum und Währung*, Stuttgart und Mainz: Kohlhammer 1979.
15. W. Lecher (1979): Unternehmensmitbestimmung und Tarifpolitik — die europäische Perspektive, in: *WSI-Mitteilungen* (1979), No. 4, pp. 178-186.
16. Ch. Lindblom (1977): *Politics and Markets. The World's Political-Economic Systems*. New York: Basic Books 1977.
17. N. Luhman (1970): *Soziologische Aufklärung. Aufsätze zur Theorie sozialer Systeme*. Köln-Opladen: Westdeutscher Verlag 1970.
18. F. S. O'Brian (1965): Industrial Conflict and Business Fluctuations, in: *Journal of Political Economy*, Dec. 1965.
19. OECD (1977a): *Economic Surveys*, Germany, July 1977.
20. OECD (1977b): *Structural Determinants of Employment and Unemployment*. Vol. 1. Paris 1977.
21. OECD (1977c): *Collective Bargaining and Inflation: New Relations between Government, Labour and Management*. Final Report on an International Management Seminar Convened by the OECD, Paris 1977.
22. A. Rees (1952): Industrial Conflict and Business Fluctuations, in: *Journal of Political Economy*, Oct. 1952. Reprinted in: A. Kornhauser, R. Dubin, A. Ross (eds.): *Industrial Conflict*, New York 1954.
23. I. Regalia, M. Regini, E. Reyneri (1978): *Labour Conflicts and Industrial Relations in Italy*, in: The Resurgence of Class Conflict in Western Europe

since 1968. Eds. C. Crouch, A. Pizzorno. Vol. 1. London: Macmillan 1978, pp. 101-158.

24. G. Schmid (1978): Strukturelle Arbeitslosigkeit in der BRD. Beiträge zur Problemanalyse der Unterbeschäftigung und Überlegungen zu arbeitsmarkpolitischen Konsequenzen. *IIM papers* 77-6, Wissenschaftszentrum Berlin, August 1978.

25. Philippe C. Schmitter (1979): *Exchange Theories of Integration: 'Exit', 'Voice' and 'Suffrance' as Strategies in Regional Organizations.* Paper presented at the Colloquium on "New Economic Approaches to the Study of International Integration: Appliactions of Economic Analysis to Political Decision-Making", Florence 1979.

26. R. N. Stern (1978): Methodological Issues in Quantitative Strike Analysis, in: *Industrial Relations* 17 (1978), No. 1, pp. 32-42.

27. A. W. J. Thomson (1979): Trade Unions and the Corporate State in Britain, in: *Industrial and Labor Relations Review* 33 (1979), No. 1, pp. 36-54.

28. R. Vaubel (1979): *International Coordination or Competition of National Stabilization Policies? A Welfare-Economic Approach.* Paper presented at the Colloquium on "New Economic Approaches to the Study of International Integration: Applications of Economic Analysis to Political Decision-Making". European University Institute, Florence, 31 May-2 June 1979.

29. M. Weber (1951): *Gesammelte Politische Schriften.* Ed. J. Winckelmann. Tübingen 1951.

30. R. J. Willey (1974): Trade Unions and Political Parties in the Federal Republic of Germany, in: *Industrial and Labor Relations Review* 28 (1974), No. 1, pp. 38-59.

LIST OF PARTICIPANTS

Oliver CLARKE, O.E.C.D., Director Division Manpower and Social Affairs, Paris.

Yves DE RICAUD, Centre d'Etudes Economiques et Juridiques de l'Emploi, Université di Toulouse.

Henry ERGAN, O.E.C.D., Division Science, Technology, and Industry, Paris.

John HUGHES, Vice Principal, The Trade Union Research Centre, Ruskin College, Oxford.

Jürgen KÜHL, Institut für Arbeitsmarkt- und Berufsforschung, Nürnberg

Wolfgang LECHER, WSI/DGB, Düsseldorf.

Giancarlo MAZZOCCHI, Università Cattolica del Sacro Cuore, Milano.

Walther MÜLLER-JENTSCH, Institut für Sozialforschung, Frankfurt/Main.

Michael J. PIORE, Massachusetts Institute for Technology, Cambridge.

Christopher SAUNDERS, The University of Sussex. Centre for Contemporary European Studies, Brighton.

Paolo SAVONA, Direttore Generale Confindustria, Rome.

Georges TAPINOS Institut d'Etudes Politiques de Paris.

Andrew W. J. THOMSON, The University of Glasgow.

Vittorio VALLI, Bocconi University, Milano.

and the staff of the European University Institute, Florence:

Louis DUQUESNE DE LA VINELLE
Pierre SALMON
Andrew SHONFIELD
Ezio TARANTELLI
Gerhard WILLKE

STAMPATO A FIRENZE
NEGLI STABILIMENTI TIPOGRAFICI
« E. ARIANI » E « L'ARTE DELLA STAMPA »
FEBBRAIO 1981